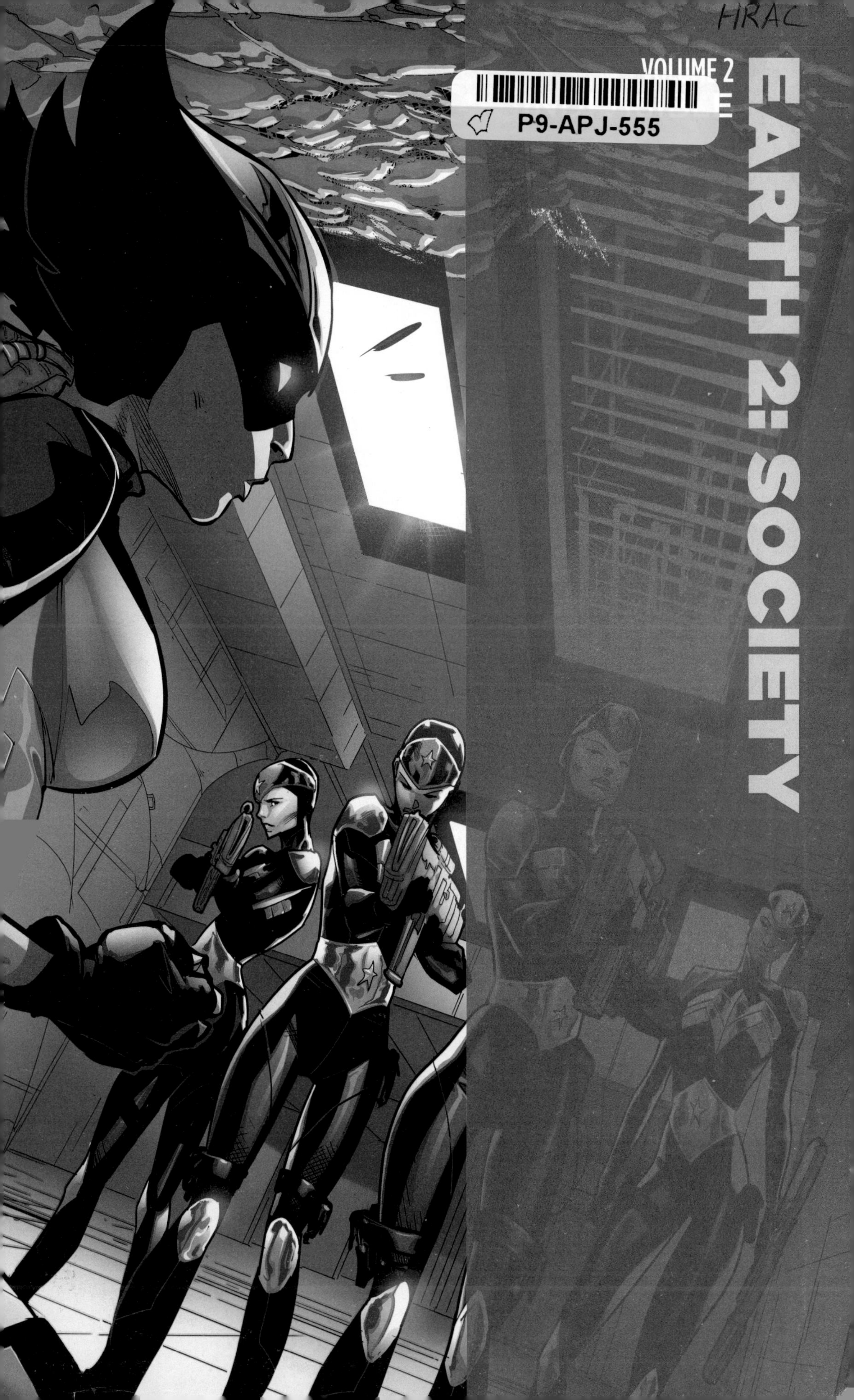
VOLUME 2
EARTH 2: SOCIETY

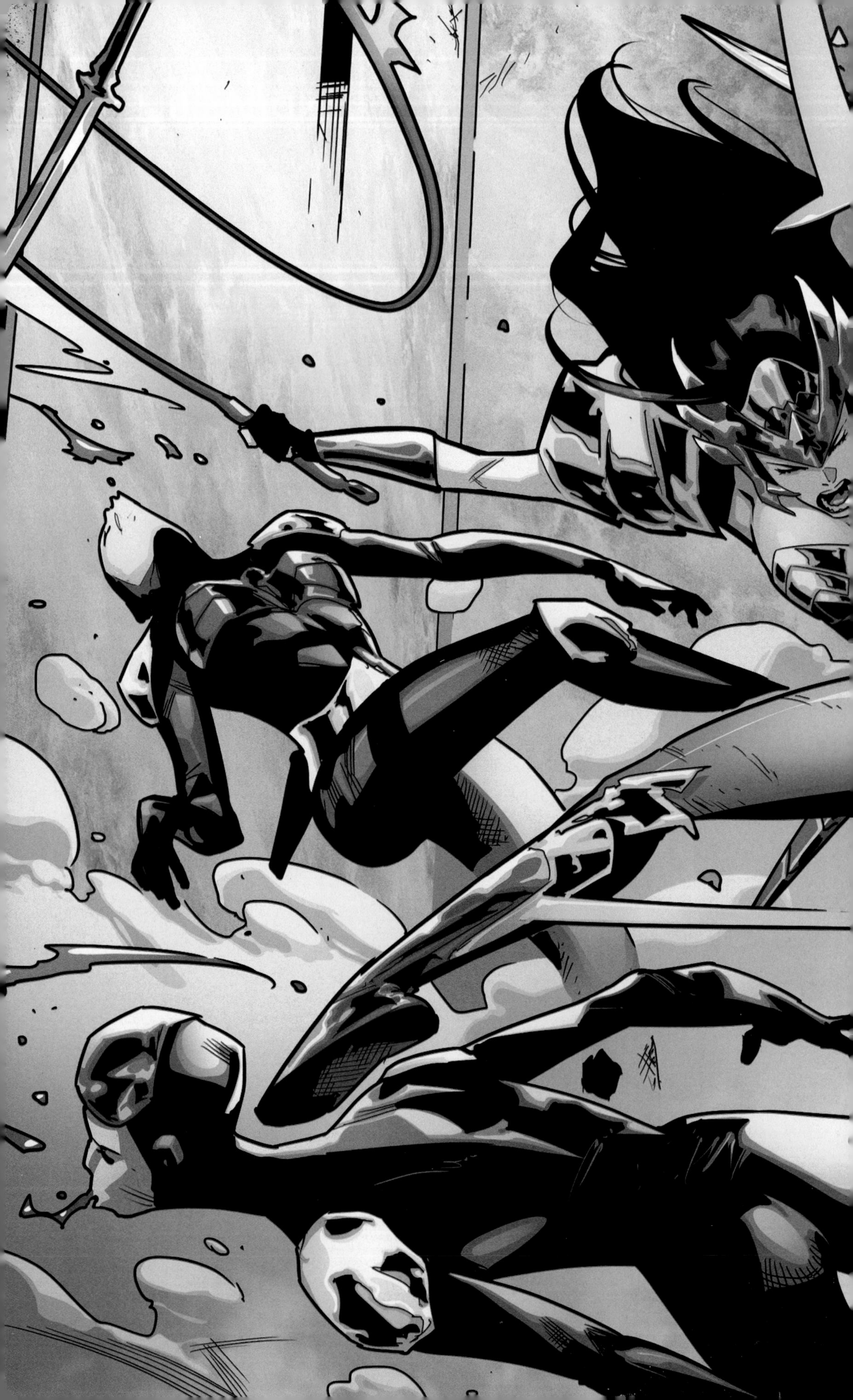

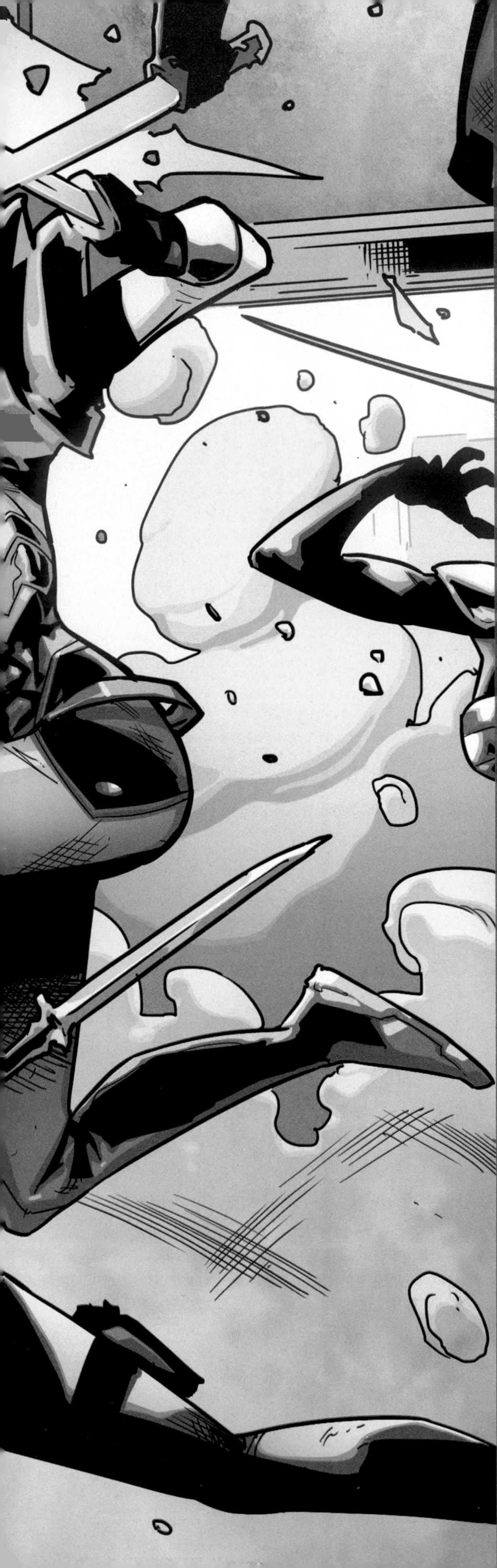

EARTH 2: SOCIETY

VOLUME 2
INDIVISIBLE

WRITTEN BY
DAN ABNETT

ART BY
JORGE JIMÉNEZ
FEDERICO DALLOCCHIO
IBAN COELLO

COLOR BY
ALEJANDRO SANCHEZ
DAVID CALDERON

LETTERS BY
TRAVIS LANHAM

COLLECTION COVER ART BY
JORGE JIMÉNEZ
& ALEJANDRO SANCHEZ

SUPERMAN CREATED BY
JERRY SIEGEL &
JOE SHUSTER
BY SPECIAL ARRANGEMENT
WITH THE JERRY SIEGEL FAMILY

MIKE COTTON JIM CHADWICK Editors – Original Series
PAUL KAMINSKI Associate Editor – Original Series
JEB WOODARD Group Editor – Collected Editions
LIZ ERICKSON Editor – Collected Edition
STEVE COOK Design Director – Books
DAMIAN RYLAND Publication Design

BOB HARRAS Senior VP – Editor-in-Chief, DC Comics

DIANE NELSON President
DAN DIDIO and JIM LEE Co-Publishers
GEOFF JOHNS Chief Creative Officer
AMIT DESAI Senior VP – Marketing & Global Franchise Management
NAIRI GARDINER Senior VP – Finance
SAM ADES VP – Digital Marketing
BOBBIE CHASE VP – Talent Development
MARK CHIARELLO Senior VP – Art, Design & Collected Editions
JOHN CUNNINGHAM VP – Content Strategy
ANNE DEPIES VP – Strategy Planning & Reporting
DON FALLETTI VP – Manufacturing Operations
LAWRENCE GANEM VP – Editorial Administration & Talent Relations
ALISON GILL Senior VP – Manufacturing & Operations
HANK KANALZ Senior VP – Editorial Strategy & Administration
JAY KOGAN VP – Legal Affairs
DEREK MADDALENA Senior VP – Sales & Business Development
JACK MAHAN VP – Business Affairs
DAN MIRON VP – Sales Planning & Trade Development
NICK NAPOLITANO VP – Manufacturing Administration
CAROL ROEDER VP – Marketing
EDDIE SCANNELL VP – Mass Account & Digital Sales
COURTNEY SIMMONS Senior VP – Publicity & Communications
JIM (SKI) SOKOLOWSKI VP – Comic Book Specialty & Newsstand Sales
SANDY YI Senior VP – Global Franchise Management

EARTH 2: SOCIETY VOLUME 2: INDIVISIBLE

Published by DC Comics. Compilation and all new material Copyright © 2016 DC Comics. All Rights Reserved.

Originally published in single magazine form in EARTH 2: SOCIETY 8-12 Copyright © 2016 DC Comics. All Rights Reserved. All characters, their distinctive likenesses and related elements featured in this publication are trademarks of DC Comics. The stories, characters and incidents featured in this publication are entirely fictional. DC Comics does not read or accept unsolicited ideas, stories or artwork.

DC Comics, 2900 West Alameda Ave., Burbank, CA 91505
Printed by RR Donnelley, Owensville, MO, USA. 7/22/16. First Printing.
ISBN: 978-1-4012-6471-0

Library of Congress Cataloging-in-Publication Data is available.

PEFC Certified

Printed on paper from
sustainably managed
forests and controlled
sources

PEFC/29-31-75   www.pefc.org

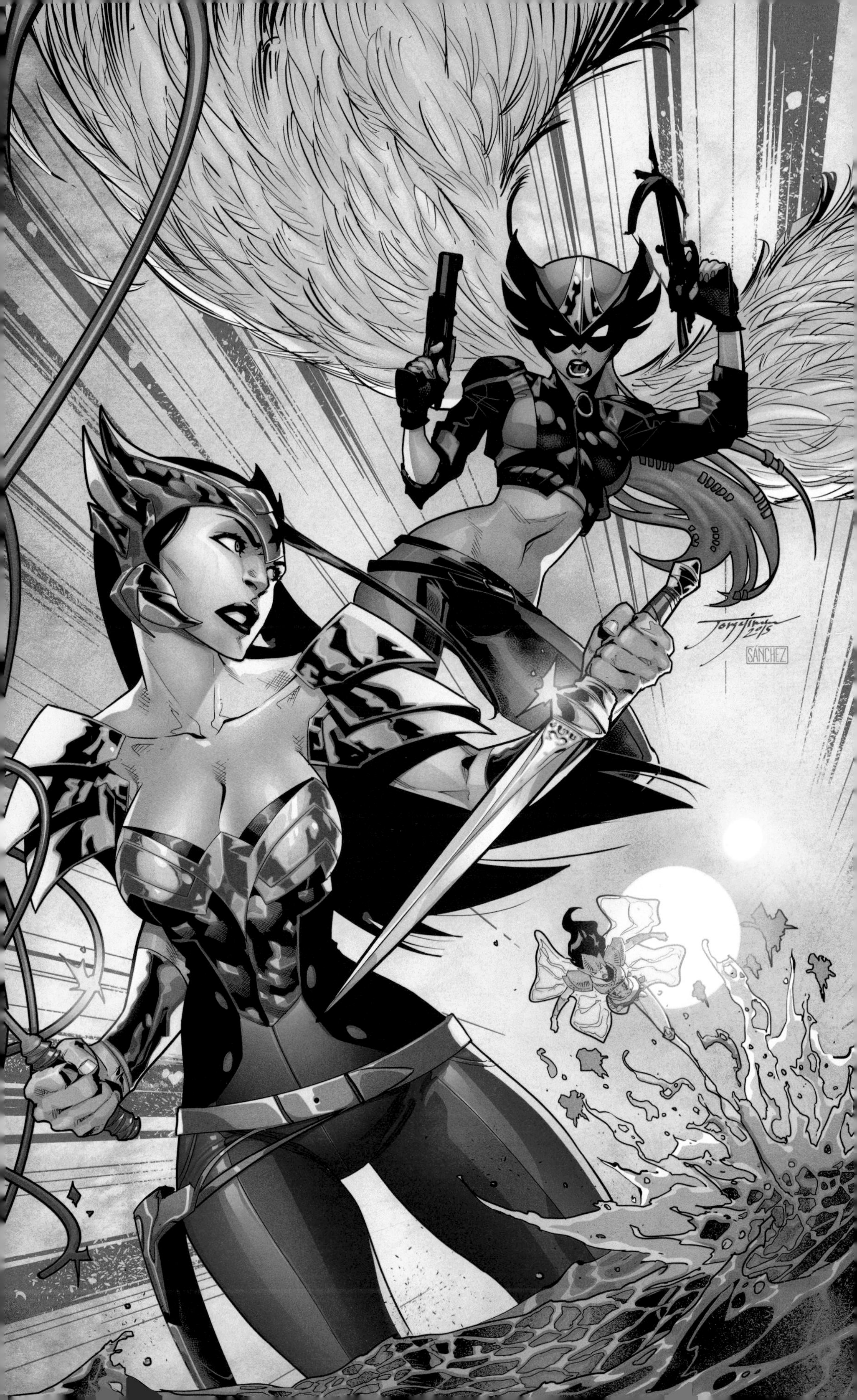
SANCHEZ

ONE NATION, INDIVISIBLE CHAPTER ONE: POWER STRUGGLES

DAN ABNETT writer JORGE JIMÉNEZ artist ALEJANDRO SANCHEZ colorist TRAVIS LANHAM letterer cover by JIMÉNEZ & SANCHEZ

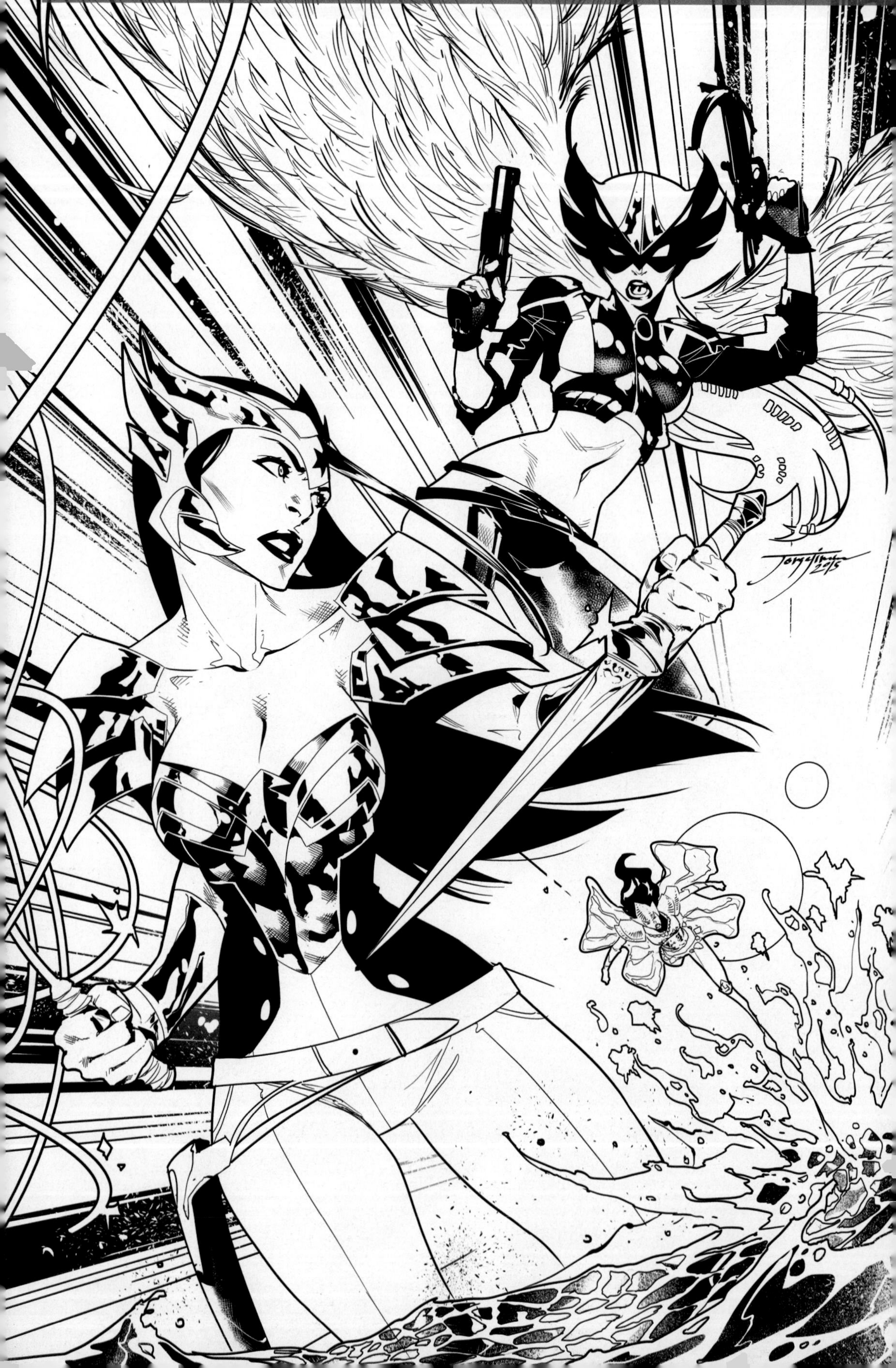

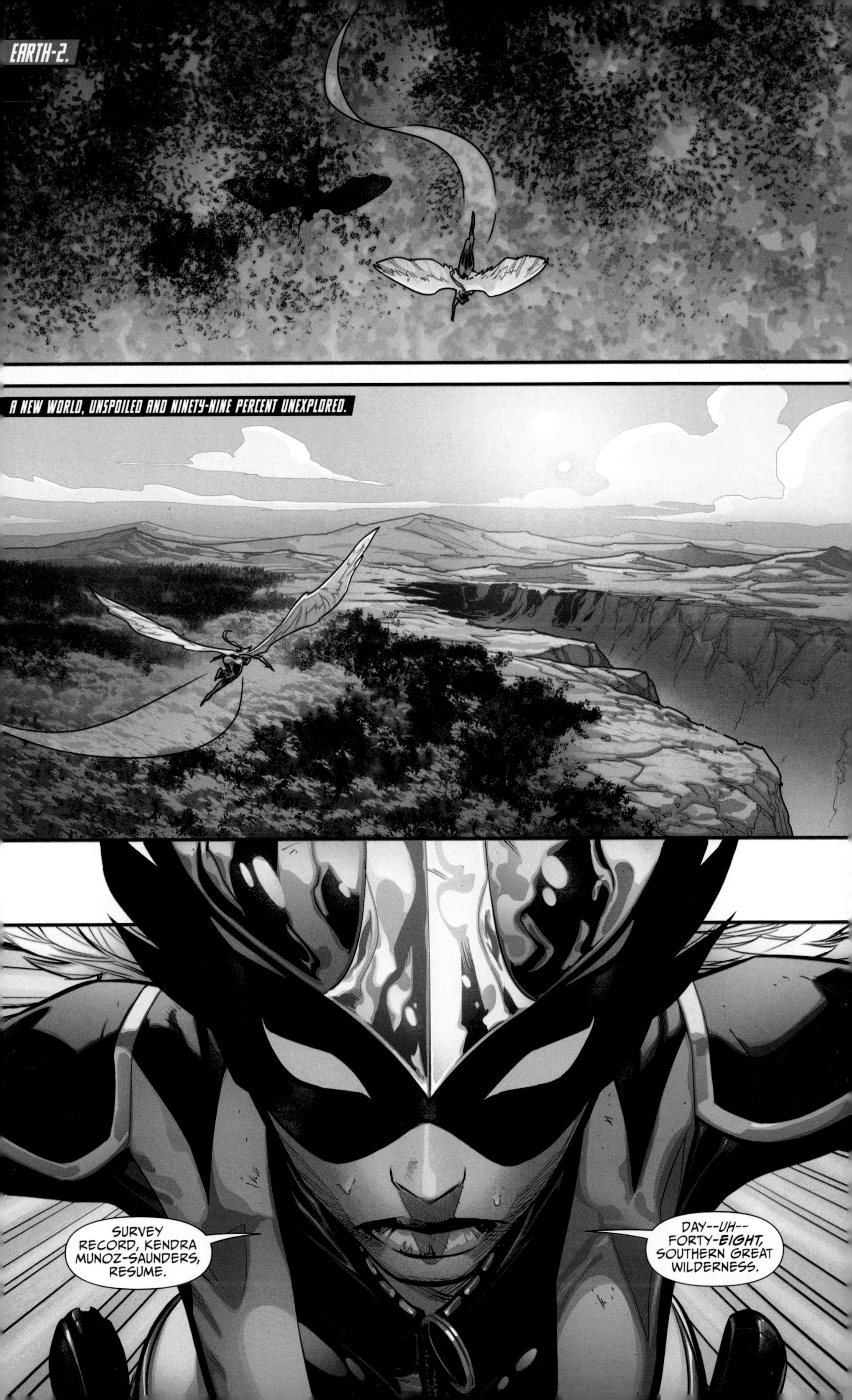
EARTH-2.
A NEW WORLD, UNSPOILED AND NINETY-NINE PERCENT UNEXPLORED.
SURVEY RECORD, KENDRA MUNOZ-SAUNDERS, RESUME.
DAY--UH--FORTY-EIGHT, SOUTHERN GREAT WILDERNESS.

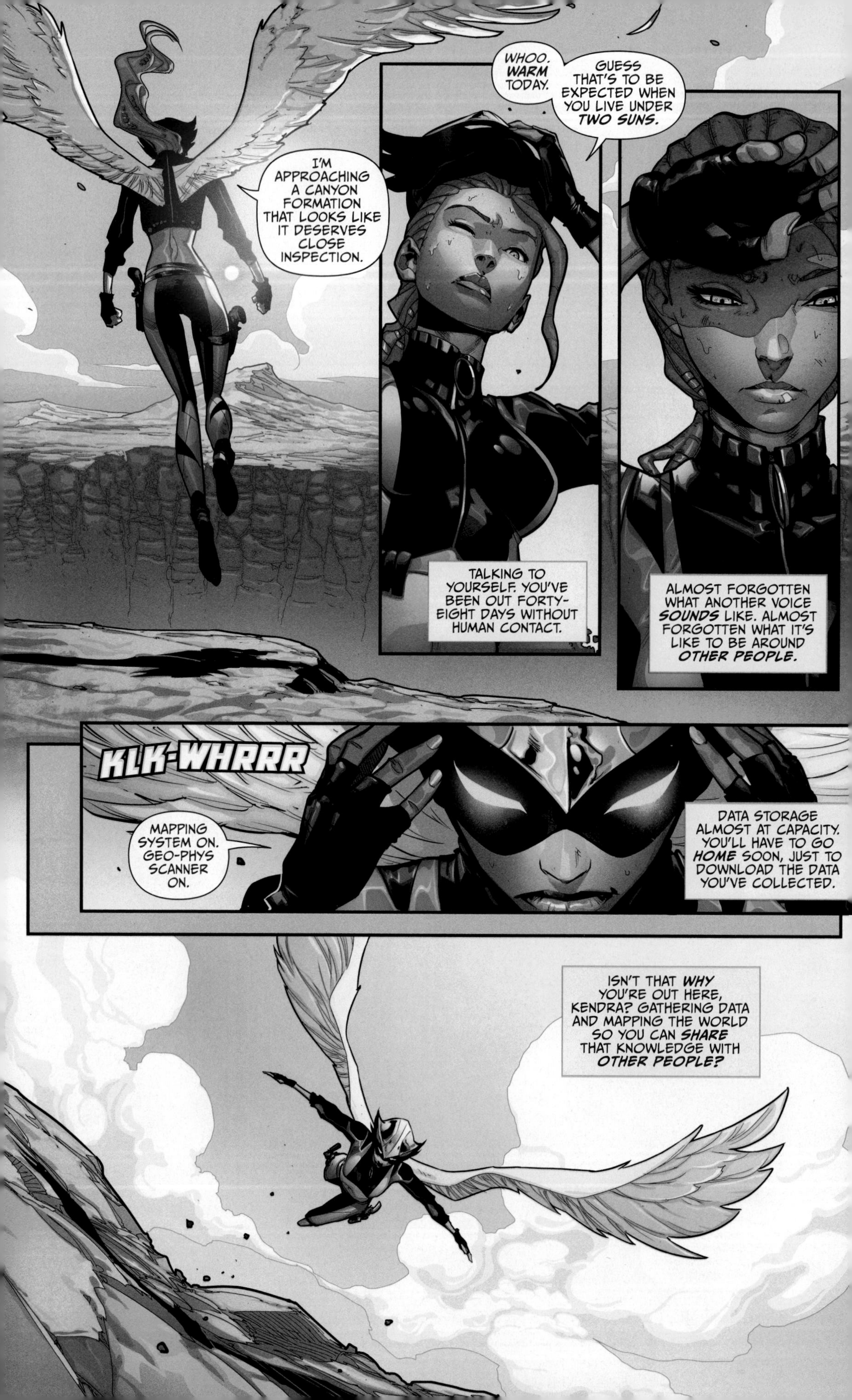
I'M APPROACHING A CANYON FORMATION THAT LOOKS LIKE IT DESERVES CLOSE INSPECTION.
WHOO. WARM TODAY.
GUESS THAT'S TO BE EXPECTED WHEN YOU LIVE UNDER TWO SUNS.
TALKING TO YOURSELF. YOU'VE BEEN OUT FORTY-EIGHT DAYS WITHOUT HUMAN CONTACT.
ALMOST FORGOTTEN WHAT ANOTHER VOICE SOUNDS LIKE. ALMOST FORGOTTEN WHAT IT'S LIKE TO BE AROUND OTHER PEOPLE.
KLK-WHRRR
MAPPING SYSTEM ON. GEO-PHYS SCANNER ON.
DATA STORAGE ALMOST AT CAPACITY. YOU'LL HAVE TO GO HOME SOON, JUST TO DOWNLOAD THE DATA YOU'VE COLLECTED.
ISN'T THAT WHY YOU'RE OUT HERE, KENDRA? GATHERING DATA AND MAPPING THE WORLD SO YOU CAN SHARE THAT KNOWLEDGE WITH OTHER PEOPLE?

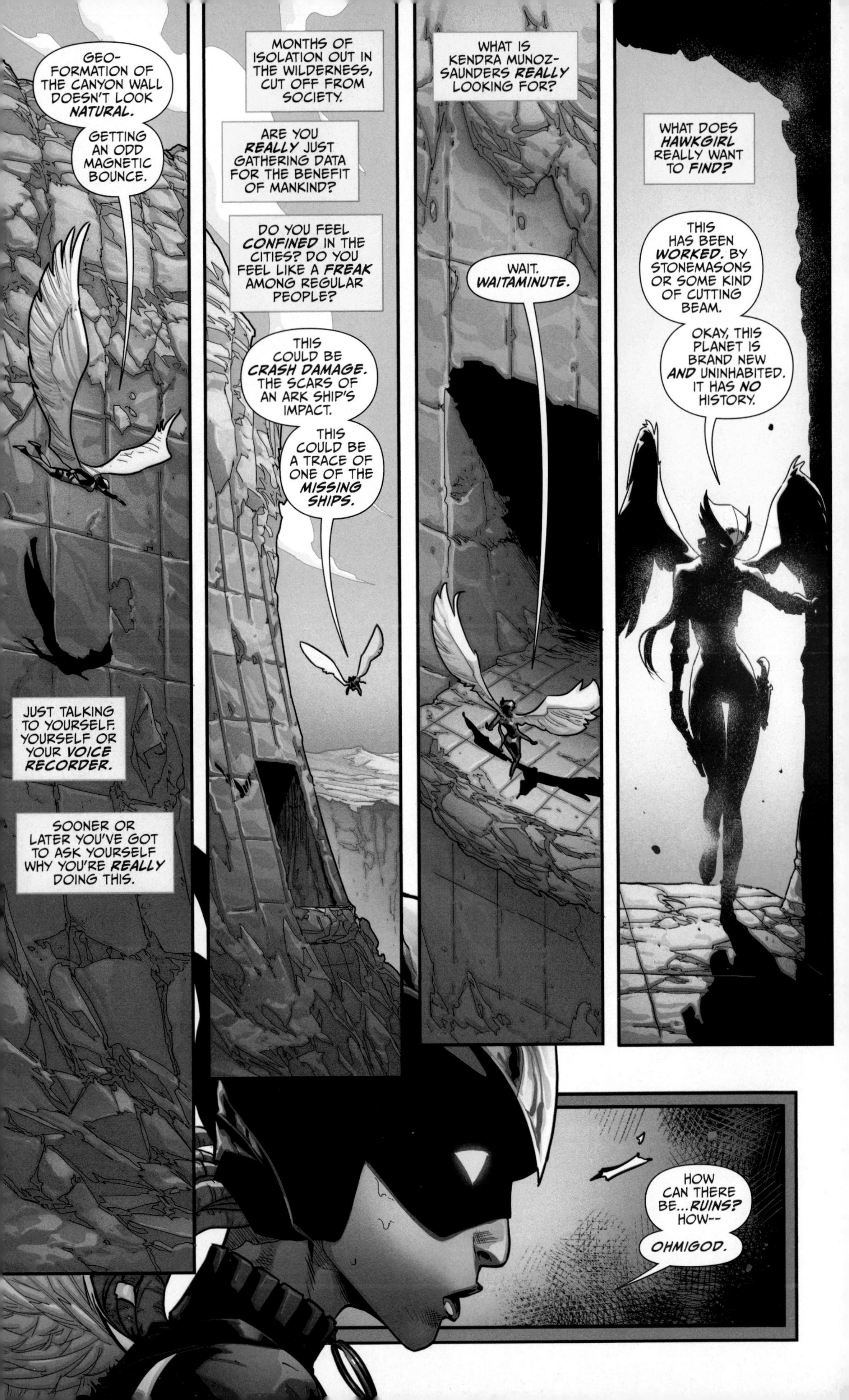
GEO-FORMATION OF THE CANYON WALL DOESN'T LOOK NATURAL.
GETTING AN ODD MAGNETIC BOUNCE.
JUST TALKING TO YOURSELF. YOURSELF OR YOUR VOICE RECORDER.
SOONER OR LATER YOU'VE GOT TO ASK YOURSELF WHY YOU'RE REALLY DOING THIS.
MONTHS OF ISOLATION OUT IN THE WILDERNESS, CUT OFF FROM SOCIETY.
ARE YOU REALLY JUST GATHERING DATA FOR THE BENEFIT OF MANKIND?
DO YOU FEEL CONFINED IN THE CITIES? DO YOU FEEL LIKE A FREAK AMONG REGULAR PEOPLE?
THIS COULD BE CRASH DAMAGE. THE SCARS OF AN ARK SHIP'S IMPACT.
THIS COULD BE A TRACE OF ONE OF THE MISSING SHIPS.
WHAT IS KENDRA MUNOZ-SAUNDERS REALLY LOOKING FOR?
WAIT. WAITAMINUTE.
WHAT DOES HAWKGIRL REALLY WANT TO FIND?
THIS HAS BEEN WORKED. BY STONEMASONS OR SOME KIND OF CUTTING BEAM.
OKAY, THIS PLANET IS BRAND NEW AND UNINHABITED. IT HAS NO HISTORY.
HOW CAN THERE BE...RUINS? HOW--
OHMIGOD.

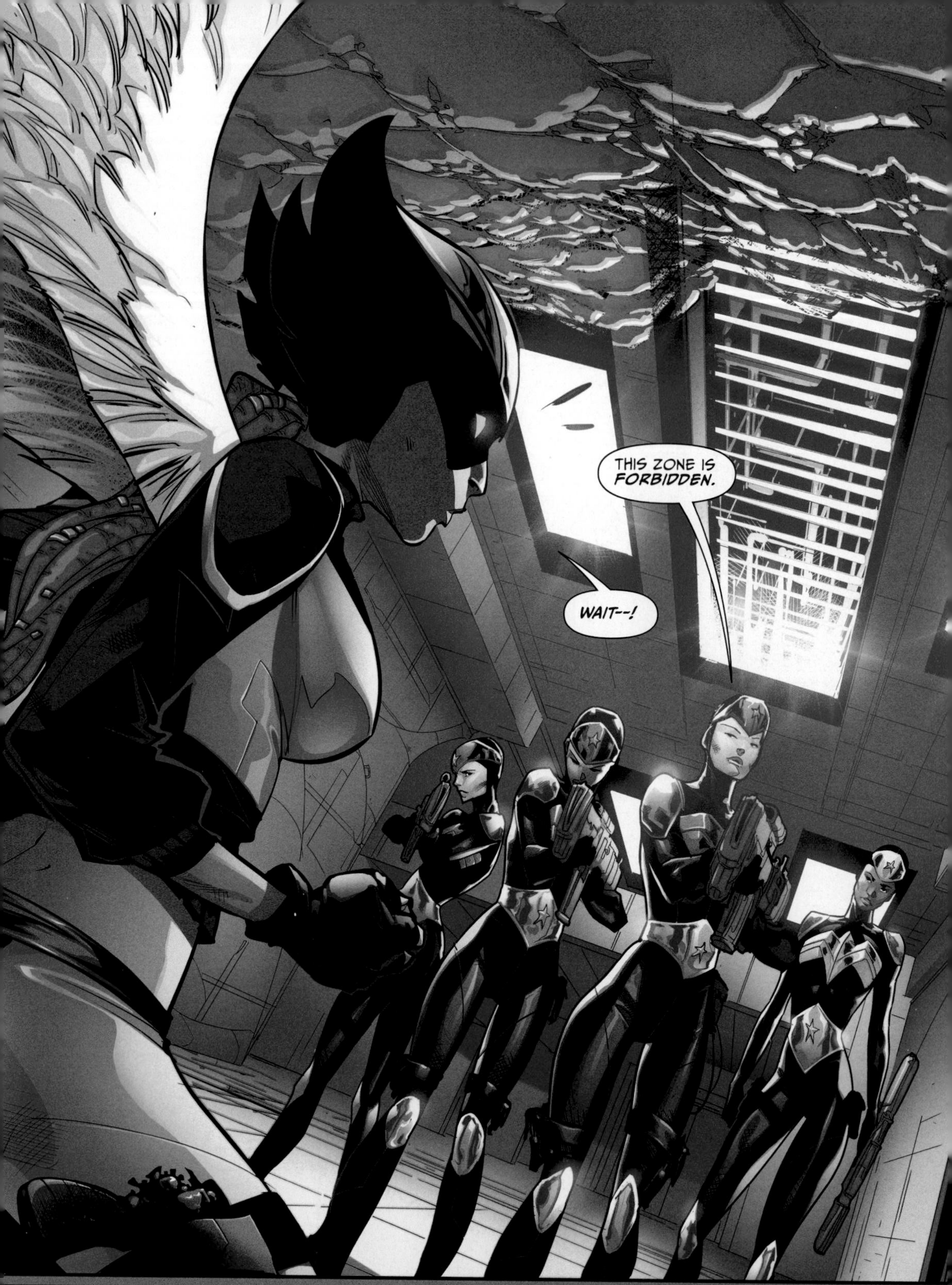
THIS ZONE IS FORBIDDEN.
WAIT--!

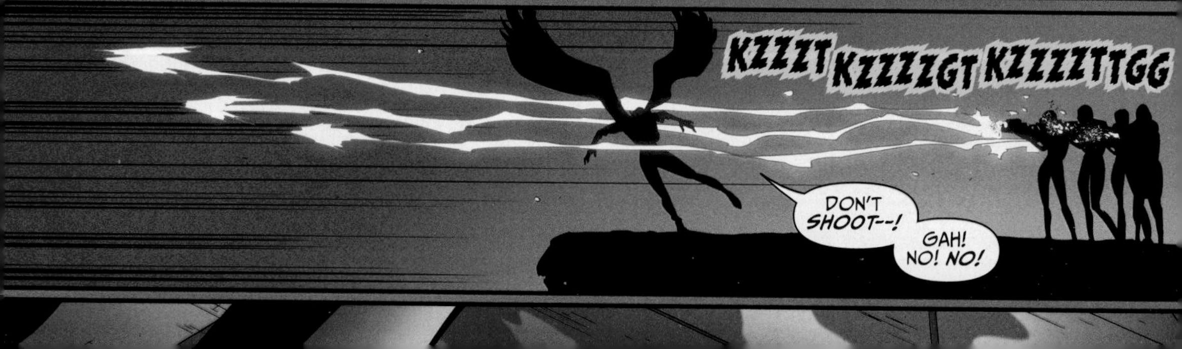
KZZZT KZZZZGT KZZZZTTGG
DON'T SHOOT--!
GAH! NO! NO!

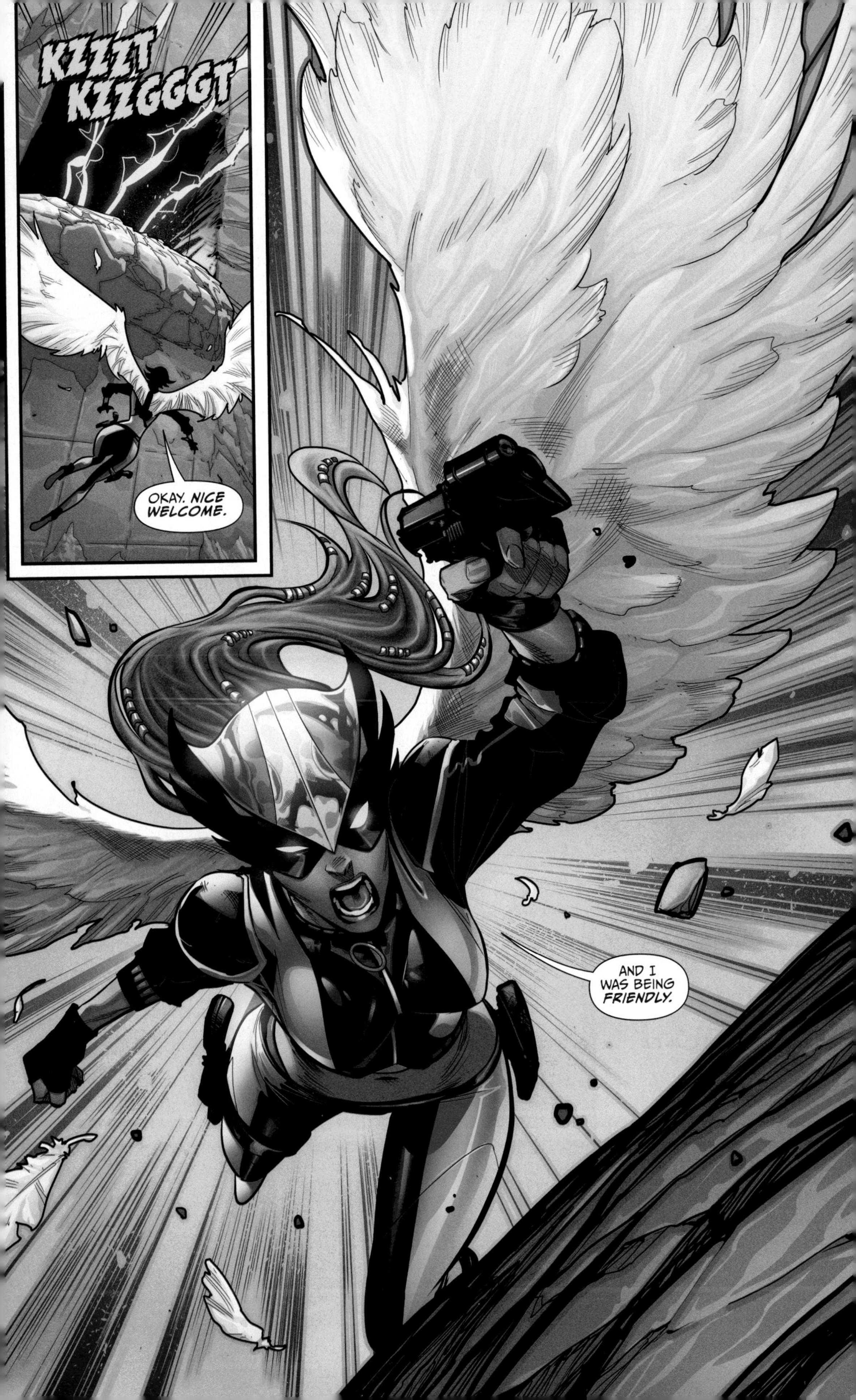
KZZZT KZZGGGT
OKAY. NICE WELCOME.
AND I WAS BEING FRIENDLY.

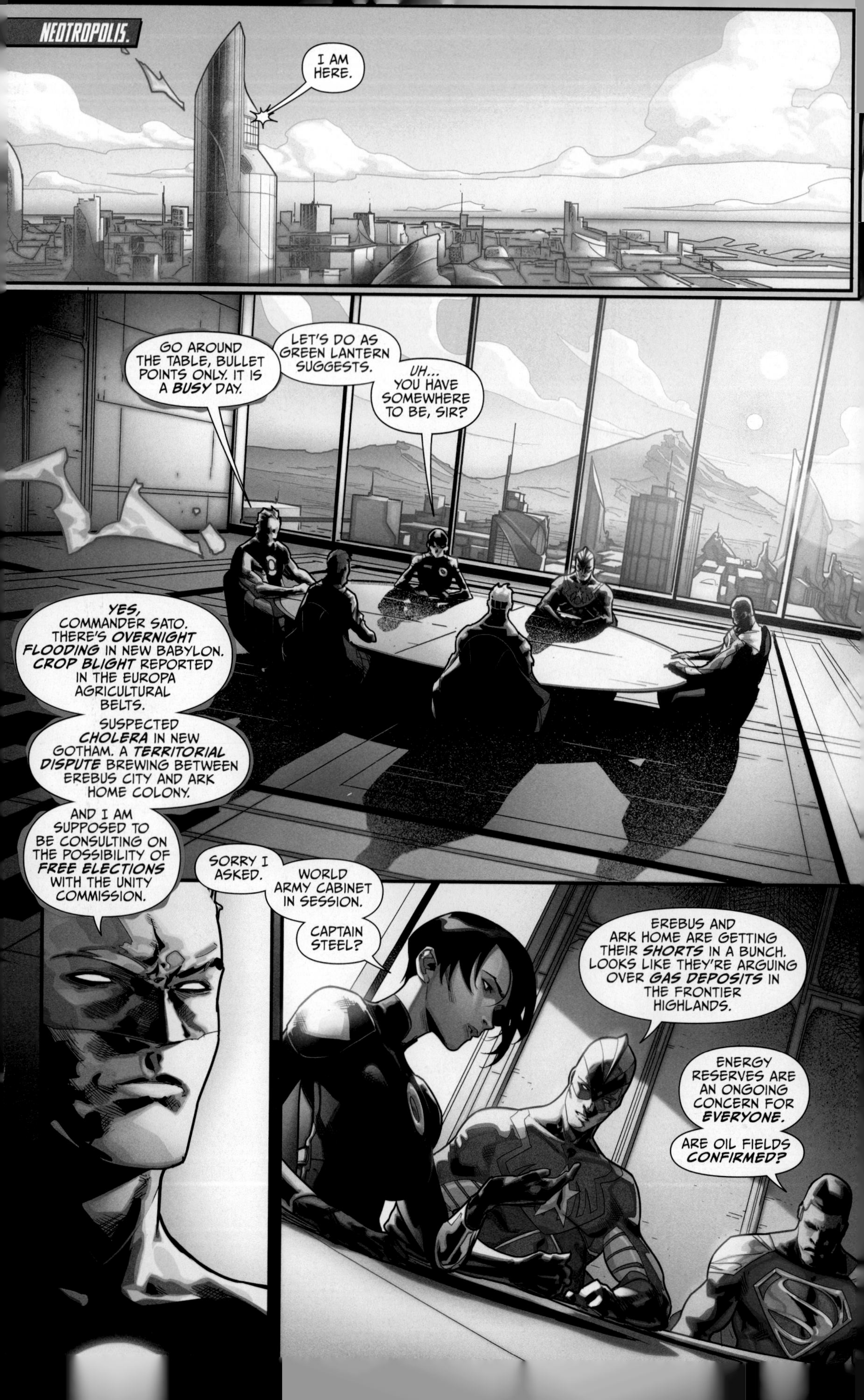
NEOTROPOLIS.
I AM HERE.
GO AROUND THE TABLE, BULLET POINTS ONLY. IT IS A BUSY DAY.
LET'S DO AS GREEN LANTERN SUGGESTS.
UH... YOU HAVE SOMEWHERE TO BE, SIR?
YES, COMMANDER SATO. THERE'S OVERNIGHT FLOODING IN NEW BABYLON. CROP BLIGHT REPORTED IN THE EUROPA AGRICULTURAL BELTS.
SUSPECTED CHOLERA IN NEW GOTHAM. A TERRITORIAL DISPUTE BREWING BETWEEN EREBUS CITY AND ARK HOME COLONY.
AND I AM SUPPOSED TO BE CONSULTING ON THE POSSIBILITY OF FREE ELECTIONS WITH THE UNITY COMMISSION.
SORRY I ASKED.
WORLD ARMY CABINET IN SESSION.
CAPTAIN STEEL?
EREBUS AND ARK HOME ARE GETTING THEIR SHORTS IN A BUNCH. LOOKS LIKE THEY'RE ARGUING OVER GAS DEPOSITS IN THE FRONTIER HIGHLANDS.
ENERGY RESERVES ARE AN ONGOING CONCERN FOR EVERYONE.
ARE OIL FIELDS CONFIRMED?

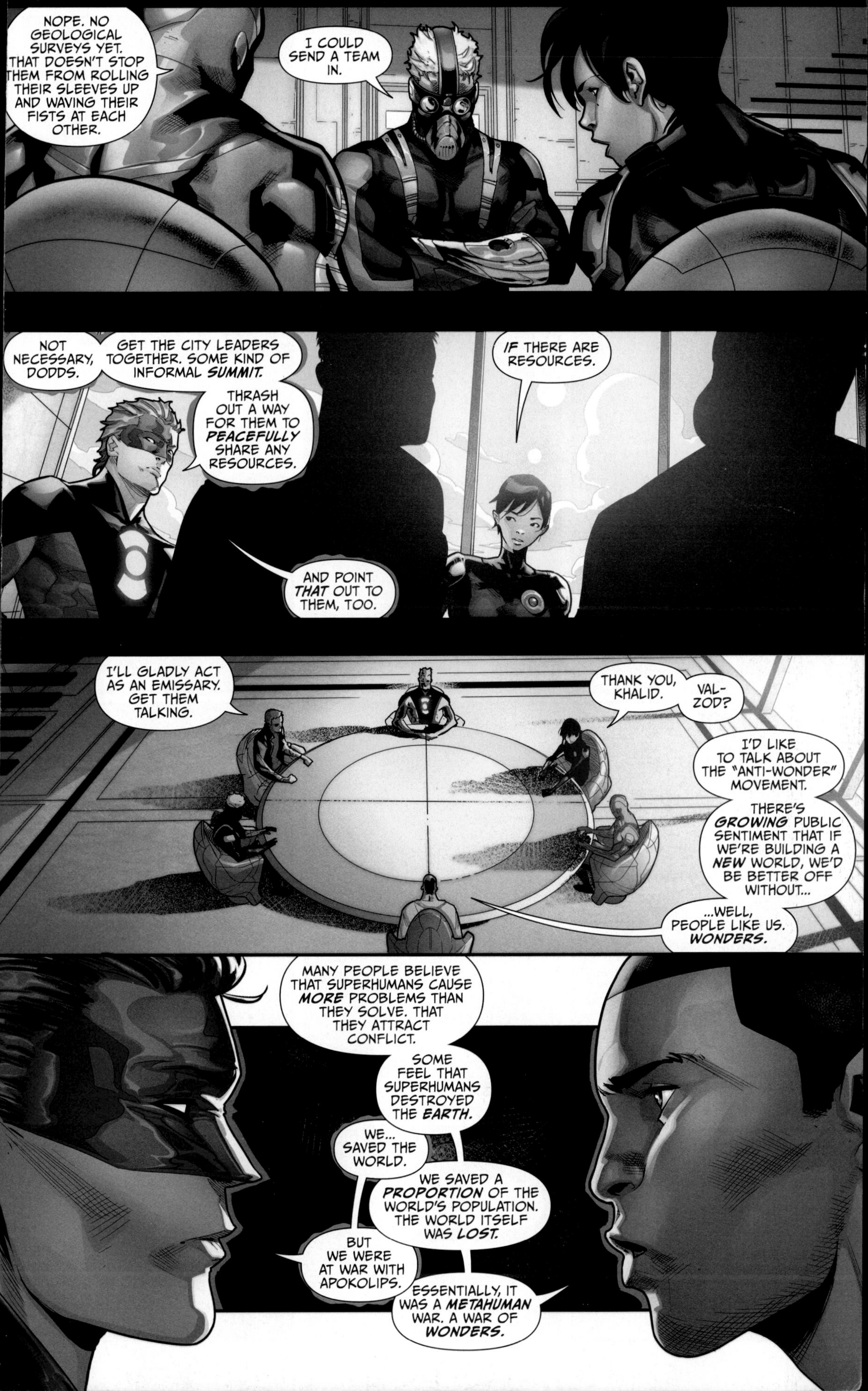
NOPE. NO GEOLOGICAL SURVEYS YET. THAT DOESN'T STOP THEM FROM ROLLING THEIR SLEEVES UP AND WAVING THEIR FISTS AT EACH OTHER.
I COULD SEND A TEAM IN.
NOT NECESSARY, DODDS.
GET THE CITY LEADERS TOGETHER. SOME KIND OF INFORMAL *SUMMIT.*
THRASH OUT A WAY FOR THEM TO *PEACEFULLY* SHARE ANY RESOURCES.
IF THERE ARE RESOURCES.
AND POINT *THAT* OUT TO THEM, TOO.
I'LL GLADLY ACT AS AN EMISSARY. GET THEM TALKING.
THANK YOU, KHALID.
VAL-ZOD?
I'D LIKE TO TALK ABOUT THE "ANTI-WONDER" MOVEMENT.
THERE'S *GROWING* PUBLIC SENTIMENT THAT IF WE'RE BUILDING A *NEW* WORLD, WE'D BE BETTER OFF WITHOUT...
...WELL, PEOPLE LIKE US. *WONDERS.*
MANY PEOPLE BELIEVE THAT SUPERHUMANS CAUSE *MORE* PROBLEMS THAN THEY SOLVE. THAT THEY ATTRACT CONFLICT.
SOME FEEL THAT SUPERHUMANS DESTROYED THE *EARTH.*
WE... SAVED THE WORLD.
WE SAVED A *PROPORTION* OF THE WORLD'S POPULATION. THE WORLD ITSELF WAS *LOST.*
BUT WE WERE AT WAR WITH APOKOLIPS.
ESSENTIALLY, IT WAS A *METAHUMAN* WAR. A WAR OF *WONDERS.*

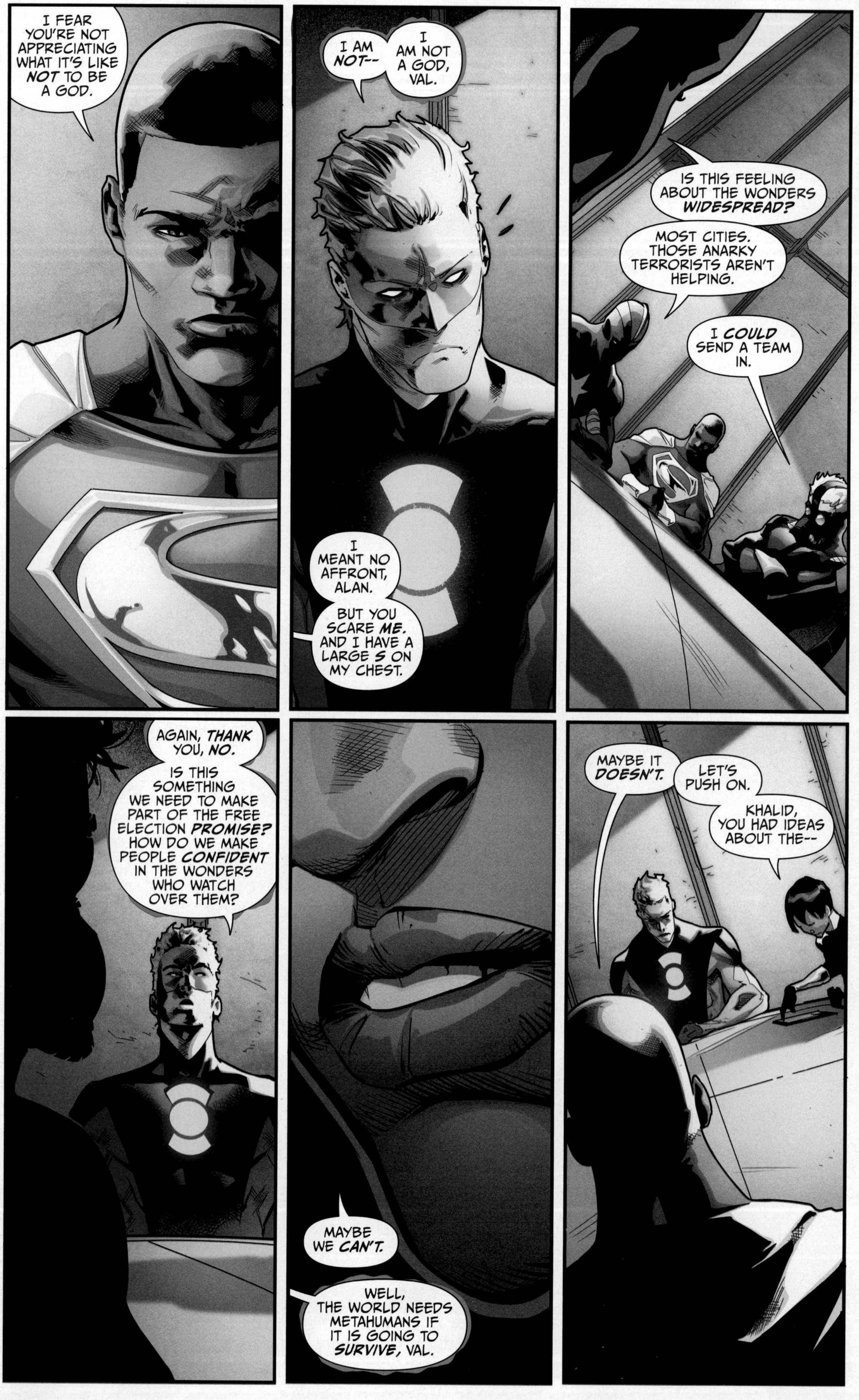
I FEAR YOU'RE NOT APPRECIATING WHAT IT'S LIKE NOT TO BE A GOD.
I AM NOT--
I AM NOT A GOD, VAL.
I MEANT NO AFFRONT, ALAN.
BUT YOU SCARE ME. AND I HAVE A LARGE S ON MY CHEST.
IS THIS FEELING ABOUT THE WONDERS WIDESPREAD?
MOST CITIES. THOSE ANARKY TERRORISTS AREN'T HELPING.
I COULD SEND A TEAM IN.
AGAIN, THANK YOU, NO.
IS THIS SOMETHING WE NEED TO MAKE PART OF THE FREE ELECTION PROMISE? HOW DO WE MAKE PEOPLE CONFIDENT IN THE WONDERS WHO WATCH OVER THEM?
MAYBE WE CAN'T.
WELL, THE WORLD NEEDS METAHUMANS IF IT IS GOING TO SURVIVE, VAL.
MAYBE IT DOESN'T.
LET'S PUSH ON.
KHALID, YOU HAD IDEAS ABOUT THE--

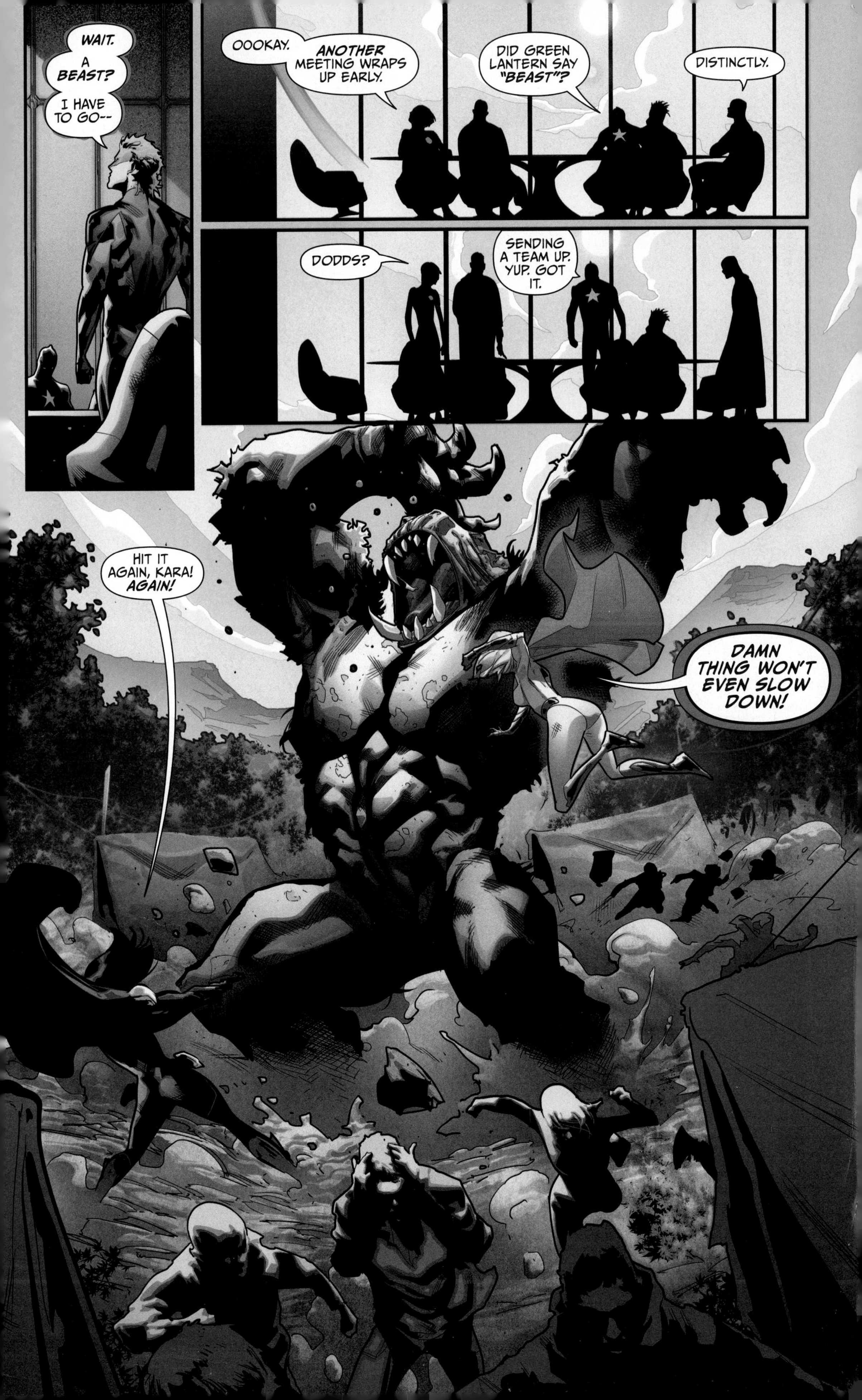
WAIT. A BEAST?
I HAVE TO GO--
OOOKAY.
ANOTHER MEETING WRAPS UP EARLY.
DID GREEN LANTERN SAY "BEAST"?
DISTINCTLY.
DODDS?
SENDING A TEAM UP. YUP. GOT IT.
HIT IT AGAIN, KARA! AGAIN!
DAMN THING WON'T EVEN SLOW DOWN!

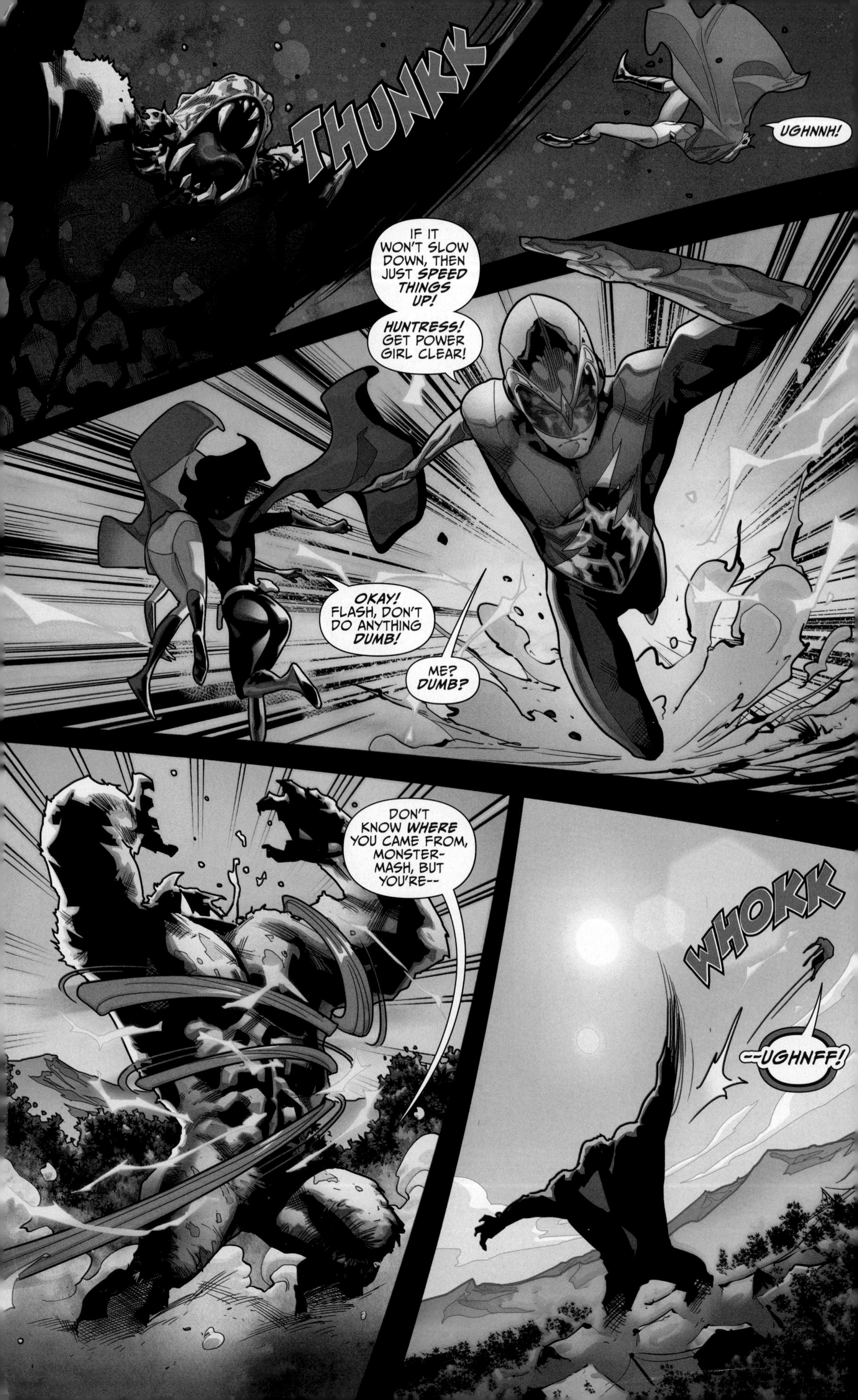
THUNKK
UGHNNH!
IF IT WON'T SLOW DOWN, THEN JUST SPEED THINGS UP!
HUNTRESS! GET POWER GIRL CLEAR!
OKAY! FLASH, DON'T DO ANYTHING DUMB!
ME? DUMB?
DON'T KNOW WHERE YOU CAME FROM, MONSTER-MASH, BUT YOU'RE--
WHOKK
--UGHNFF!

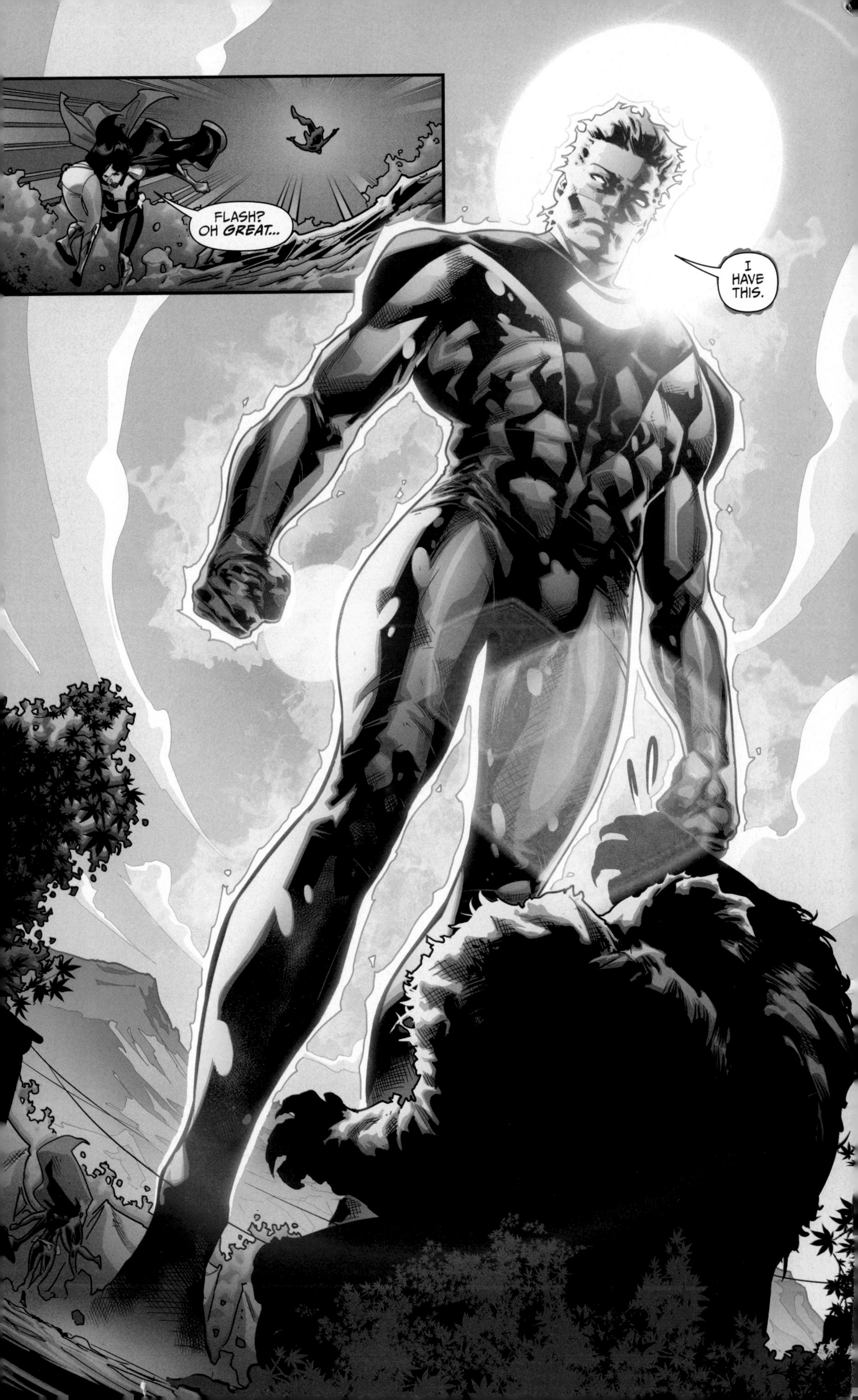
FLASH?
OH GREAT...
I HAVE THIS.

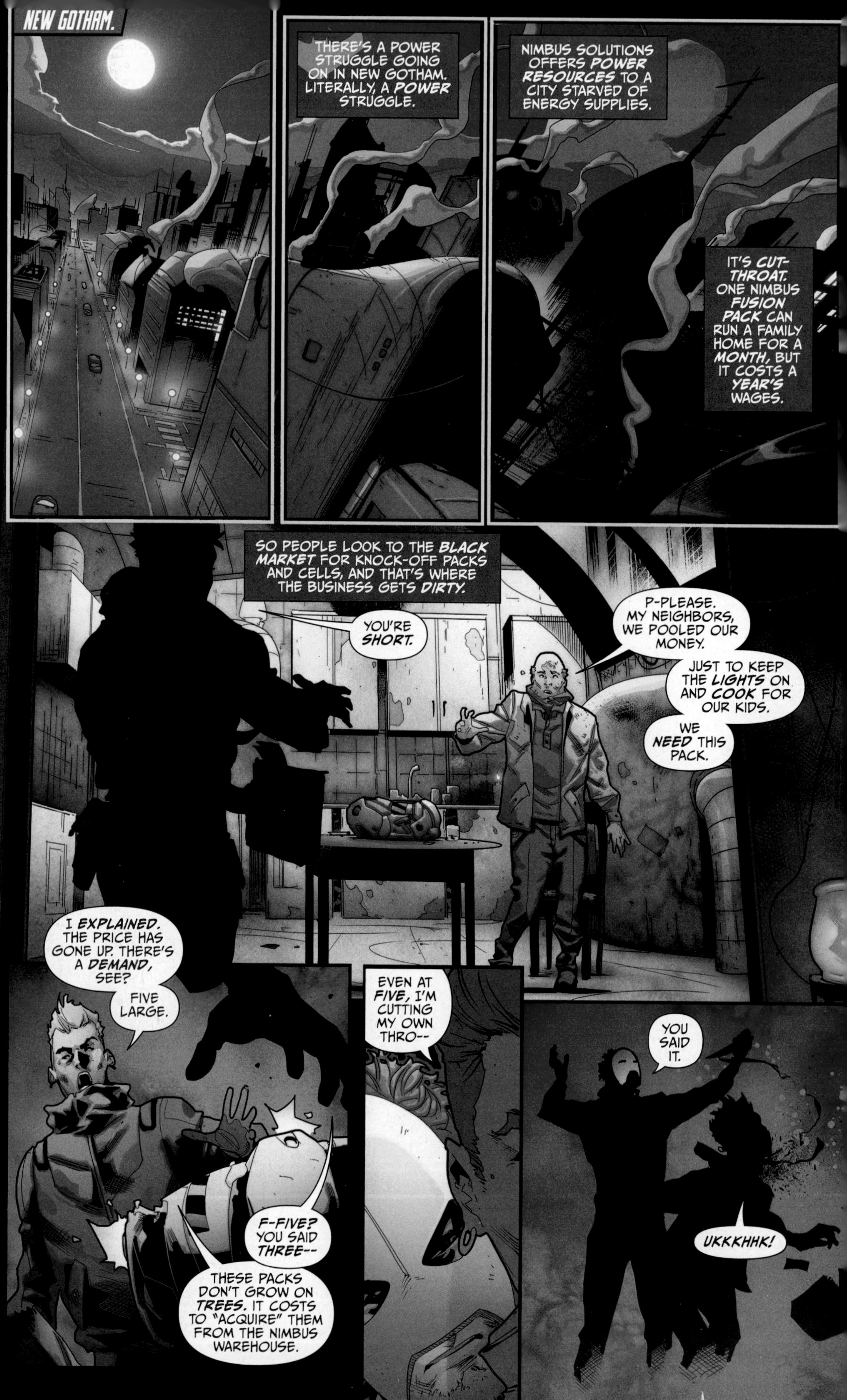

NEW GOTHAM.
THERE'S A POWER STRUGGLE GOING ON IN NEW GOTHAM. LITERALLY, A POWER STRUGGLE.
NIMBUS SOLUTIONS OFFERS POWER RESOURCES TO A CITY STARVED OF ENERGY SUPPLIES.
IT'S CUT-THROAT. ONE NIMBUS FUSION PACK CAN RUN A FAMILY HOME FOR A MONTH, BUT IT COSTS A YEAR'S WAGES.
SO PEOPLE LOOK TO THE BLACK MARKET FOR KNOCK-OFF PACKS AND CELLS, AND THAT'S WHERE THE BUSINESS GETS DIRTY.
YOU'RE SHORT.
P-PLEASE. MY NEIGHBORS, WE POOLED OUR MONEY.
JUST TO KEEP THE LIGHTS ON AND COOK FOR OUR KIDS.
WE NEED THIS PACK.
I EXPLAINED. THE PRICE HAS GONE UP. THERE'S A DEMAND, SEE?
FIVE LARGE.
F-FIVE? YOU SAID THREE--
THESE PACKS DON'T GROW ON TREES. IT COSTS TO "ACQUIRE" THEM FROM THE NIMBUS WAREHOUSE.
EVEN AT FIVE, I'M CUTTING MY OWN THRO--
YOU SAID IT.
UKKKHHK!

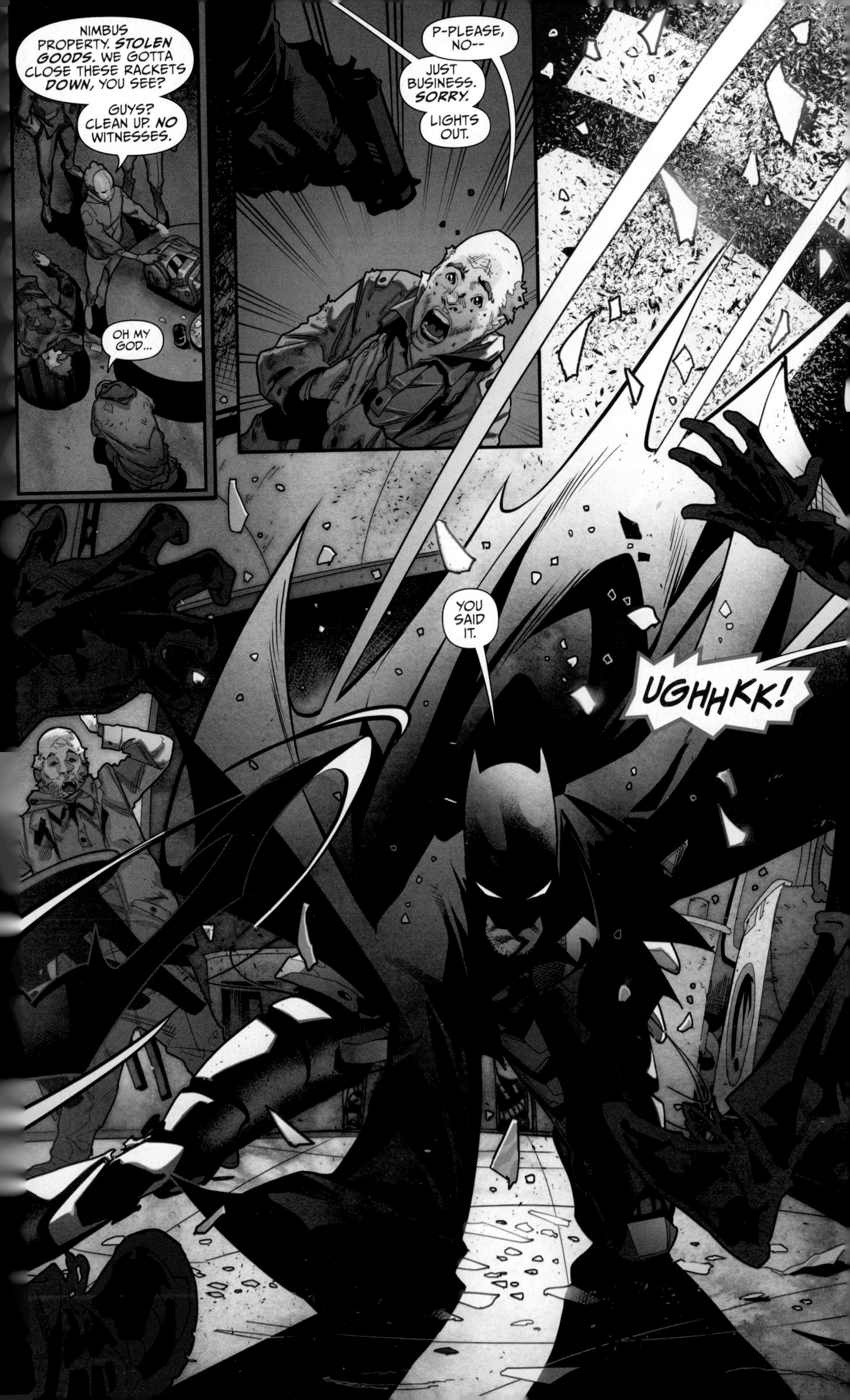
NIMBUS PROPERTY. STOLEN GOODS. WE GOTTA CLOSE THESE RACKETS DOWN, YOU SEE?
GUYS? CLEAN UP. NO WITNESSES.
OH MY GOD...
P-PLEASE, NO--
JUST BUSINESS. SORRY.
LIGHTS OUT.
YOU SAID IT.
UGHHKK!

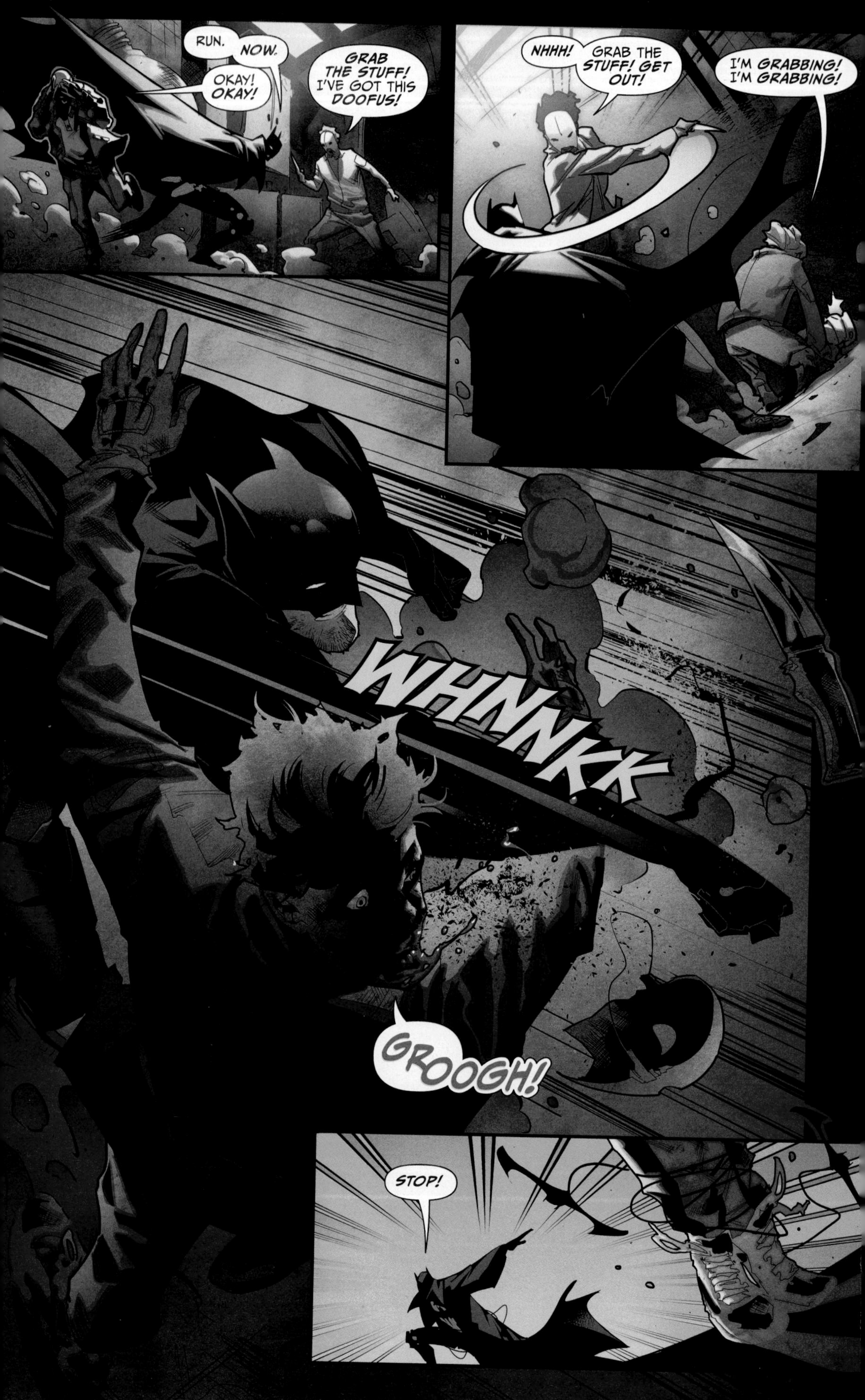
RUN.
NOW.
OKAY! OKAY!
GRAB THE STUFF! I'VE GOT THIS DOOFUS!
NHHH!
GRAB THE STUFF! GET OUT!
I'M GRABBING! I'M GRABBING!
WHNNKK
GROOGH!
STOP!

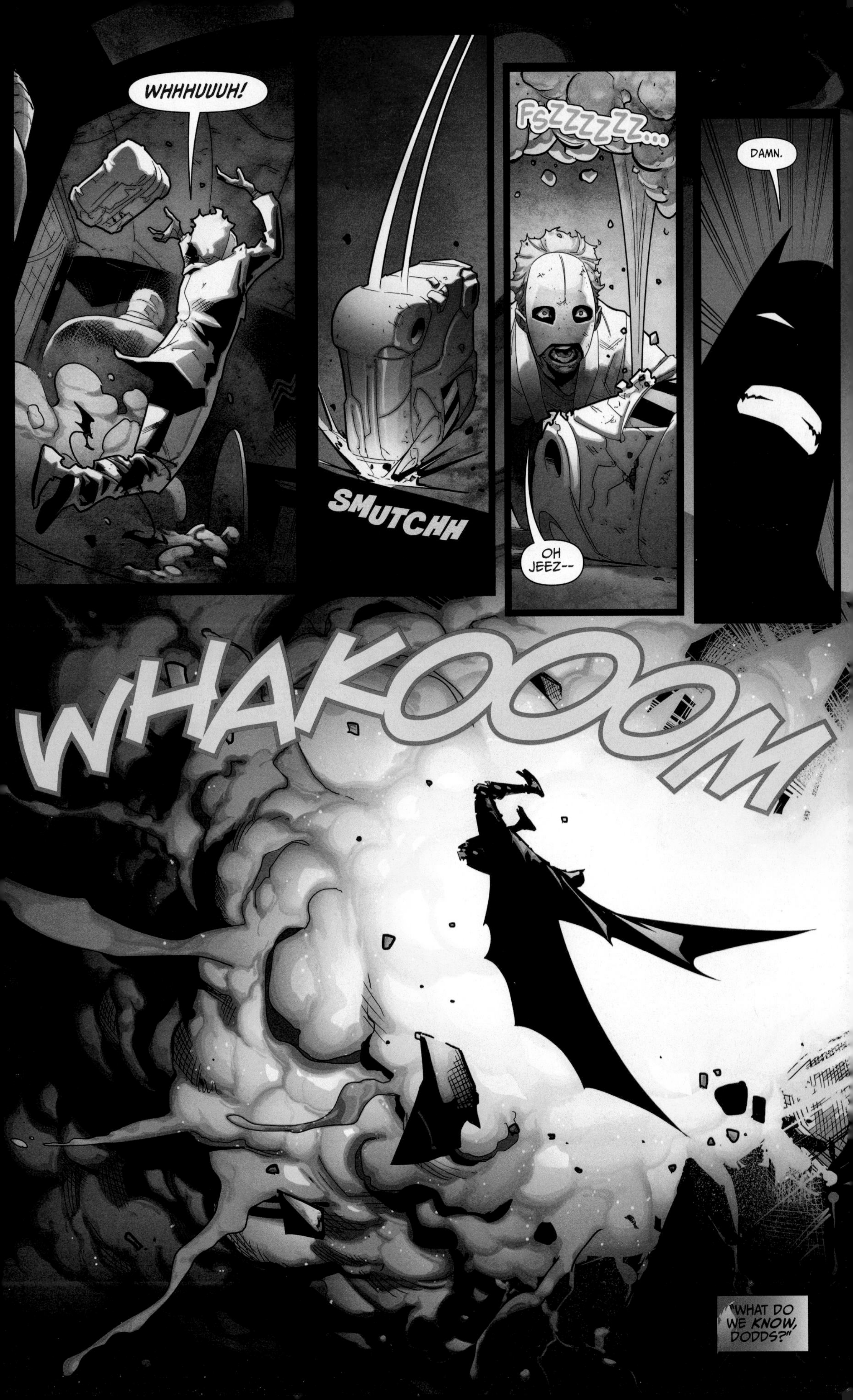
WHHHUUUH!
SMUTCHH
FSZZZZZZ...
OH JEEZ--
DAMN.
WHAKOOOM
"WHAT DO WE KNOW, DODDS?"

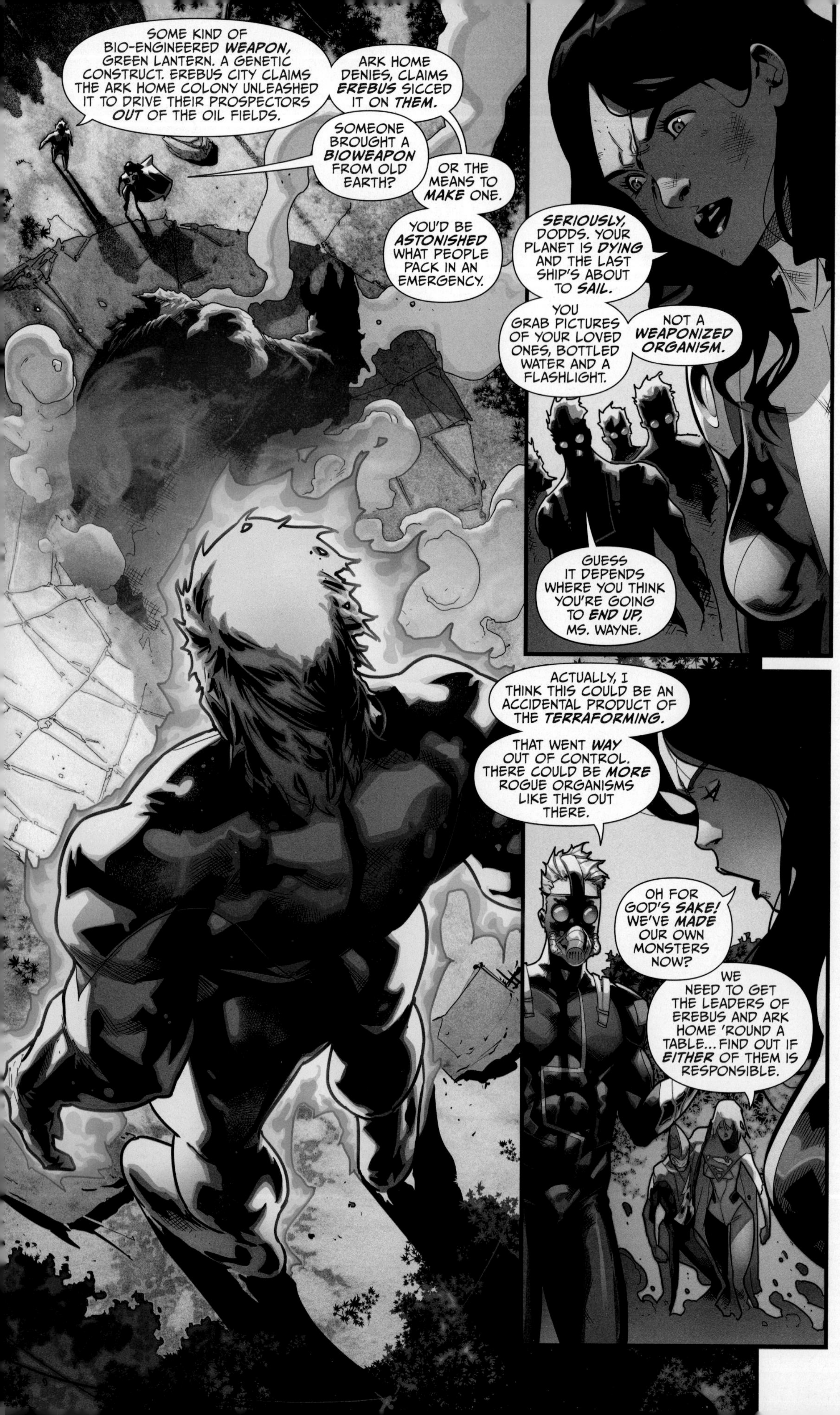
SOME KIND OF BIO-ENGINEERED WEAPON, GREEN LANTERN. A GENETIC CONSTRUCT. EREBUS CITY CLAIMS THE ARK HOME COLONY UNLEASHED IT TO DRIVE THEIR PROSPECTORS OUT OF THE OIL FIELDS.
ARK HOME DENIES, CLAIMS EREBUS SICCED IT ON THEM.
SOMEONE BROUGHT A BIOWEAPON FROM OLD EARTH?
OR THE MEANS TO MAKE ONE.
YOU'D BE ASTONISHED WHAT PEOPLE PACK IN AN EMERGENCY.
SERIOUSLY, DODDS. YOUR PLANET IS DYING AND THE LAST SHIP'S ABOUT TO SAIL.
YOU GRAB PICTURES OF YOUR LOVED ONES, BOTTLED WATER AND A FLASHLIGHT.
NOT A WEAPONIZED ORGANISM.
GUESS IT DEPENDS WHERE YOU THINK YOU'RE GOING TO END UP, MS. WAYNE.
ACTUALLY, I THINK THIS COULD BE AN ACCIDENTAL PRODUCT OF THE TERRAFORMING.
THAT WENT WAY OUT OF CONTROL. THERE COULD BE MORE ROGUE ORGANISMS LIKE THIS OUT THERE.
OH FOR GOD'S SAKE! WE'VE MADE OUR OWN MONSTERS NOW?
WE NEED TO GET THE LEADERS OF EREBUS AND ARK HOME 'ROUND A TABLE... FIND OUT IF EITHER OF THEM IS RESPONSIBLE.

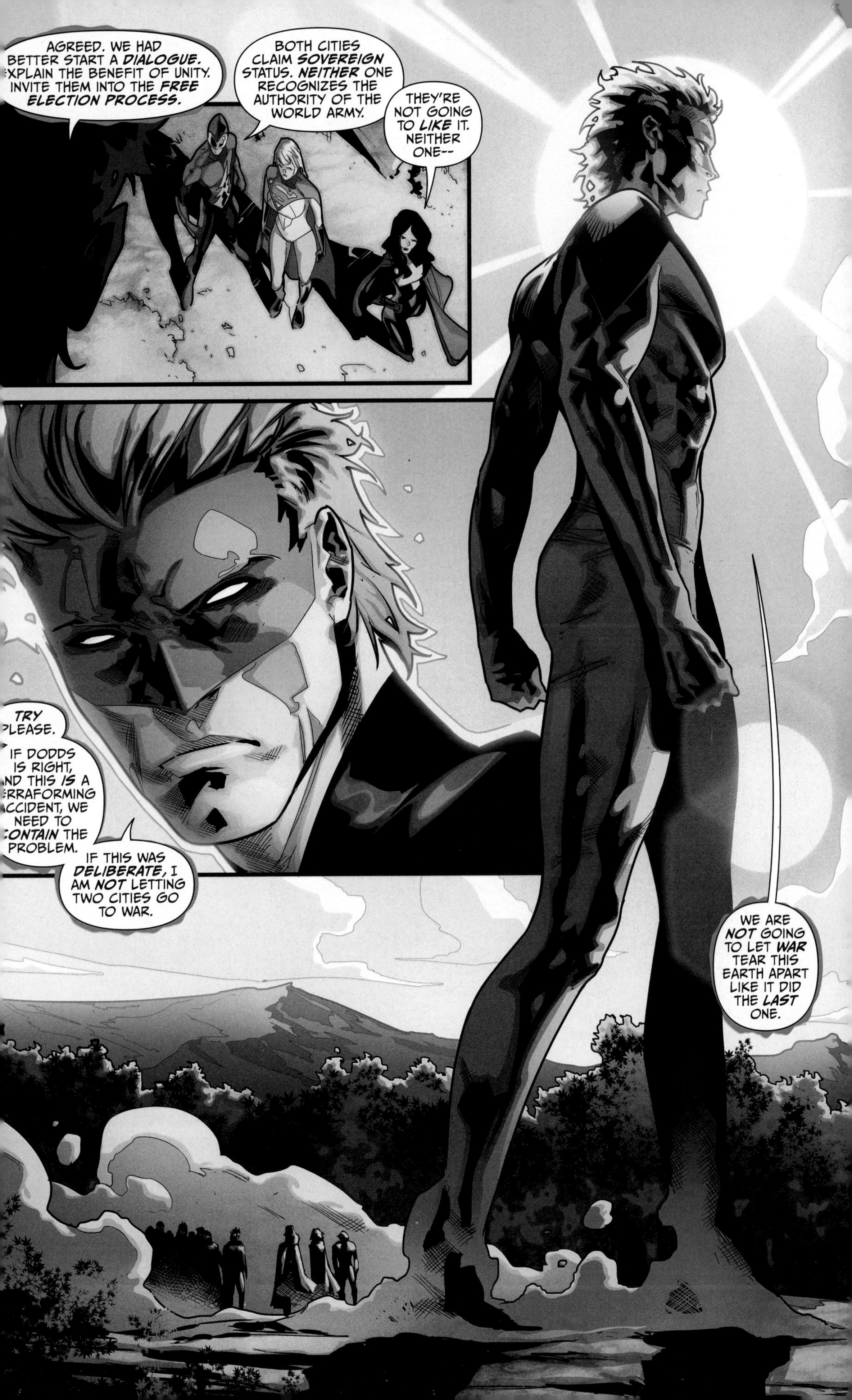
AGREED. WE HAD BETTER START A DIALOGUE. EXPLAIN THE BENEFIT OF UNITY. INVITE THEM INTO THE FREE ELECTION PROCESS.
BOTH CITIES CLAIM SOVEREIGN STATUS. NEITHER ONE RECOGNIZES THE AUTHORITY OF THE WORLD ARMY.
THEY'RE NOT GOING TO LIKE IT. NEITHER ONE--
TRY PLEASE.
IF DODDS IS RIGHT, AND THIS IS A TERRAFORMING ACCIDENT, WE NEED TO CONTAIN THE PROBLEM.
IF THIS WAS DELIBERATE, I AM NOT LETTING TWO CITIES GO TO WAR.
WE ARE NOT GOING TO LET WAR TEAR THIS EARTH APART LIKE IT DID THE LAST ONE.

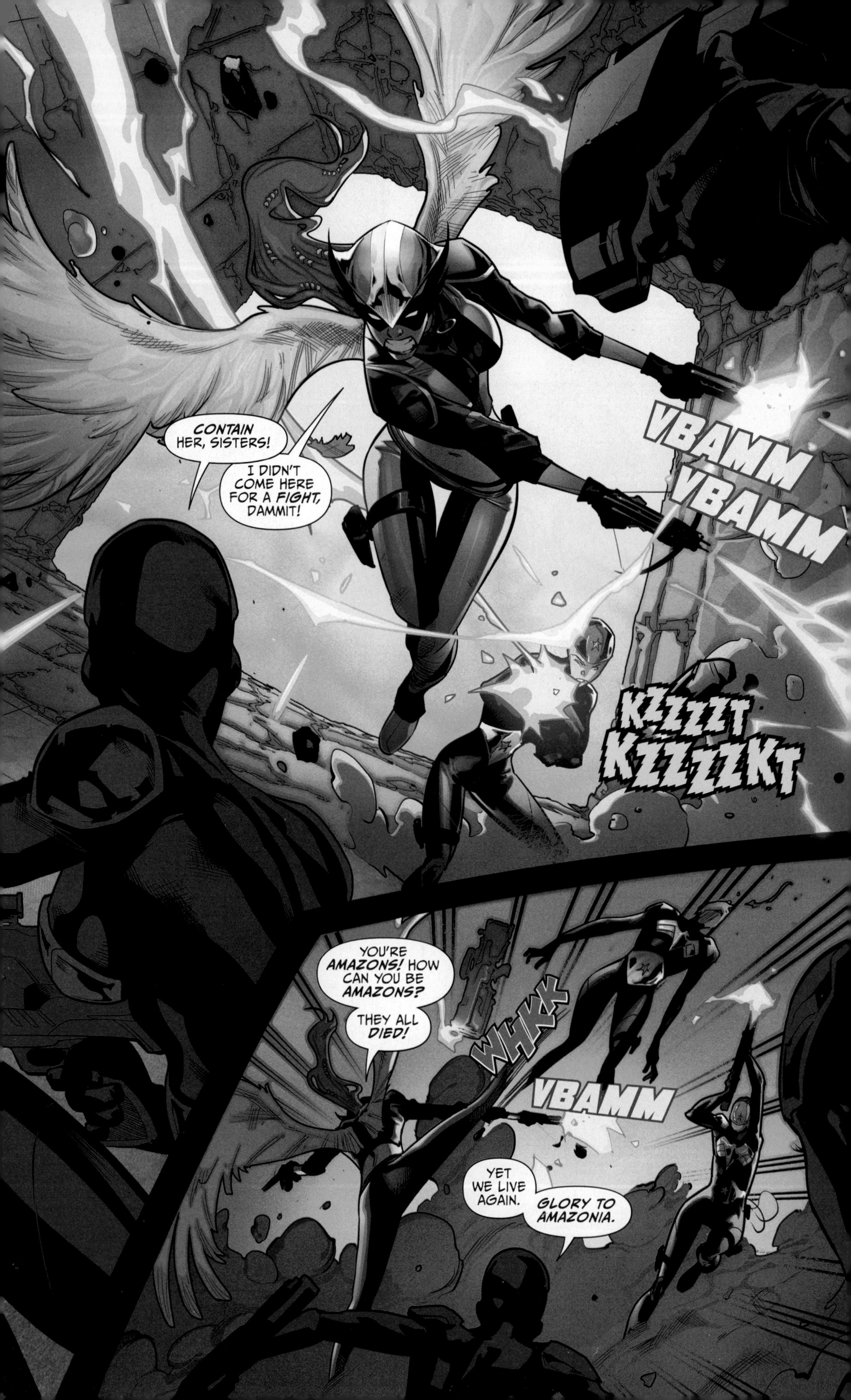
CONTAIN HER, SISTERS!
I DIDN'T COME HERE FOR A FIGHT, DAMMIT!
VBAMM VBAMM
KZZZZT KZZZZZKT
YOU'RE AMAZONS! HOW CAN YOU BE AMAZONS?
THEY ALL DIED!
WHKK
VBAMM
YET WE LIVE AGAIN.
GLORY TO AMAZONIA.

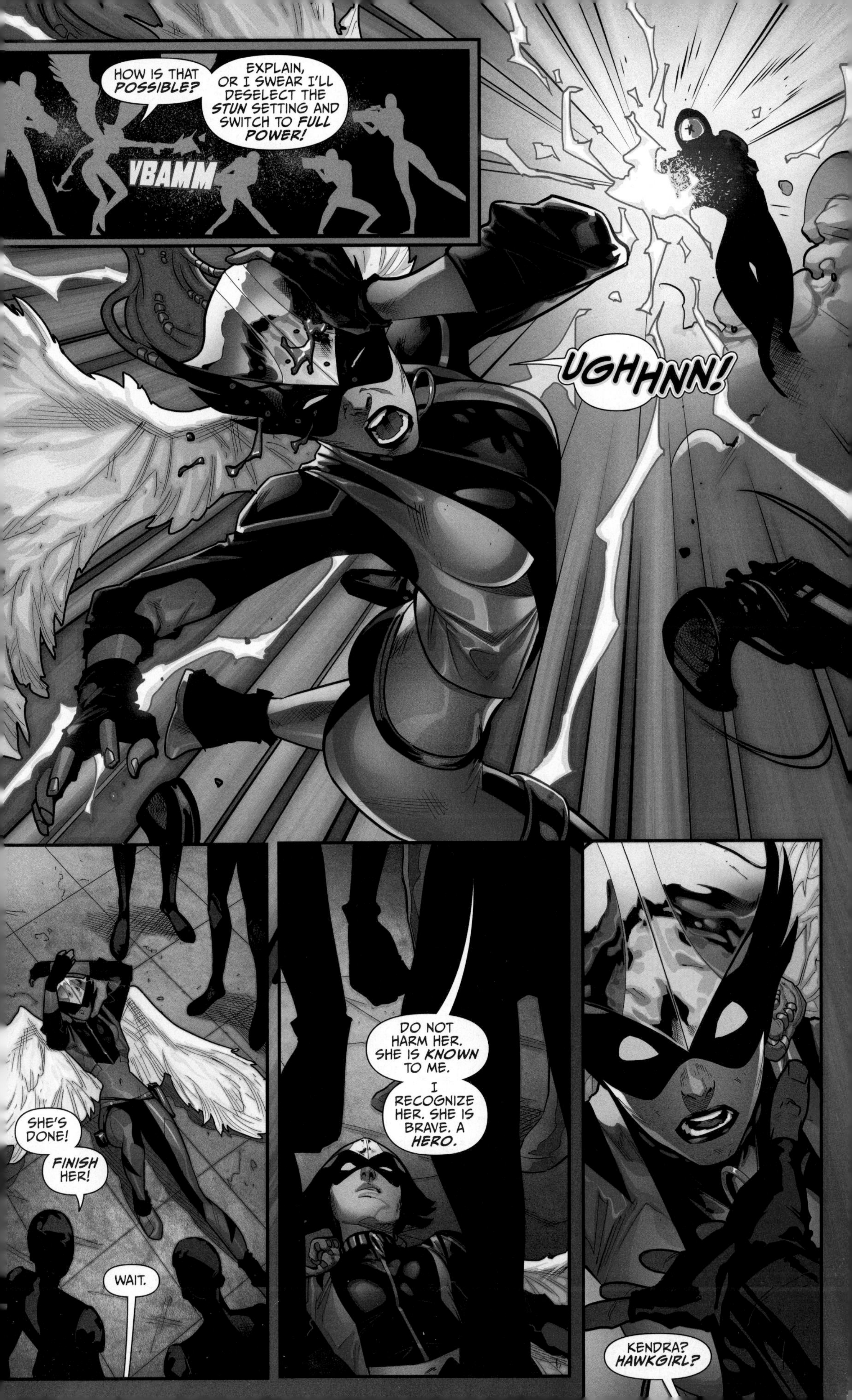
HOW IS THAT POSSIBLE?
EXPLAIN, OR I SWEAR I'LL DESELECT THE STUN SETTING AND SWITCH TO FULL POWER!
VBAMM
UGHHNN!
SHE'S DONE!
FINISH HER!
WAIT.
DO NOT HARM HER. SHE IS KNOWN TO ME.
I RECOGNIZE HER. SHE IS BRAVE. A HERO.
KENDRA? HAWKGIRL?

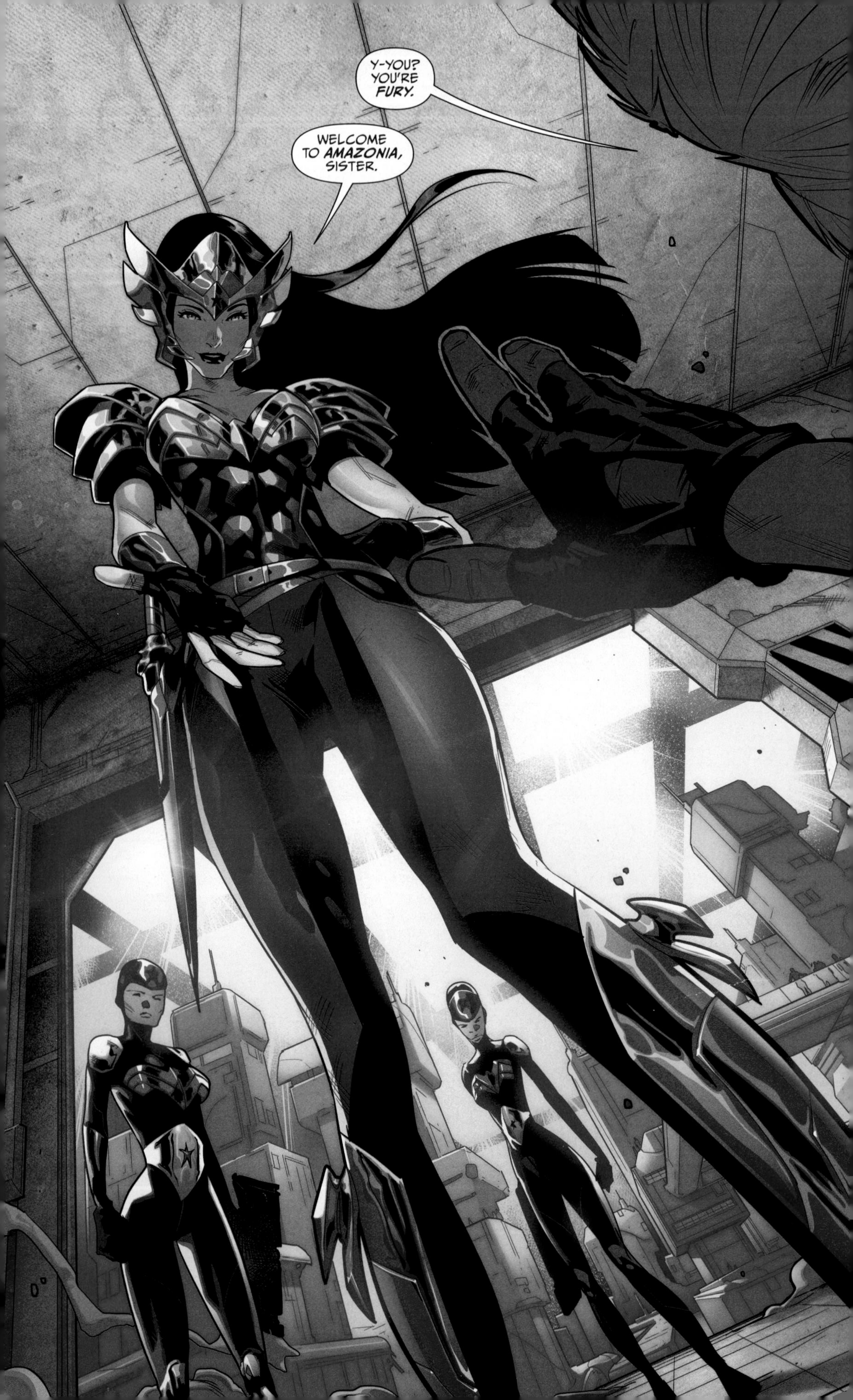
Y-YOU? YOU'RE FURY.
WELCOME TO AMAZONIA, SISTER.

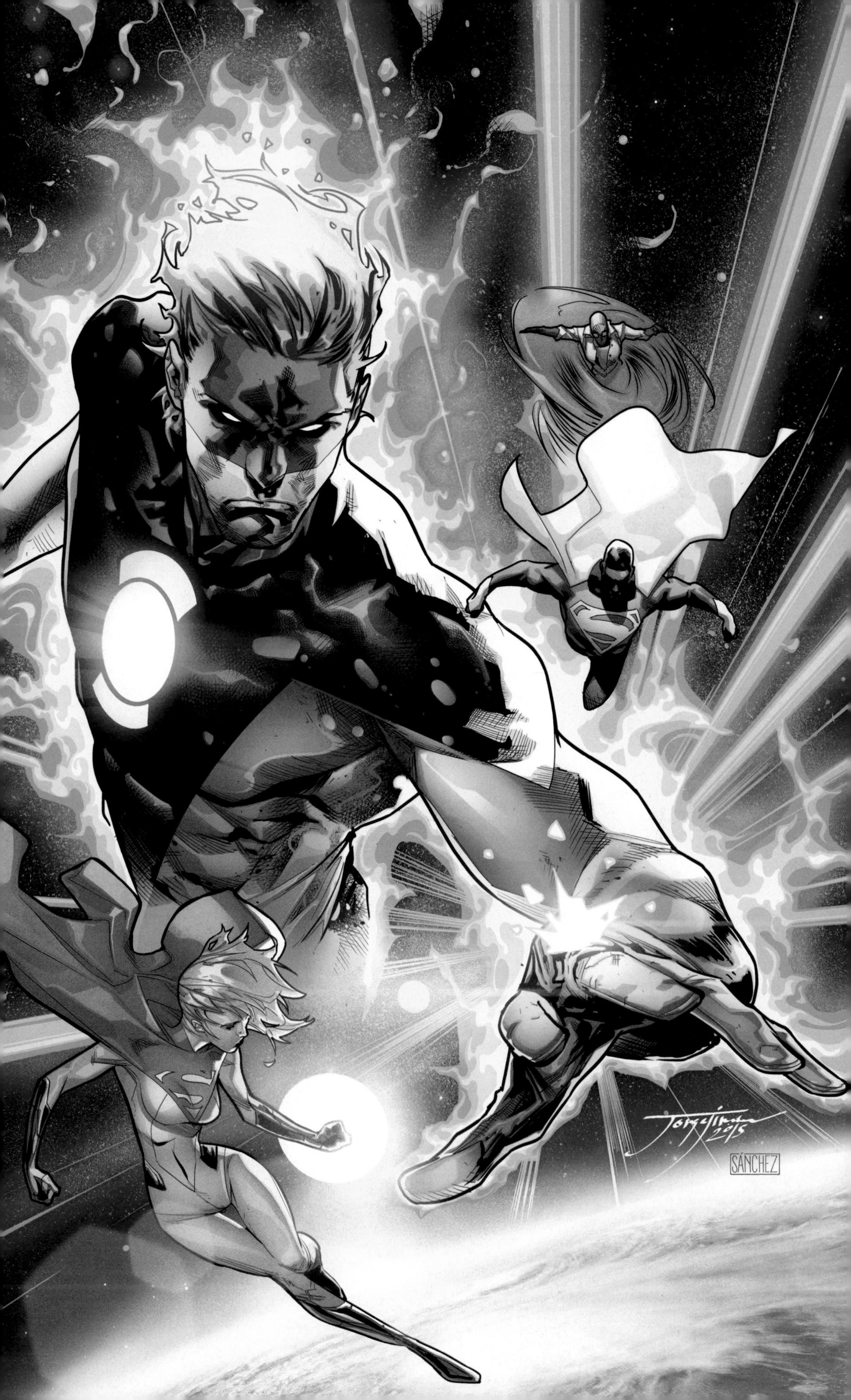
SÁNCHEZ

ONE NATION, INDIVISIBLE CHAPTER TWO: WORLD-LEADER PRETEND

DAN ABNETT writer **JORGE JIMÉNEZ** artist **ALEJANDRO SANCHEZ** colorist **TRAVIS LANHAM** letterer cover by **JIMÉNEZ & SANCHEZ**

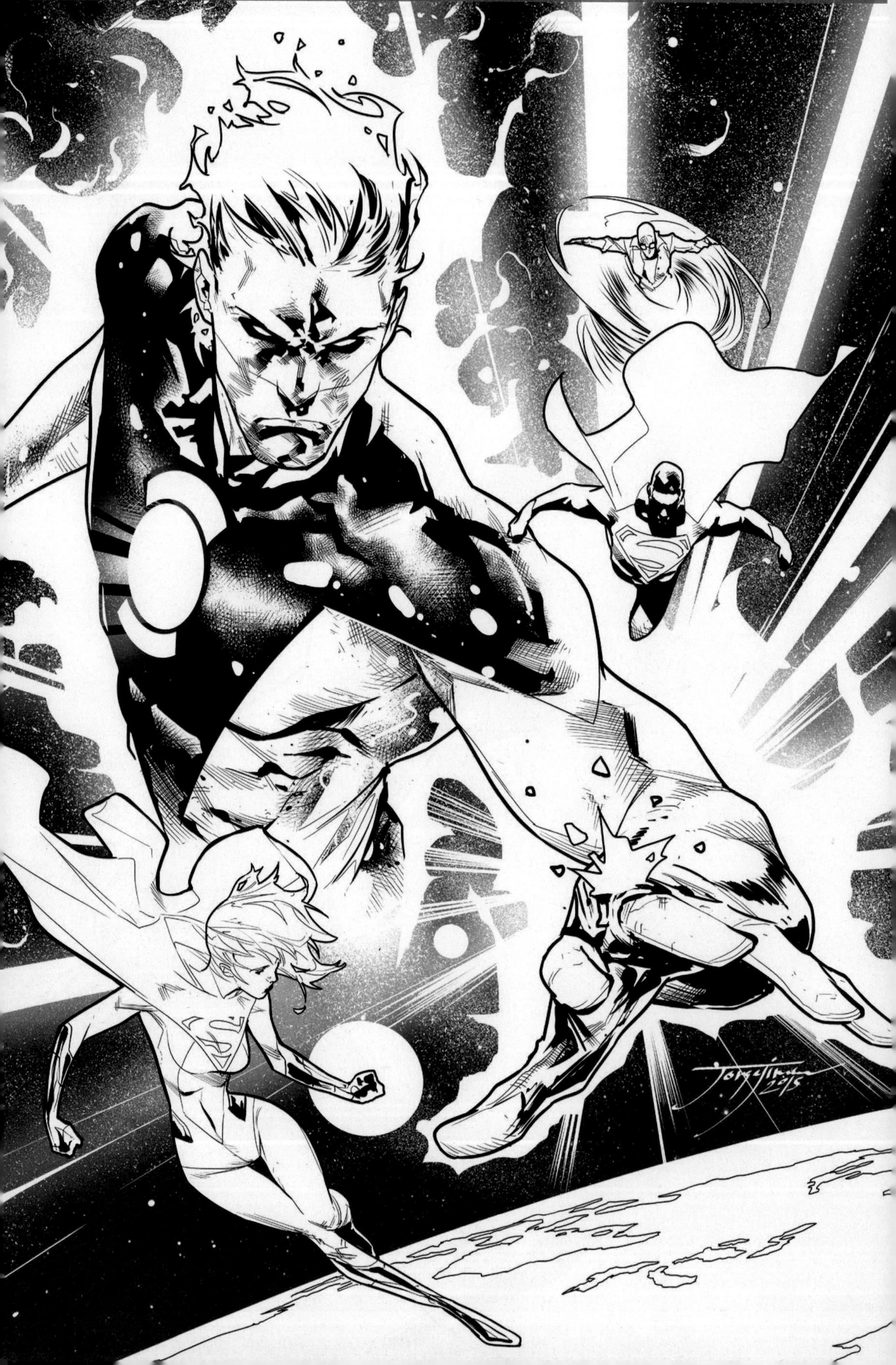

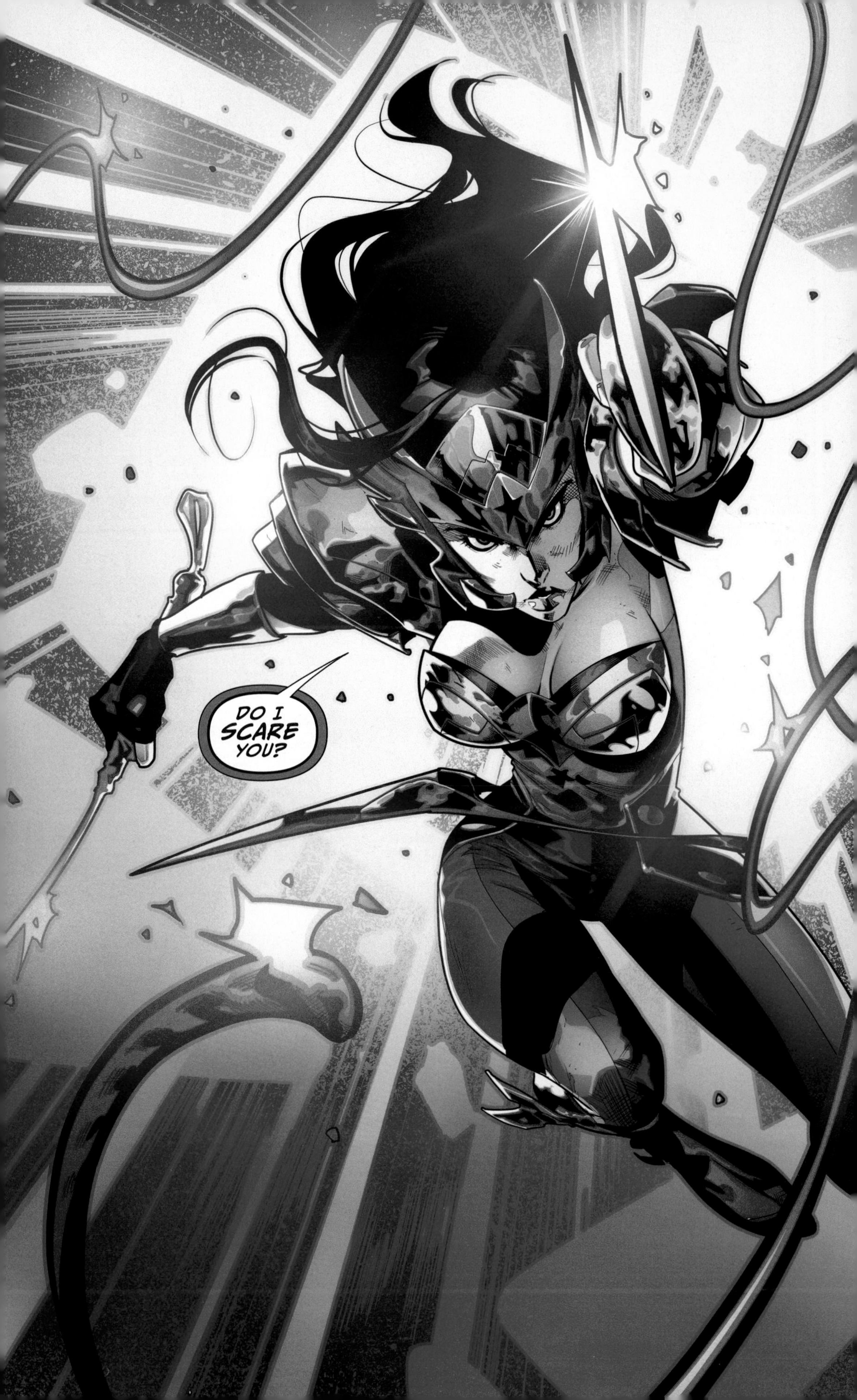
DO I SCARE YOU?

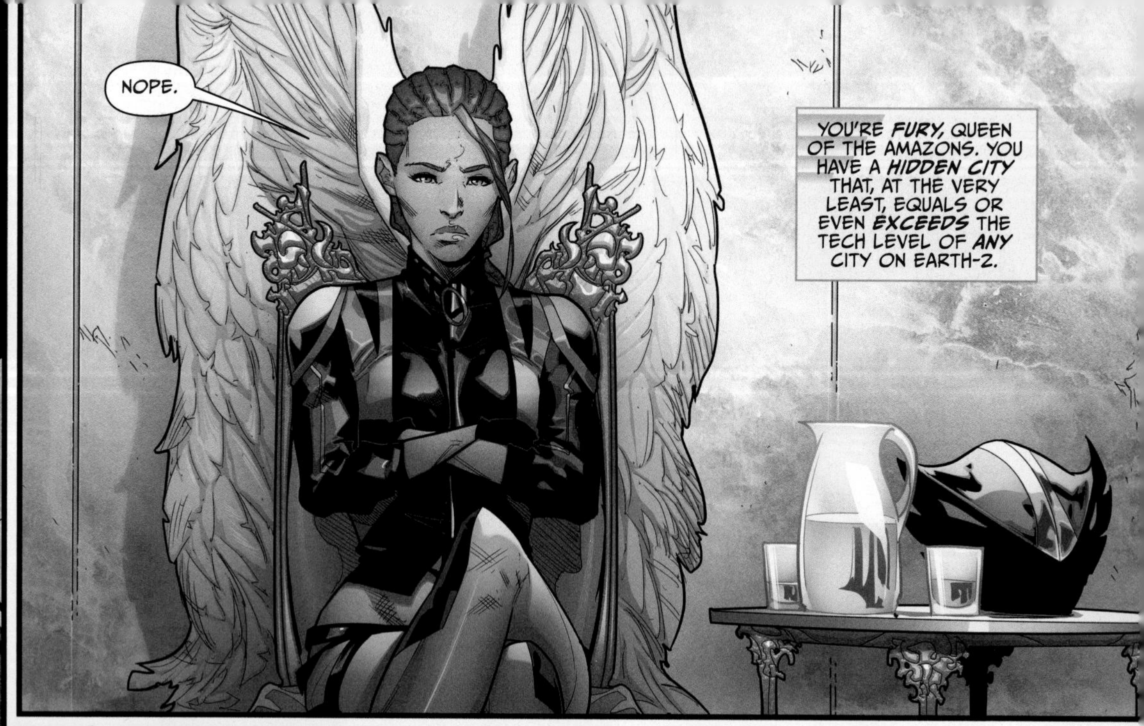
NOPE.
YOU'RE FURY, QUEEN OF THE AMAZONS. YOU HAVE A HIDDEN CITY THAT, AT THE VERY LEAST, EQUALS OR EVEN EXCEEDS THE TECH LEVEL OF ANY CITY ON EARTH-2.
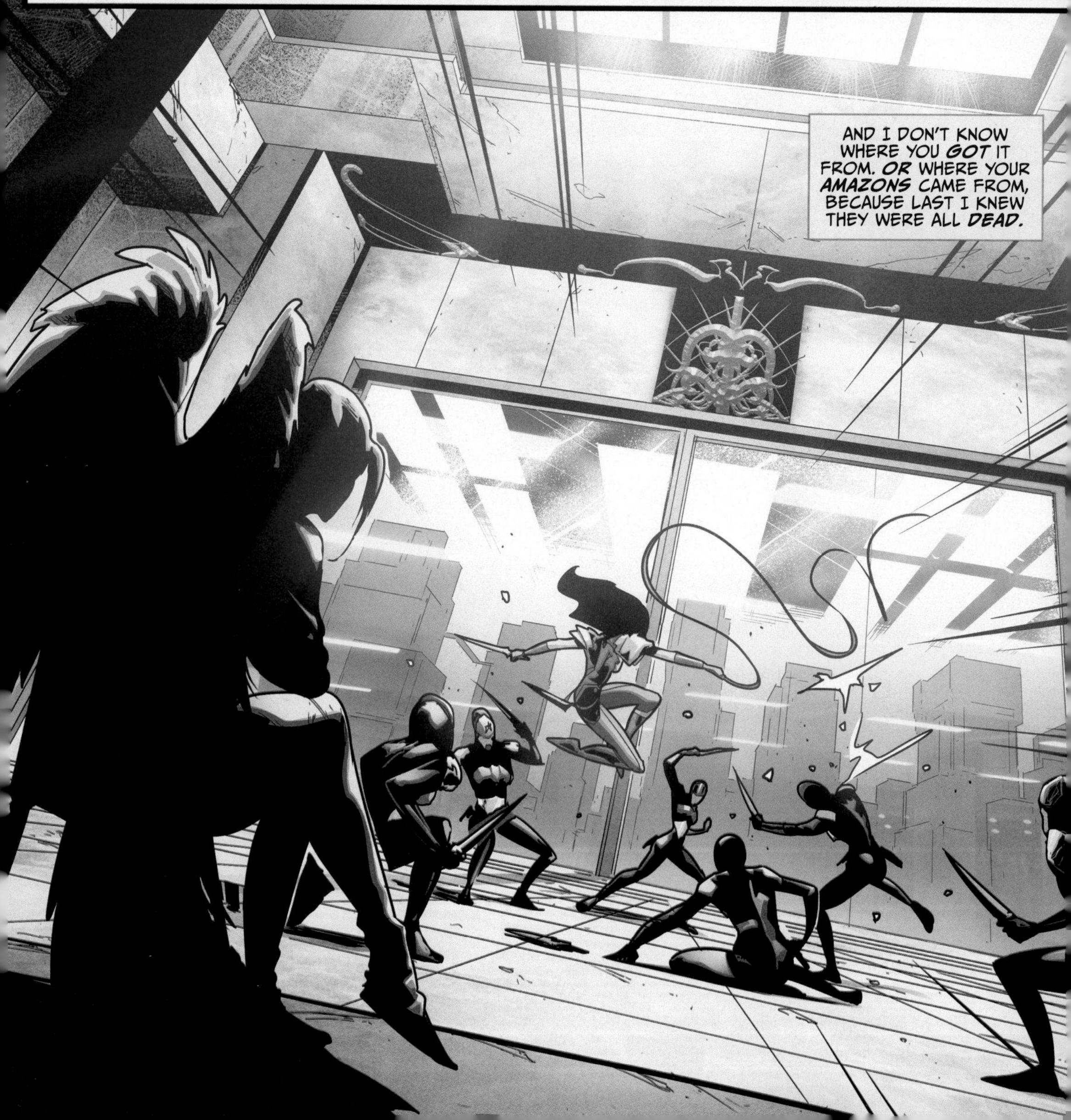
AND I DON'T KNOW WHERE YOU GOT IT FROM. OR WHERE YOUR AMAZONS CAME FROM, BECAUSE LAST I KNEW THEY WERE ALL DEAD.

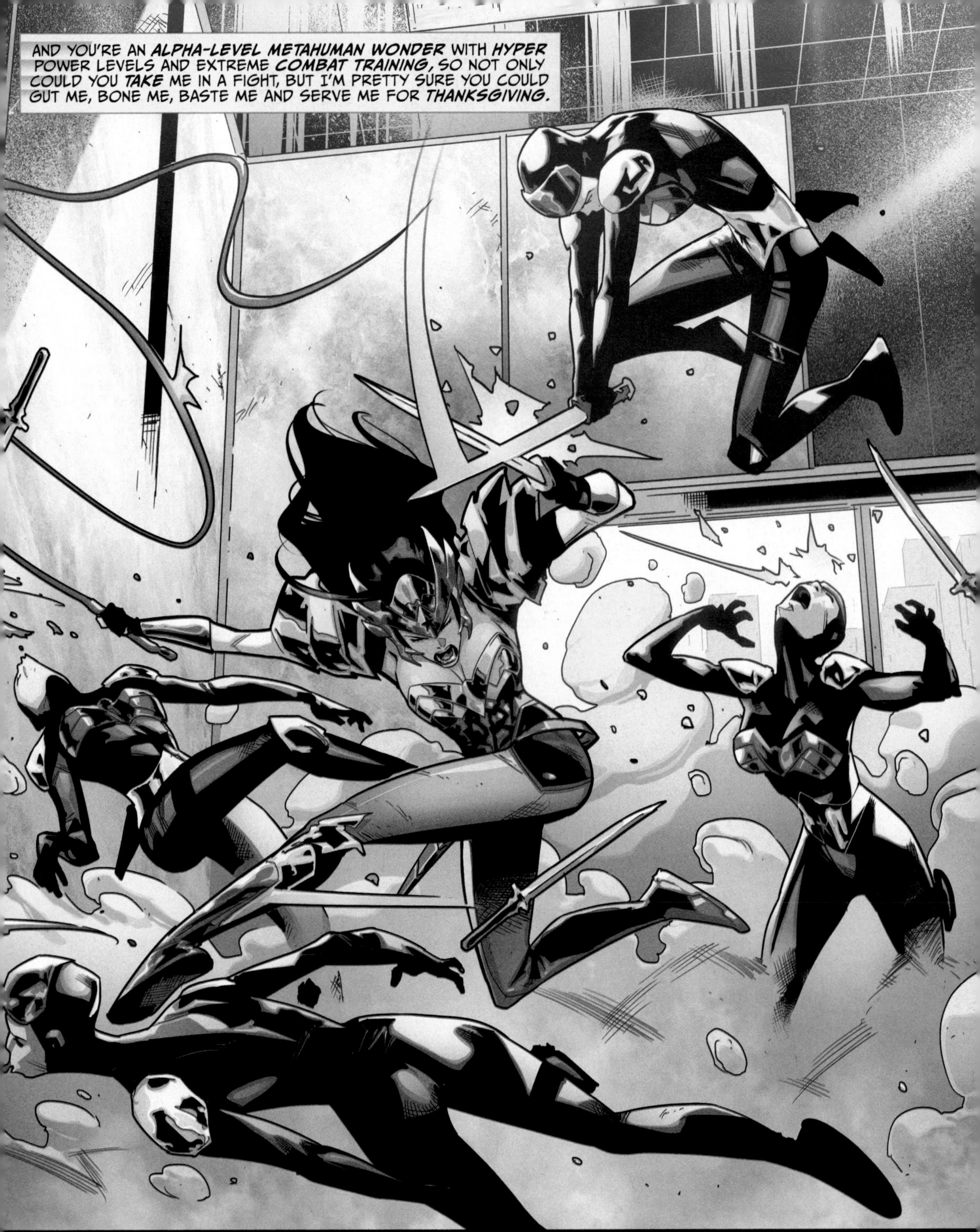
AND YOU'RE AN ALPHA-LEVEL METAHUMAN WONDER WITH HYPER POWER LEVELS AND EXTREME COMBAT TRAINING, SO NOT ONLY COULD YOU TAKE ME IN A FIGHT, BUT I'M PRETTY SURE YOU COULD GUT ME, BONE ME, BASTE ME AND SERVE ME FOR THANKSGIVING.

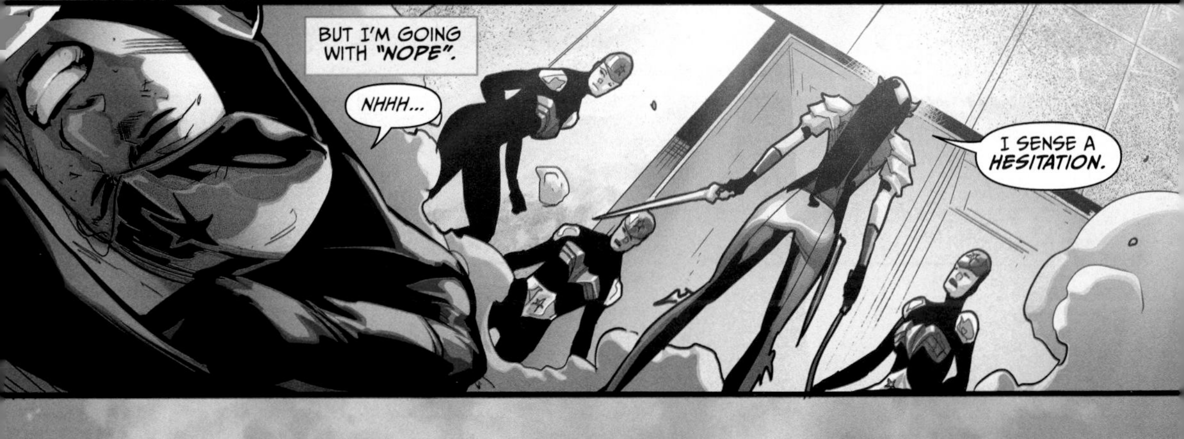
BUT I'M GOING WITH "NOPE".
NHHH...
I SENSE A HESITATION.

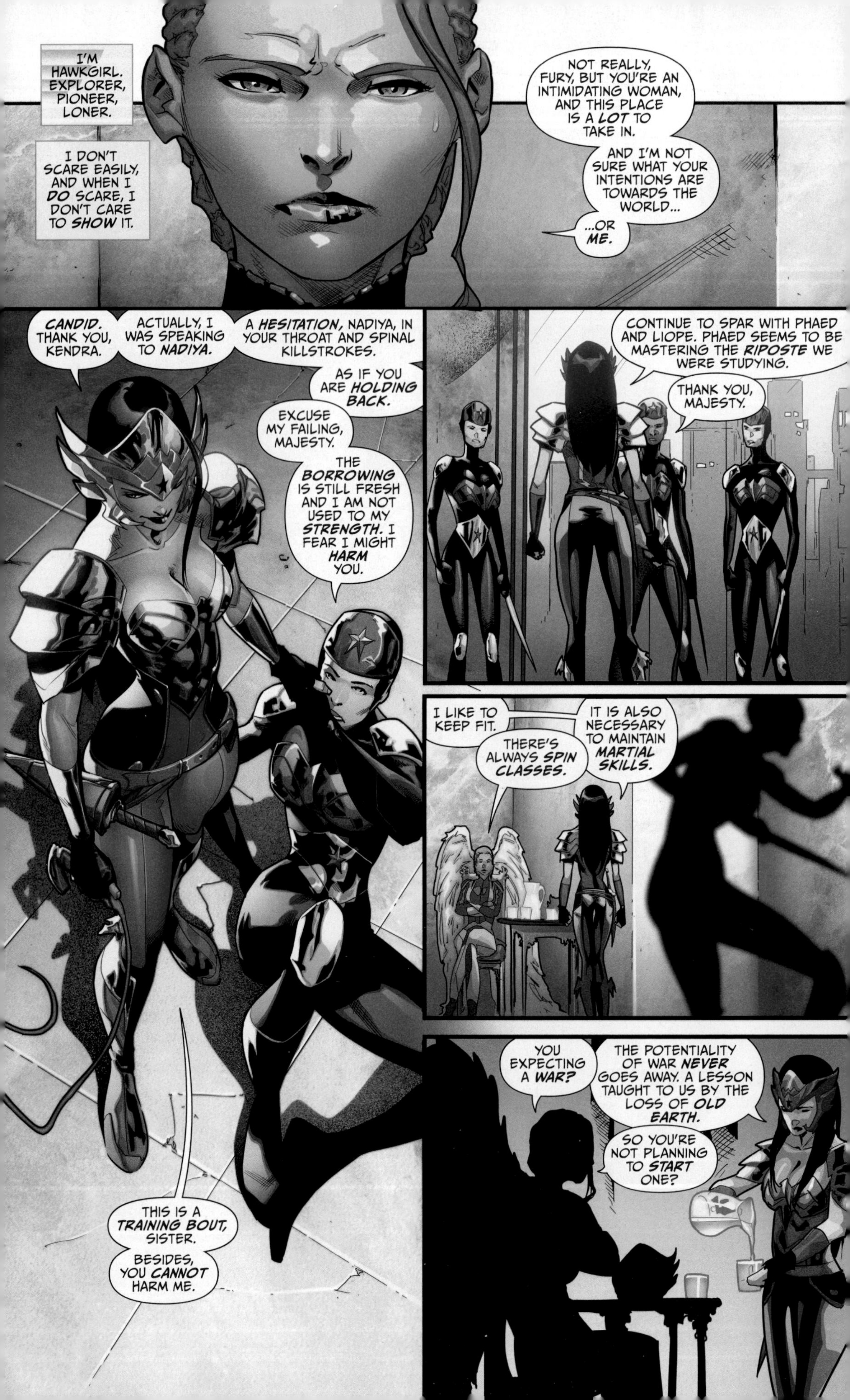
I'M HAWKGIRL. EXPLORER, PIONEER, LONER.
I DON'T SCARE EASILY, AND WHEN I DO SCARE, I DON'T CARE TO SHOW IT.
NOT REALLY, FURY, BUT YOU'RE AN INTIMIDATING WOMAN, AND THIS PLACE IS A LOT TO TAKE IN.
AND I'M NOT SURE WHAT YOUR INTENTIONS ARE TOWARDS THE WORLD...
...OR ME.
CANDID. THANK YOU, KENDRA.
ACTUALLY, I WAS SPEAKING TO NADIYA.
A HESITATION, NADIYA, IN YOUR THROAT AND SPINAL KILLSTROKES.
AS IF YOU ARE HOLDING BACK.
EXCUSE MY FAILING, MAJESTY.
THE BORROWING IS STILL FRESH AND I AM NOT USED TO MY STRENGTH. I FEAR I MIGHT HARM YOU.
THIS IS A TRAINING BOUT, SISTER.
BESIDES, YOU CANNOT HARM ME.
CONTINUE TO SPAR WITH PHAED AND LIOPE. PHAED SEEMS TO BE MASTERING THE RIPOSTE WE WERE STUDYING.
THANK YOU, MAJESTY.
I LIKE TO KEEP FIT.
IT IS ALSO NECESSARY TO MAINTAIN MARTIAL SKILLS.
THERE'S ALWAYS SPIN CLASSES.
YOU EXPECTING A WAR?
THE POTENTIALITY OF WAR NEVER GOES AWAY. A LESSON TAUGHT TO US BY THE LOSS OF OLD EARTH.
SO YOU'RE NOT PLANNING TO START ONE?

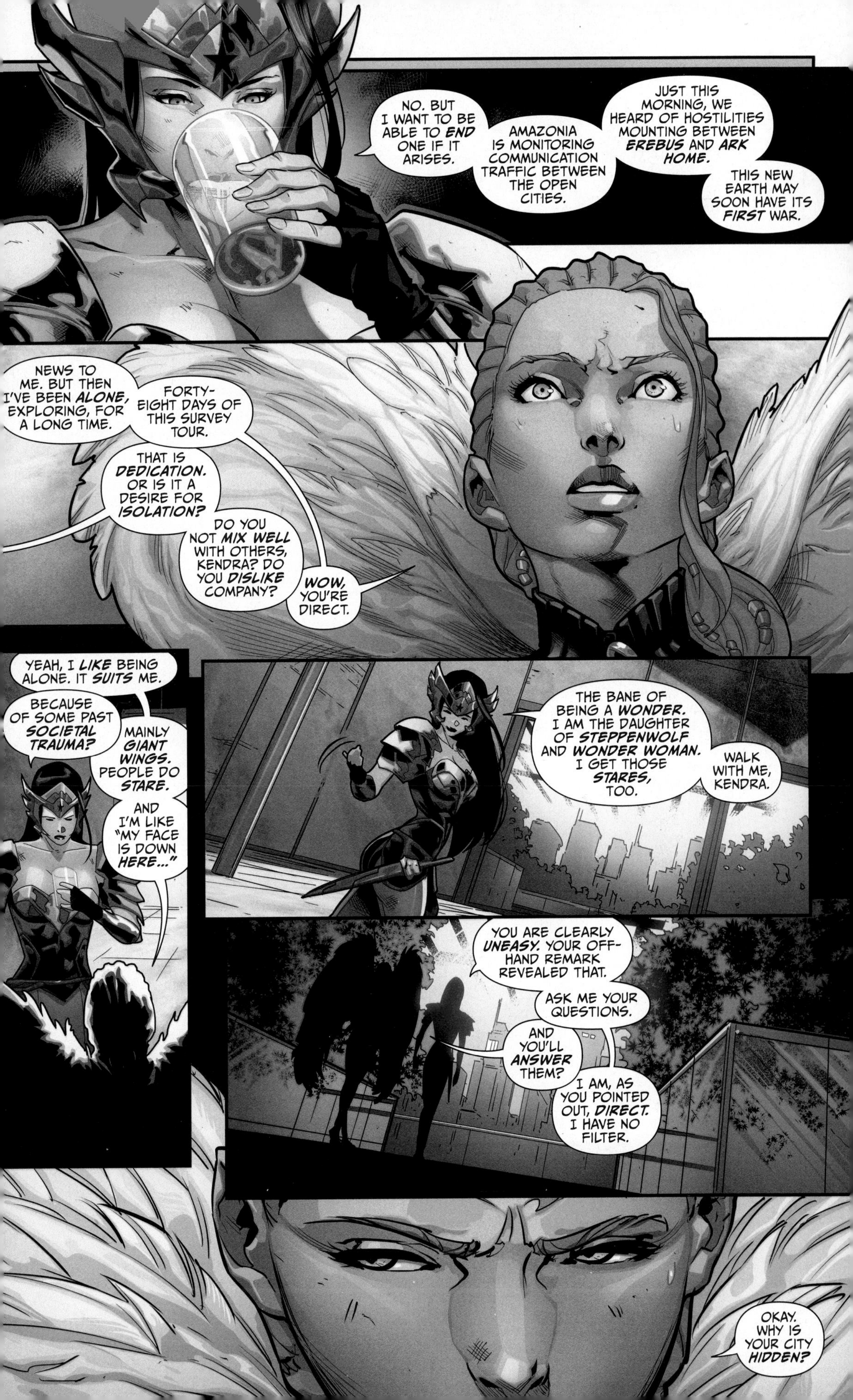
NO. BUT I WANT TO BE ABLE TO END ONE IF IT ARISES.
AMAZONIA IS MONITORING COMMUNICATION TRAFFIC BETWEEN THE OPEN CITIES.
JUST THIS MORNING, WE HEARD OF HOSTILITIES MOUNTING BETWEEN EREBUS AND ARK HOME.
THIS NEW EARTH MAY SOON HAVE ITS FIRST WAR.
NEWS TO ME. BUT THEN I'VE BEEN ALONE, EXPLORING, FOR A LONG TIME.
FORTY-EIGHT DAYS OF THIS SURVEY TOUR.
THAT IS DEDICATION. OR IS IT A DESIRE FOR ISOLATION?
DO YOU NOT MIX WELL WITH OTHERS, KENDRA? DO YOU DISLIKE COMPANY?
WOW, YOU'RE DIRECT.
YEAH, I LIKE BEING ALONE. IT SUITS ME.
BECAUSE OF SOME PAST SOCIETAL TRAUMA?
MAINLY GIANT WINGS. PEOPLE DO STARE.
AND I'M LIKE "MY FACE IS DOWN HERE..."
THE BANE OF BEING A WONDER. I AM THE DAUGHTER OF STEPPENWOLF AND WONDER WOMAN. I GET THOSE STARES, TOO.
WALK WITH ME, KENDRA.
YOU ARE CLEARLY UNEASY. YOUR OFF-HAND REMARK REVEALED THAT.
ASK ME YOUR QUESTIONS.
AND YOU'LL ANSWER THEM?
I AM, AS YOU POINTED OUT, DIRECT. I HAVE NO FILTER.
OKAY. WHY IS YOUR CITY HIDDEN?

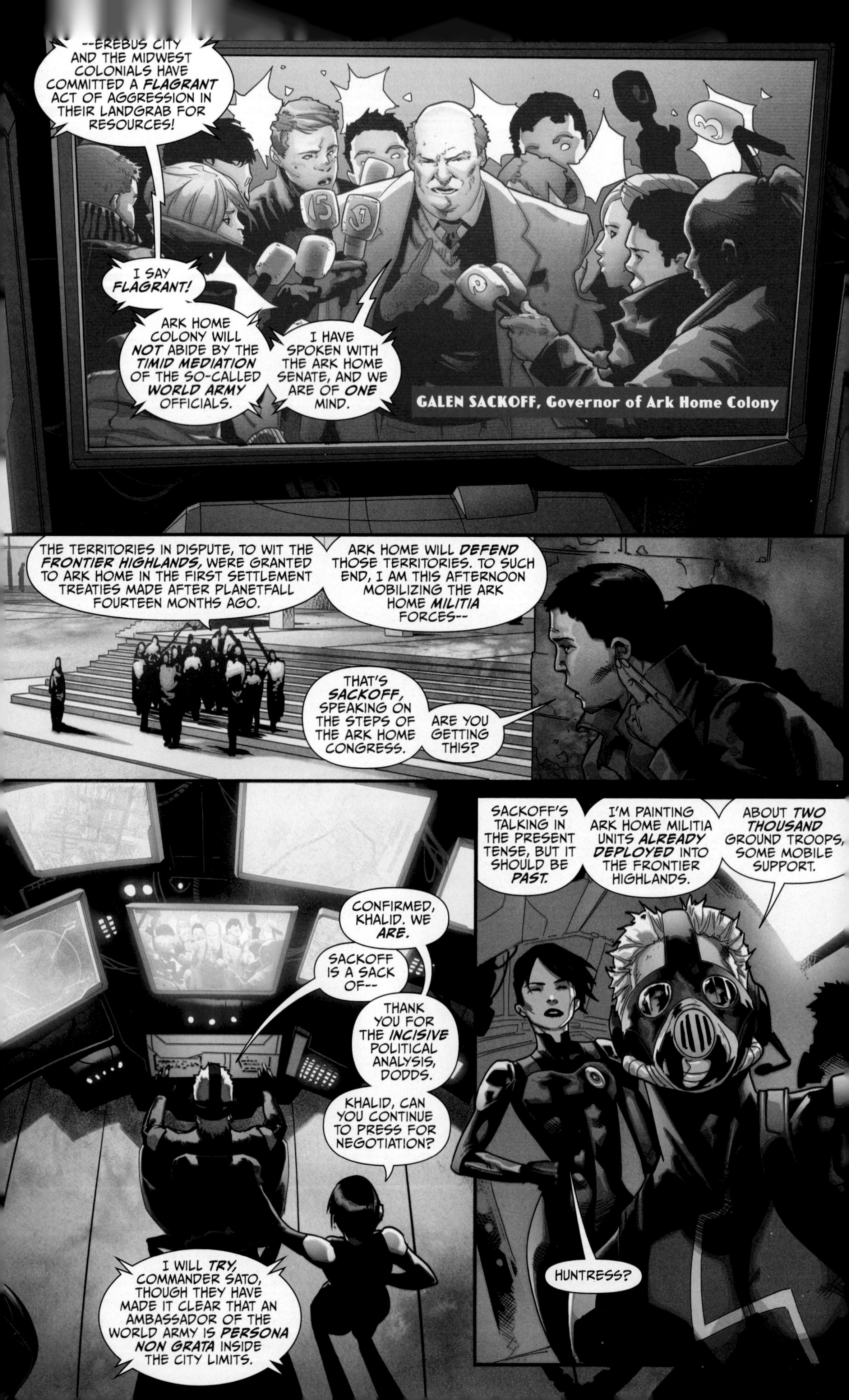
--EREBUS CITY AND THE MIDWEST COLONIALS HAVE COMMITTED A FLAGRANT ACT OF AGGRESSION IN THEIR LANDGRAB FOR RESOURCES!
I SAY FLAGRANT!
ARK HOME COLONY WILL NOT ABIDE BY THE TIMID MEDIATION OF THE SO-CALLED WORLD ARMY OFFICIALS.
I HAVE SPOKEN WITH THE ARK HOME SENATE, AND WE ARE OF ONE MIND.
GALEN SACKOFF, Governor of Ark Home Colony
THE TERRITORIES IN DISPUTE, TO WIT THE FRONTIER HIGHLANDS, WERE GRANTED TO ARK HOME IN THE FIRST SETTLEMENT TREATIES MADE AFTER PLANETFALL FOURTEEN MONTHS AGO.
ARK HOME WILL DEFEND THOSE TERRITORIES. TO SUCH END, I AM THIS AFTERNOON MOBILIZING THE ARK HOME MILITIA FORCES--
THAT'S SACKOFF, SPEAKING ON THE STEPS OF THE ARK HOME CONGRESS.
ARE YOU GETTING THIS?
CONFIRMED, KHALID. WE ARE.
SACKOFF IS A SACK OF--
THANK YOU FOR THE INCISIVE POLITICAL ANALYSIS, DODDS.
KHALID, CAN YOU CONTINUE TO PRESS FOR NEGOTIATION?
I WILL TRY, COMMANDER SATO, THOUGH THEY HAVE MADE IT CLEAR THAT AN AMBASSADOR OF THE WORLD ARMY IS PERSONA NON GRATA INSIDE THE CITY LIMITS.
SACKOFF'S TALKING IN THE PRESENT TENSE, BUT IT SHOULD BE PAST.
I'M PAINTING ARK HOME MILITIA UNITS ALREADY DEPLOYED INTO THE FRONTIER HIGHLANDS.
ABOUT TWO THOUSAND GROUND TROOPS, SOME MOBILE SUPPORT.
HUNTRESS?

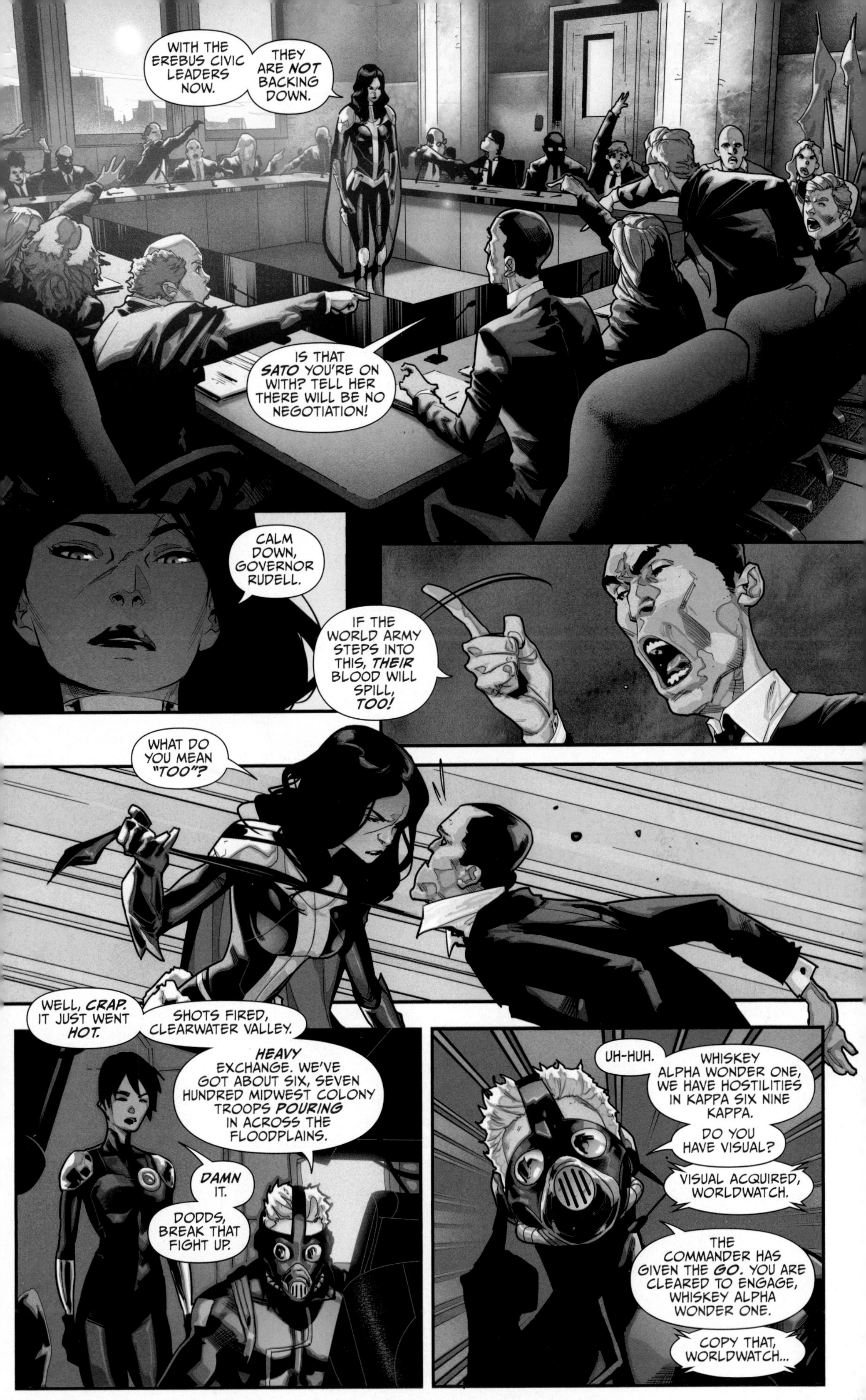
WITH THE EREBUS CIVIC LEADERS NOW.
THEY ARE NOT BACKING DOWN.
IS THAT SATO YOU'RE ON WITH? TELL HER THERE WILL BE NO NEGOTIATION!
CALM DOWN, GOVERNOR RUDELL.
IF THE WORLD ARMY STEPS INTO THIS, THEIR BLOOD WILL SPILL, TOO!
WHAT DO YOU MEAN "TOO"?
WELL, CRAP. IT JUST WENT HOT.
SHOTS FIRED, CLEARWATER VALLEY.
HEAVY EXCHANGE. WE'VE GOT ABOUT SIX, SEVEN HUNDRED MIDWEST COLONY TROOPS POURING IN ACROSS THE FLOODPLAINS.
DAMN IT.
DODDS, BREAK THAT FIGHT UP.
UH-HUH.
WHISKEY ALPHA WONDER ONE, WE HAVE HOSTILITIES IN KAPPA SIX NINE KAPPA.
DO YOU HAVE VISUAL?
VISUAL ACQUIRED, WORLDWATCH.
THE COMMANDER HAS GIVEN THE GO. YOU ARE CLEARED TO ENGAGE, WHISKEY ALPHA WONDER ONE.
COPY THAT, WORLDWATCH...

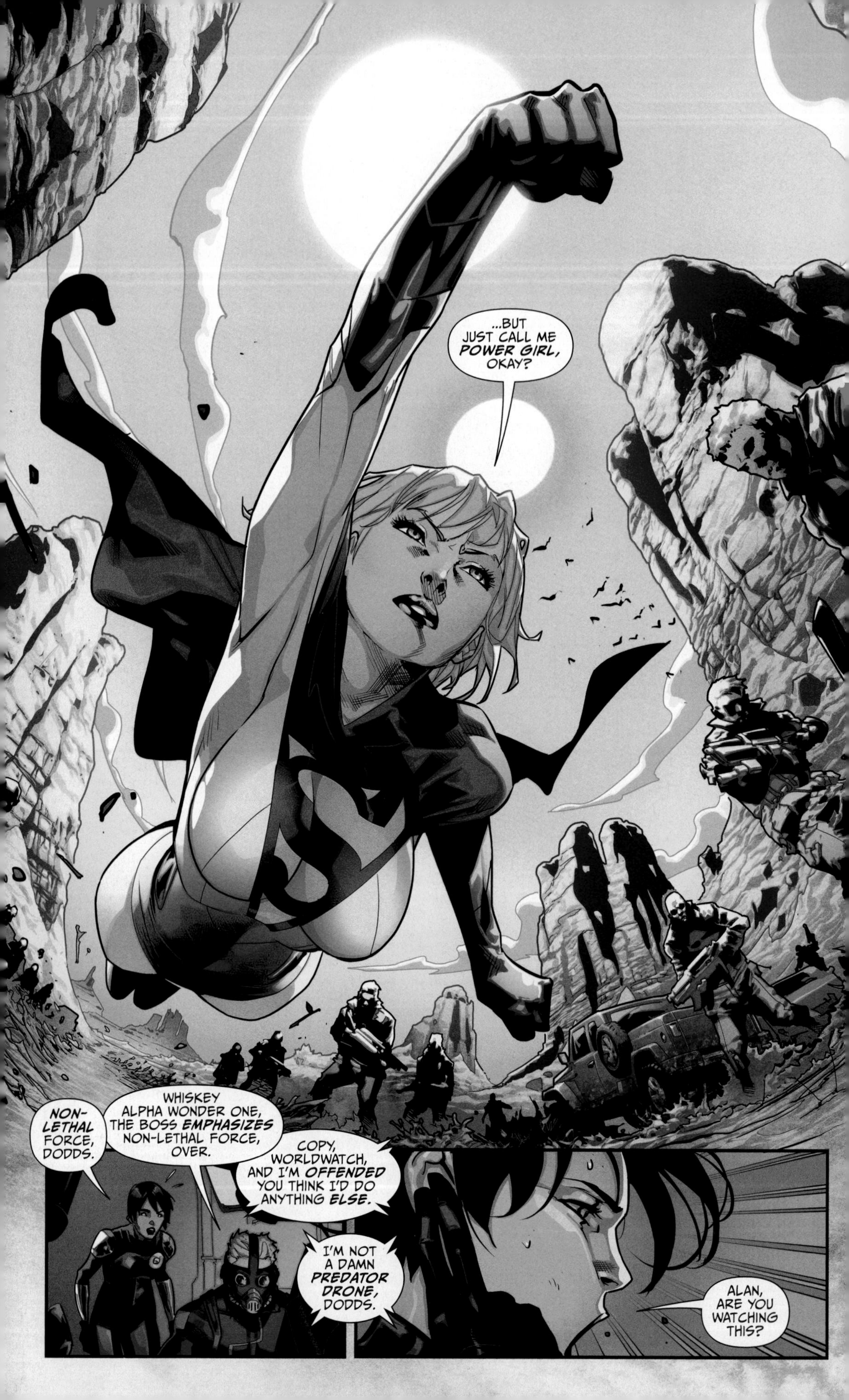
...BUT JUST CALL ME POWER GIRL, OKAY?
NON-LETHAL FORCE, DODDS.
WHISKEY ALPHA WONDER ONE, THE BOSS EMPHASIZES NON-LETHAL FORCE, OVER.
COPY, WORLDWATCH, AND I'M OFFENDED YOU THINK I'D DO ANYTHING ELSE.
I'M NOT A DAMN PREDATOR DRONE, DODDS.
ALAN, ARE YOU WATCHING THIS?

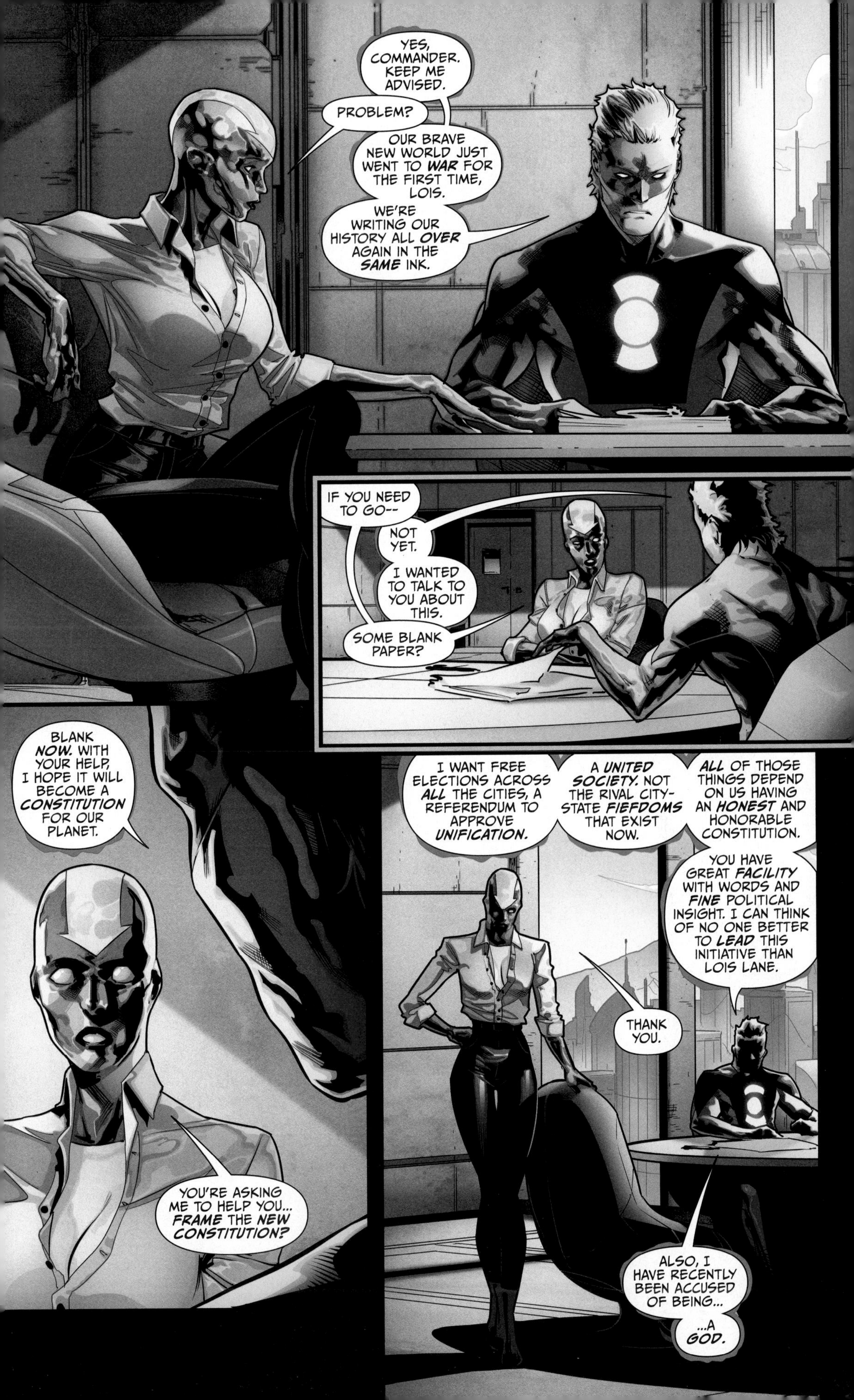
YES, COMMANDER. KEEP ME ADVISED.
PROBLEM?
OUR BRAVE NEW WORLD JUST WENT TO WAR FOR THE FIRST TIME, LOIS.
WE'RE WRITING OUR HISTORY ALL OVER AGAIN IN THE SAME INK.
IF YOU NEED TO GO--
NOT YET.
I WANTED TO TALK TO YOU ABOUT THIS.
SOME BLANK PAPER?
BLANK NOW. WITH YOUR HELP, I HOPE IT WILL BECOME A CONSTITUTION FOR OUR PLANET.
YOU'RE ASKING ME TO HELP YOU... FRAME THE NEW CONSTITUTION?
I WANT FREE ELECTIONS ACROSS ALL THE CITIES, A REFERENDUM TO APPROVE UNIFICATION.
A UNITED SOCIETY. NOT THE RIVAL CITY-STATE FIEFDOMS THAT EXIST NOW.
ALL OF THOSE THINGS DEPEND ON US HAVING AN HONEST AND HONORABLE CONSTITUTION.
YOU HAVE GREAT FACILITY WITH WORDS AND FINE POLITICAL INSIGHT. I CAN THINK OF NO ONE BETTER TO LEAD THIS INITIATIVE THAN LOIS LANE.
THANK YOU.
ALSO, I HAVE RECENTLY BEEN ACCUSED OF BEING...
...A GOD.

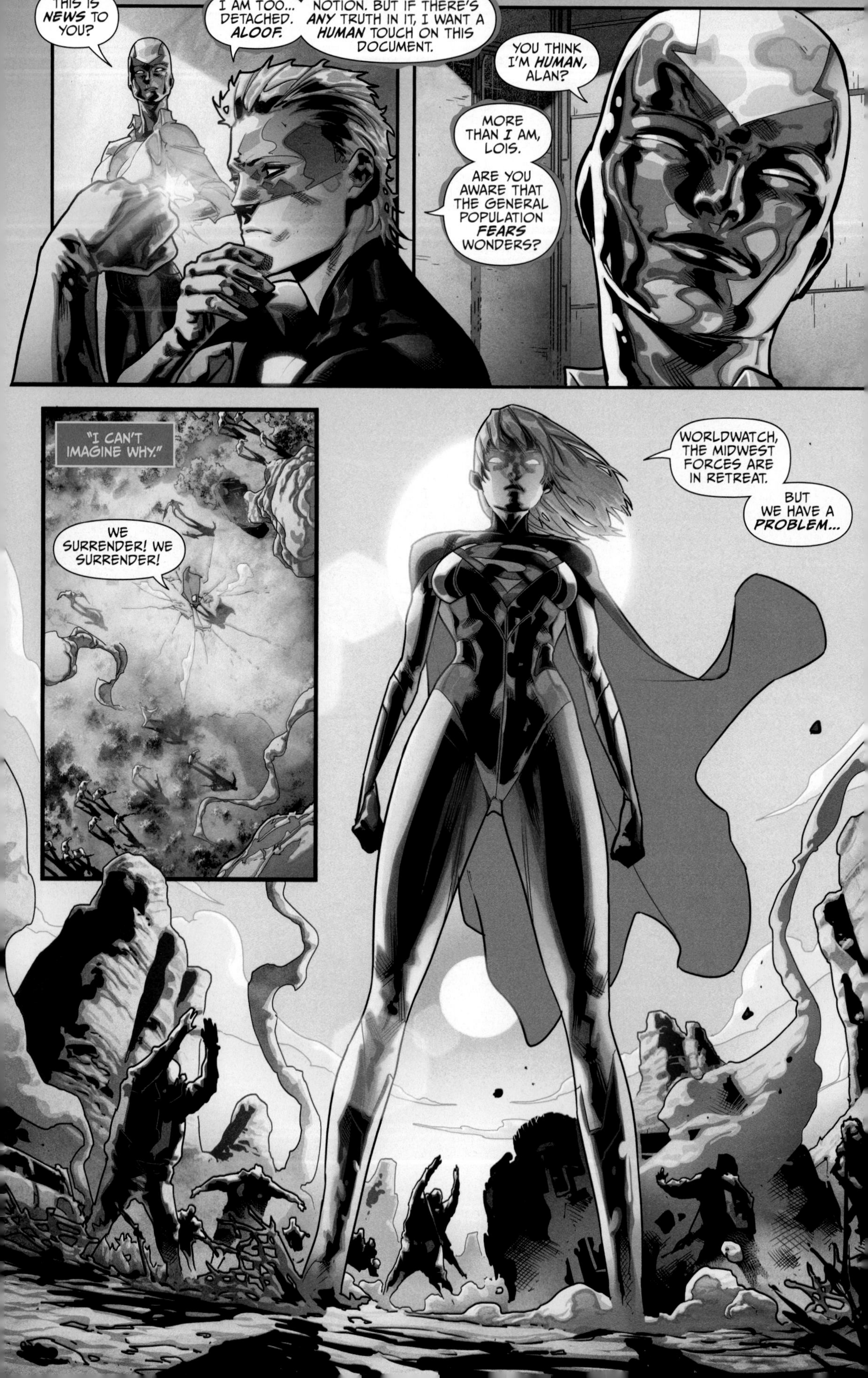
THIS IS NEWS TO YOU?
I AM TOO... DETACHED. ALOOF.
I DISLIKE THE NOTION. BUT IF THERE'S ANY TRUTH IN IT, I WANT A HUMAN TOUCH ON THIS DOCUMENT.
YOU THINK I'M HUMAN, ALAN?
MORE THAN I AM, LOIS.
ARE YOU AWARE THAT THE GENERAL POPULATION FEARS WONDERS?
"I CAN'T IMAGINE WHY."
WE SURRENDER! WE SURRENDER!
WORLDWATCH, THE MIDWEST FORCES ARE IN RETREAT.
BUT WE HAVE A PROBLEM...

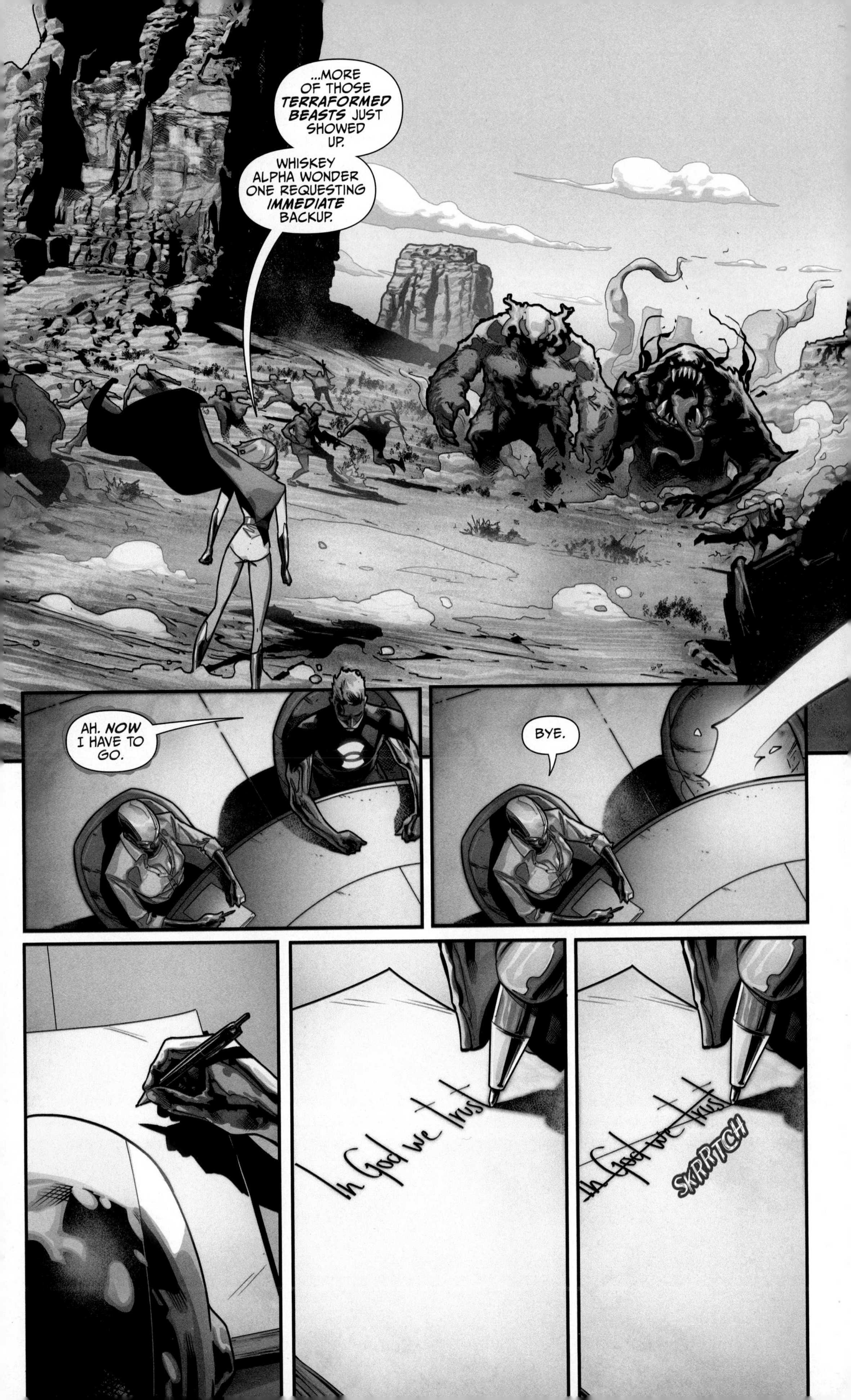
...MORE OF THOSE TERRAFORMED BEASTS JUST SHOWED UP.
WHISKEY ALPHA WONDER ONE REQUESTING IMMEDIATE BACKUP.
AH. NOW I HAVE TO GO.
BYE.
In God we trust
In God we trust
SKRRTCH

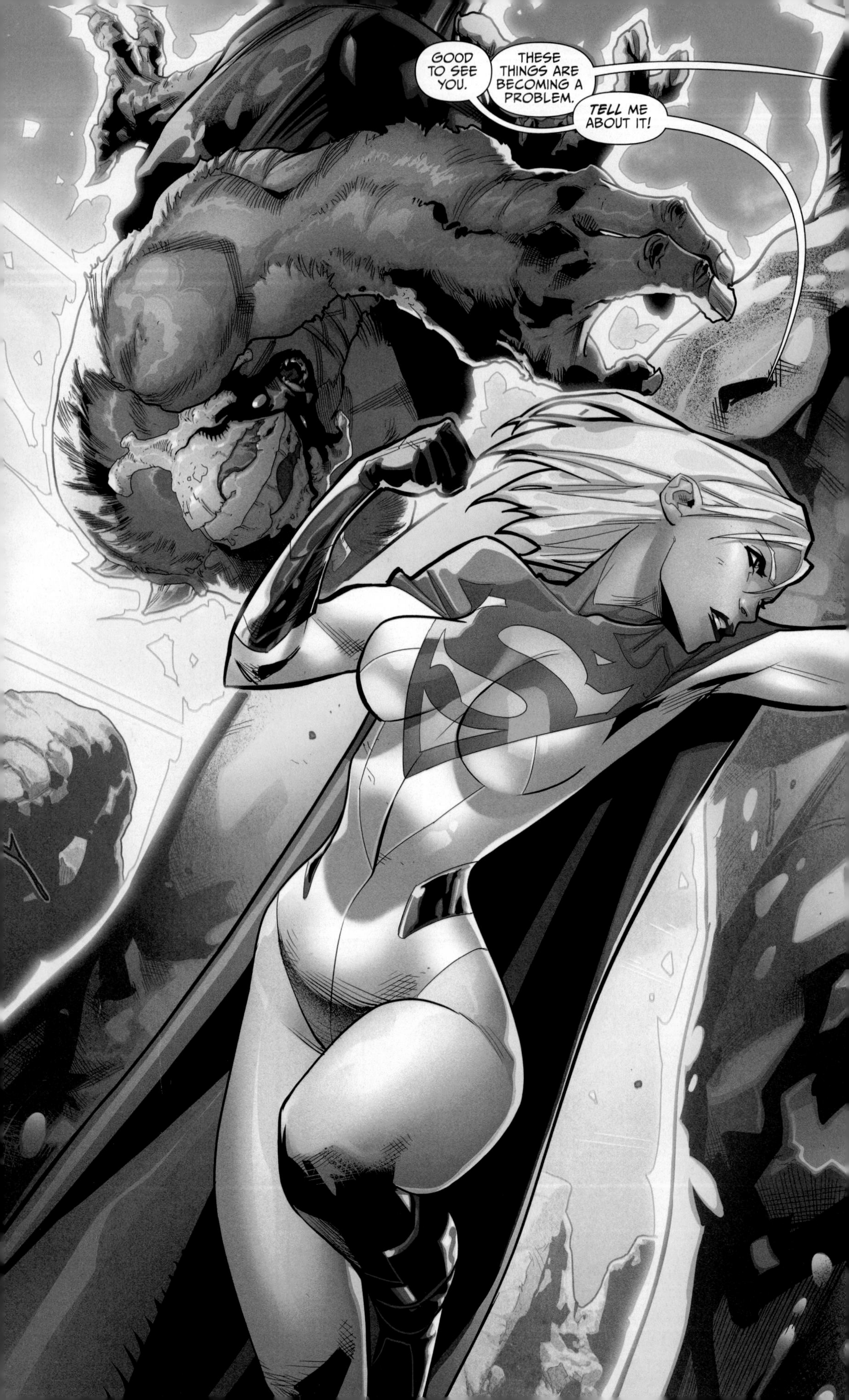
GOOD TO SEE YOU.
THESE THINGS ARE BECOMING A PROBLEM.
TELL ME ABOUT IT!

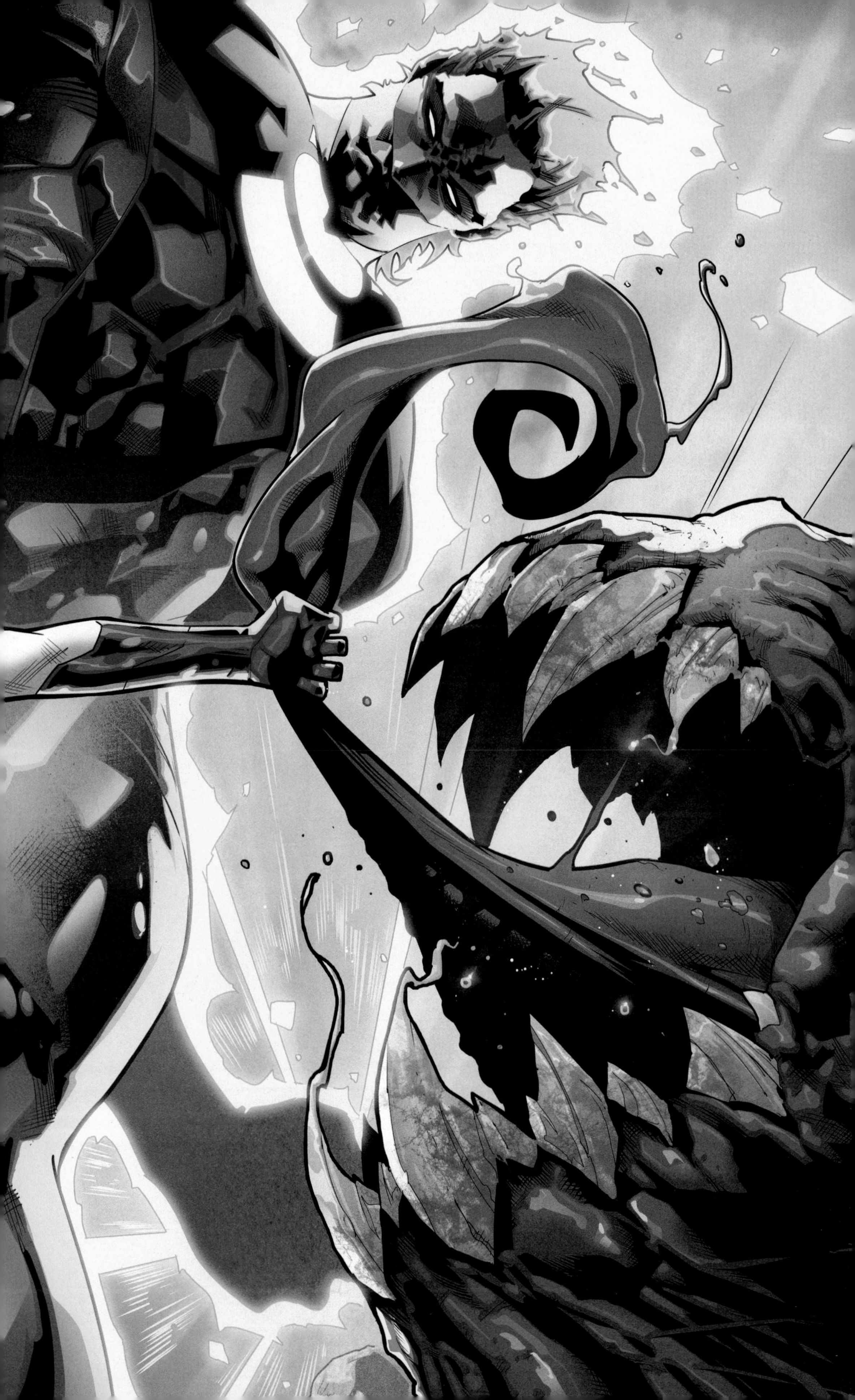

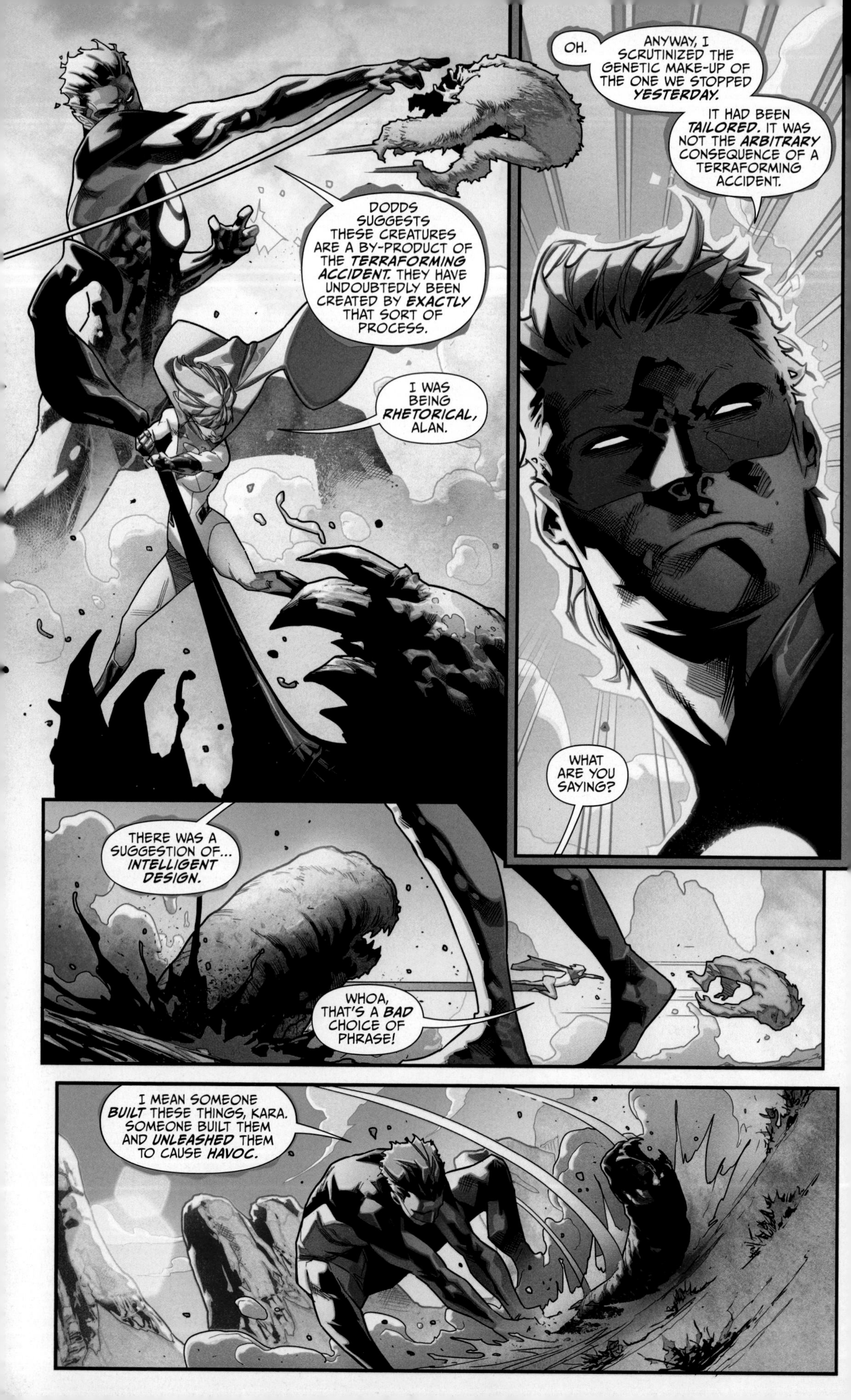
DODDS SUGGESTS THESE CREATURES ARE A BY-PRODUCT OF THE TERRAFORMING ACCIDENT. THEY HAVE UNDOUBTEDLY BEEN CREATED BY EXACTLY THAT SORT OF PROCESS.
I WAS BEING RHETORICAL, ALAN.
OH.
ANYWAY, I SCRUTINIZED THE GENETIC MAKE-UP OF THE ONE WE STOPPED YESTERDAY.
IT HAD BEEN TAILORED. IT WAS NOT THE ARBITRARY CONSEQUENCE OF A TERRAFORMING ACCIDENT.
WHAT ARE YOU SAYING?
THERE WAS A SUGGESTION OF... INTELLIGENT DESIGN.
WHOA, THAT'S A BAD CHOICE OF PHRASE!
I MEAN SOMEONE BUILT THESE THINGS, KARA. SOMEONE BUILT THEM AND UNLEASHED THEM TO CAUSE HAVOC.

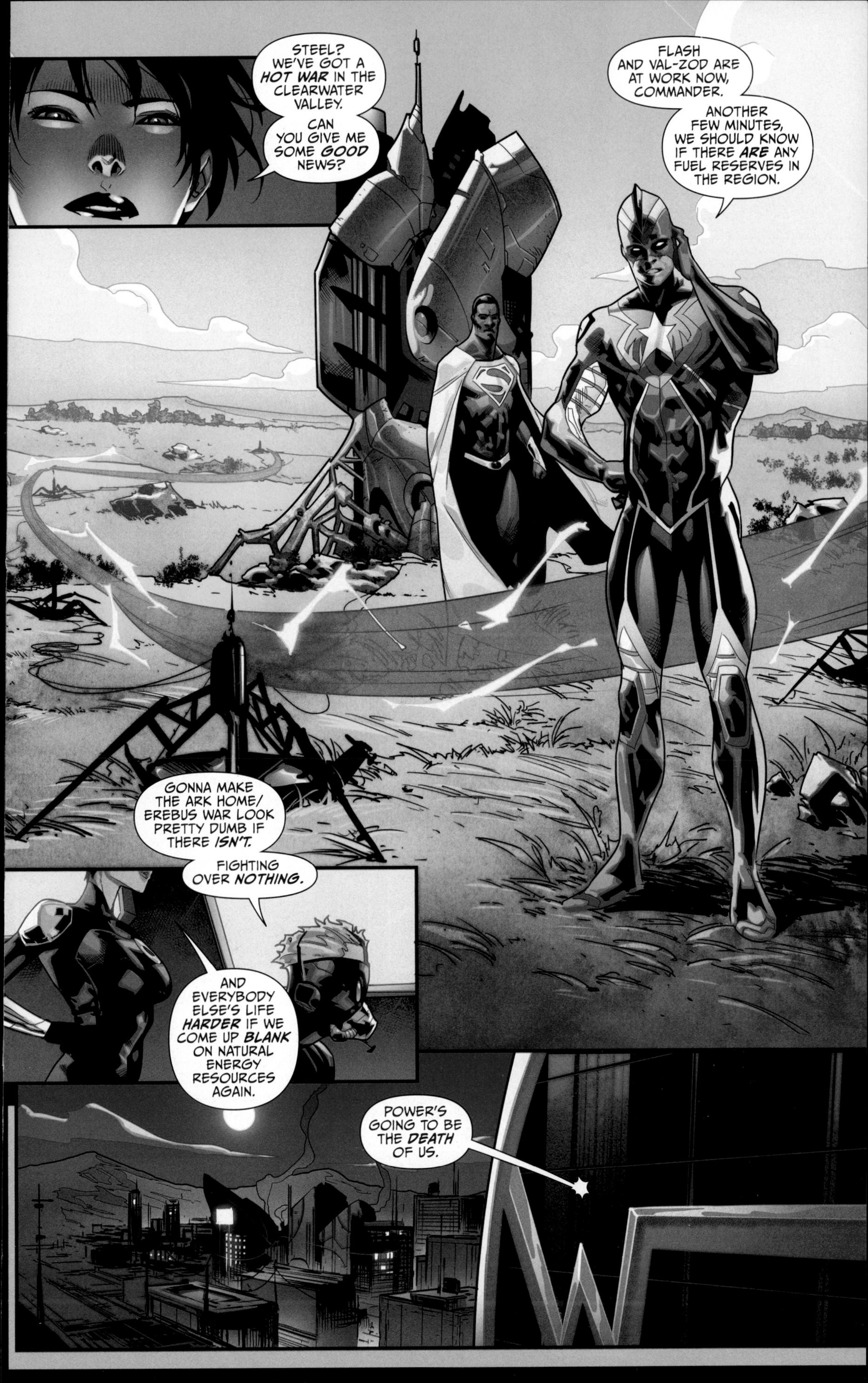
STEEL? WE'VE GOT A HOT WAR IN THE CLEARWATER VALLEY.
CAN YOU GIVE ME SOME GOOD NEWS?
FLASH AND VAL-ZOD ARE AT WORK NOW, COMMANDER.
ANOTHER FEW MINUTES, WE SHOULD KNOW IF THERE ARE ANY FUEL RESERVES IN THE REGION.
GONNA MAKE THE ARK HOME/EREBUS WAR LOOK PRETTY DUMB IF THERE ISN'T.
FIGHTING OVER NOTHING.
AND EVERYBODY ELSE'S LIFE HARDER IF WE COME UP BLANK ON NATURAL ENERGY RESOURCES AGAIN.
POWER'S GOING TO BE THE DEATH OF US.

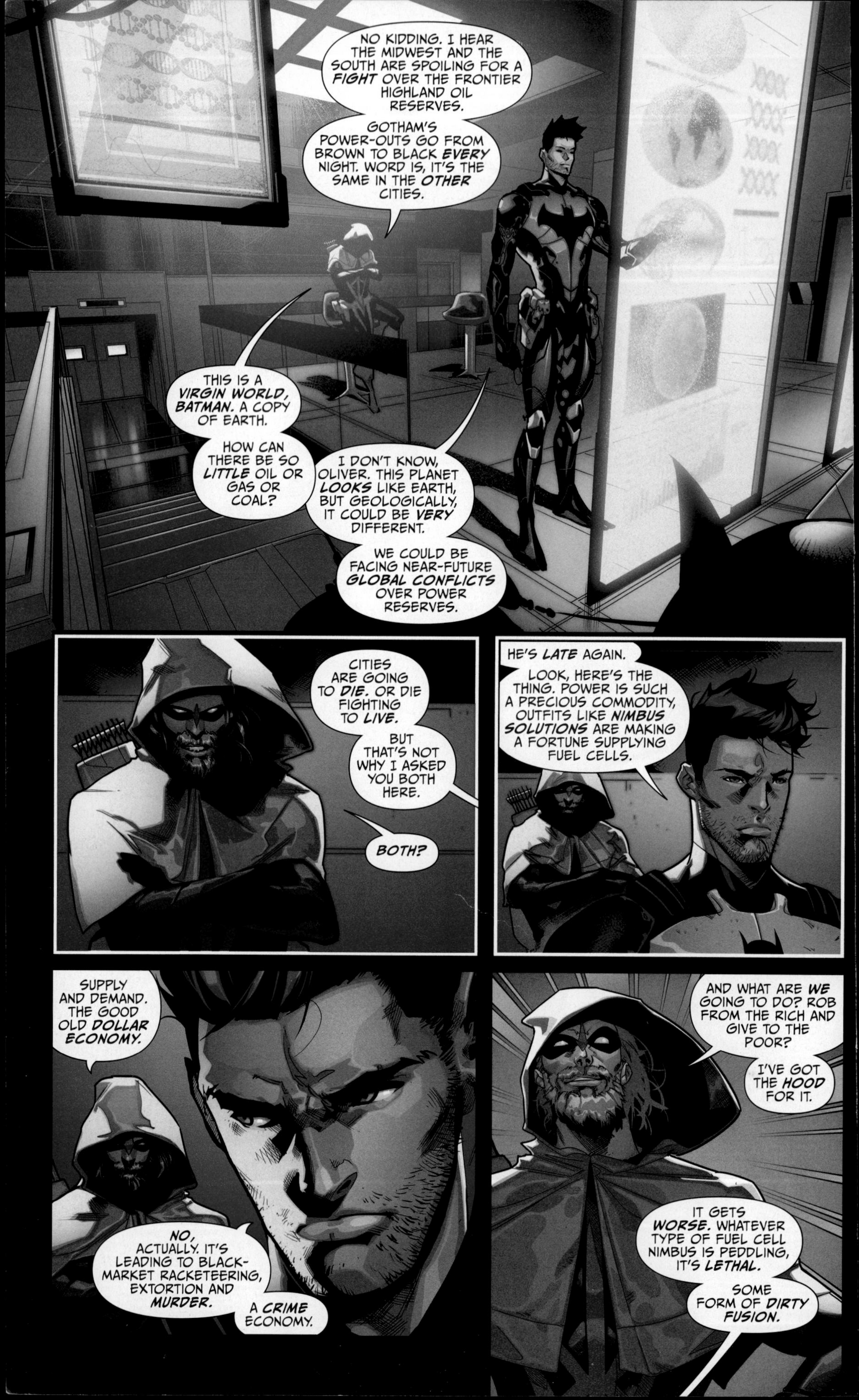
NO KIDDING. I HEAR THE MIDWEST AND THE SOUTH ARE SPOILING FOR A *FIGHT* OVER THE FRONTIER HIGHLAND OIL RESERVES.
GOTHAM'S POWER-OUTS GO FROM BROWN TO BLACK *EVERY* NIGHT. WORD IS, IT'S THE SAME IN THE *OTHER* CITIES.
THIS IS A *VIRGIN WORLD*, *BATMAN.* A COPY OF EARTH.
HOW CAN THERE BE SO *LITTLE* OIL OR GAS OR COAL?
I DON'T KNOW, OLIVER. THIS PLANET *LOOKS* LIKE EARTH, BUT GEOLOGICALLY, IT COULD BE *VERY* DIFFERENT.
WE COULD BE FACING NEAR-FUTURE *GLOBAL CONFLICTS* OVER POWER RESERVES.
CITIES ARE GOING TO *DIE*. OR DIE FIGHTING TO *LIVE*.
BUT THAT'S NOT WHY I ASKED YOU BOTH HERE.
BOTH?
HE'S *LATE* AGAIN.
LOOK, HERE'S THE THING. POWER IS SUCH A PRECIOUS COMMODITY, OUTFITS LIKE *NIMBUS SOLUTIONS* ARE MAKING A FORTUNE SUPPLYING FUEL CELLS.
SUPPLY AND DEMAND. THE GOOD OLD *DOLLAR ECONOMY.*
NO, ACTUALLY. IT'S LEADING TO BLACK-MARKET RACKETEERING, EXTORTION AND *MURDER.*
A *CRIME* ECONOMY.
AND WHAT ARE *WE* GOING TO DO? ROB FROM THE RICH AND GIVE TO THE POOR?
I'VE GOT THE *HOOD* FOR IT.
IT GETS *WORSE.* WHATEVER TYPE OF FUEL CELL NIMBUS IS PEDDLING, IT'S *LETHAL.*
SOME FORM OF *DIRTY FUSION.*

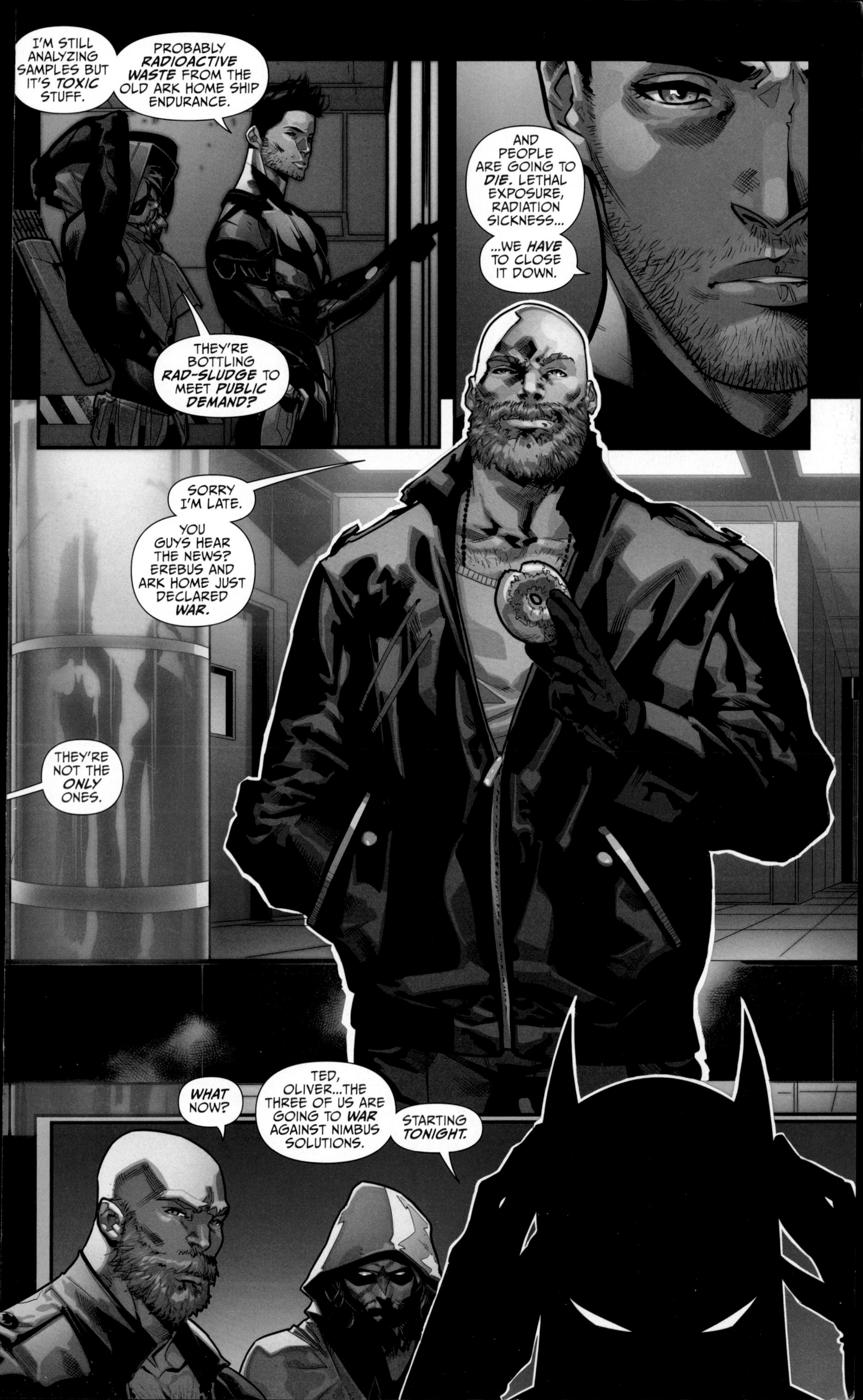
I'M STILL ANALYZING SAMPLES BUT IT'S TOXIC STUFF.
PROBABLY RADIOACTIVE WASTE FROM THE OLD ARK HOME SHIP ENDURANCE.
THEY'RE BOTTLING RAD-SLUDGE TO MEET PUBLIC DEMAND?
AND PEOPLE ARE GOING TO DIE. LETHAL EXPOSURE, RADIATION SICKNESS...
...WE HAVE TO CLOSE IT DOWN.
SORRY I'M LATE.
YOU GUYS HEAR THE NEWS? EREBUS AND ARK HOME JUST DECLARED WAR.
THEY'RE NOT THE ONLY ONES.
WHAT NOW?
TED, OLIVER...THE THREE OF US ARE GOING TO WAR AGAINST NIMBUS SOLUTIONS.
STARTING TONIGHT.

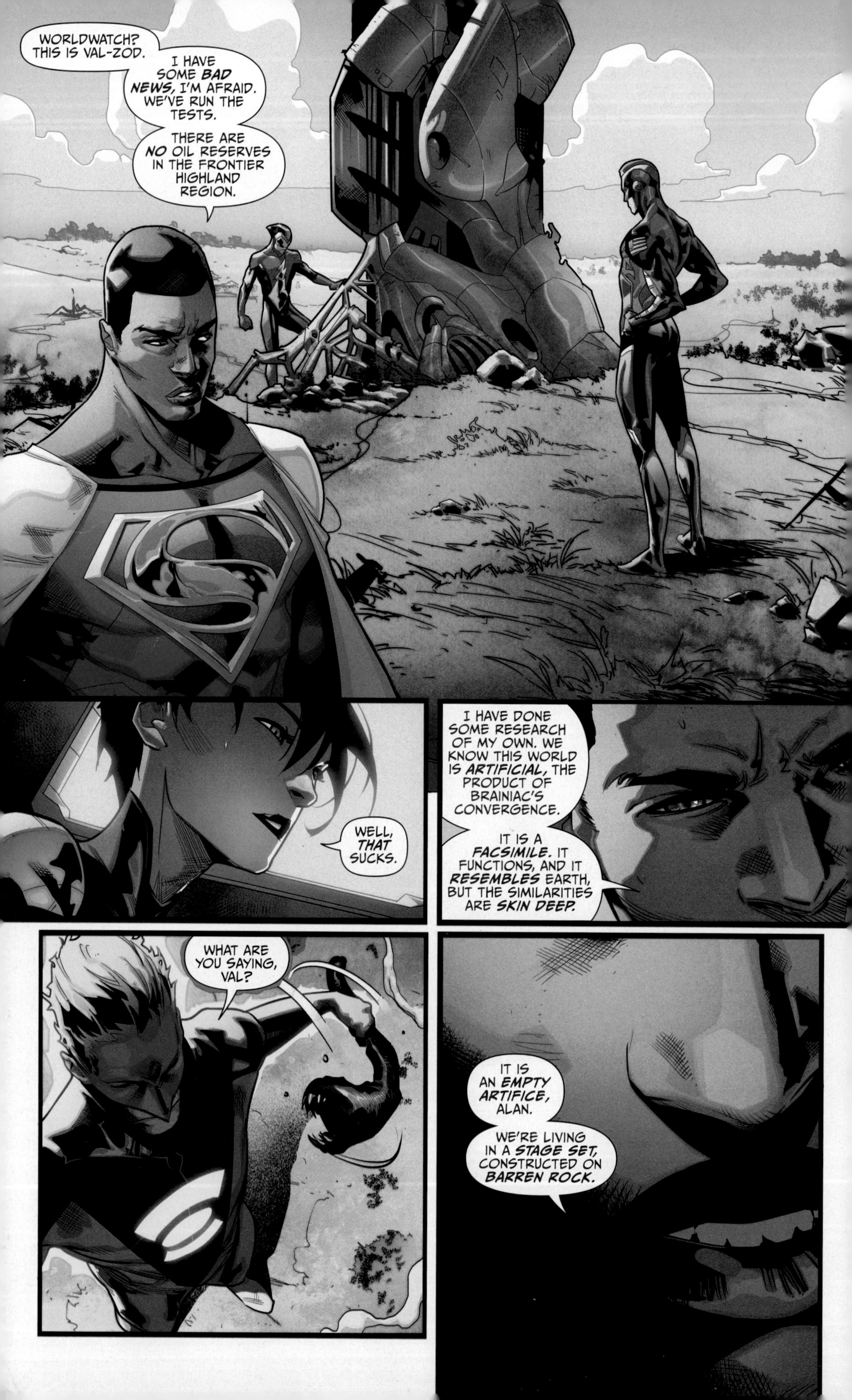
WORLDWATCH? THIS IS VAL-ZOD.
I HAVE SOME BAD NEWS, I'M AFRAID. WE'VE RUN THE TESTS.
THERE ARE NO OIL RESERVES IN THE FRONTIER HIGHLAND REGION.
WELL, THAT SUCKS.
I HAVE DONE SOME RESEARCH OF MY OWN. WE KNOW THIS WORLD IS ARTIFICIAL, THE PRODUCT OF BRAINIAC'S CONVERGENCE.
IT IS A FACSIMILE. IT FUNCTIONS, AND IT RESEMBLES EARTH, BUT THE SIMILARITIES ARE SKIN DEEP.
WHAT ARE YOU SAYING, VAL?
IT IS AN EMPTY ARTIFICE, ALAN.
WE'RE LIVING IN A STAGE SET, CONSTRUCTED ON BARREN ROCK.

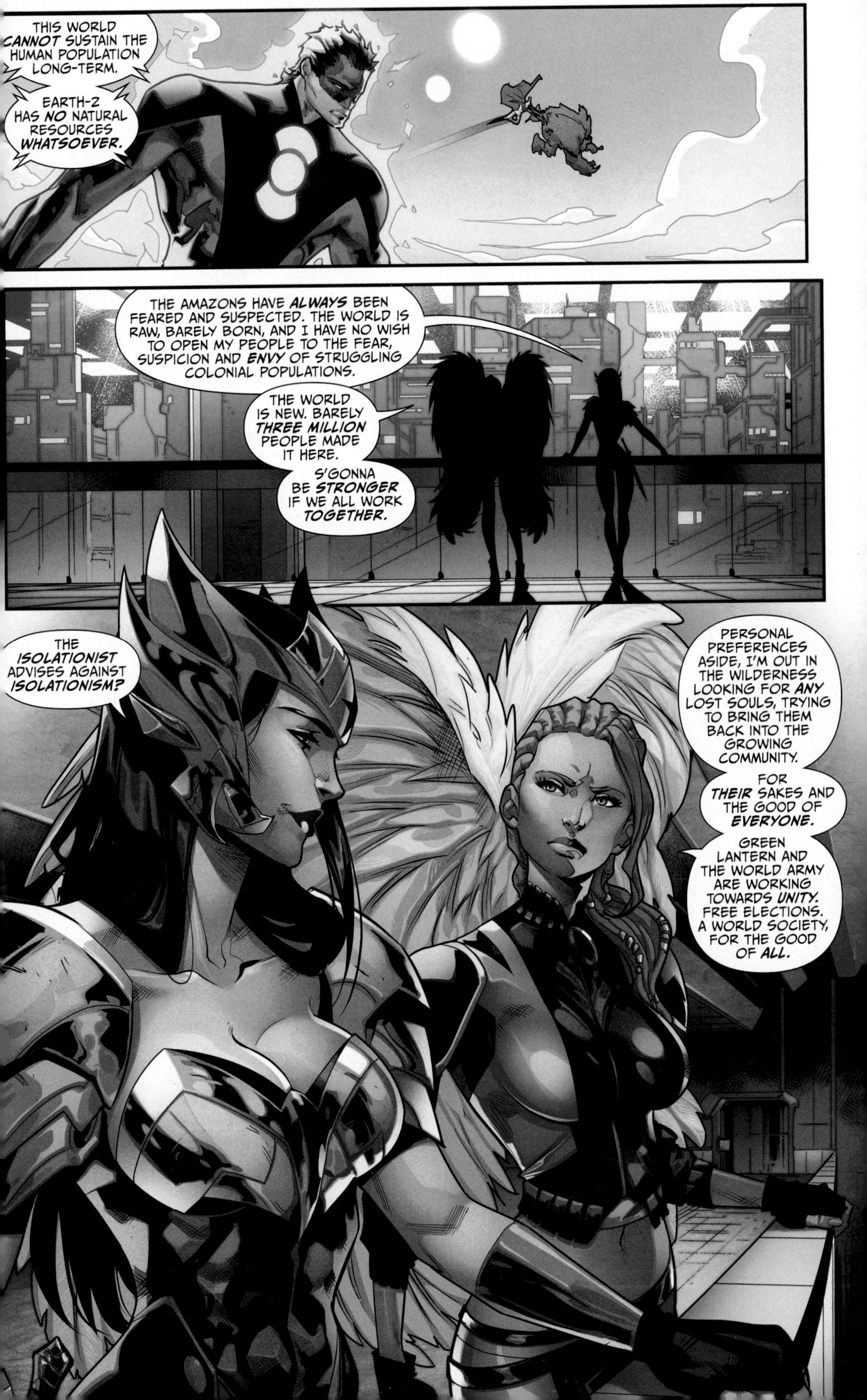

THIS WORLD CANNOT SUSTAIN THE HUMAN POPULATION LONG-TERM.
EARTH-2 HAS NO NATURAL RESOURCES WHATSOEVER.
THE AMAZONS HAVE ALWAYS BEEN FEARED AND SUSPECTED. THE WORLD IS RAW, BARELY BORN, AND I HAVE NO WISH TO OPEN MY PEOPLE TO THE FEAR, SUSPICION AND ENVY OF STRUGGLING COLONIAL POPULATIONS.
THE WORLD IS NEW. BARELY THREE MILLION PEOPLE MADE IT HERE.
S'GONNA BE STRONGER IF WE ALL WORK TOGETHER.
THE ISOLATIONIST ADVISES AGAINST ISOLATIONISM?
PERSONAL PREFERENCES ASIDE, I'M OUT IN THE WILDERNESS LOOKING FOR ANY LOST SOULS, TRYING TO BRING THEM BACK INTO THE GROWING COMMUNITY.
FOR THEIR SAKES AND THE GOOD OF EVERYONE.
GREEN LANTERN AND THE WORLD ARMY ARE WORKING TOWARDS UNITY. FREE ELECTIONS. A WORLD SOCIETY, FOR THE GOOD OF ALL.

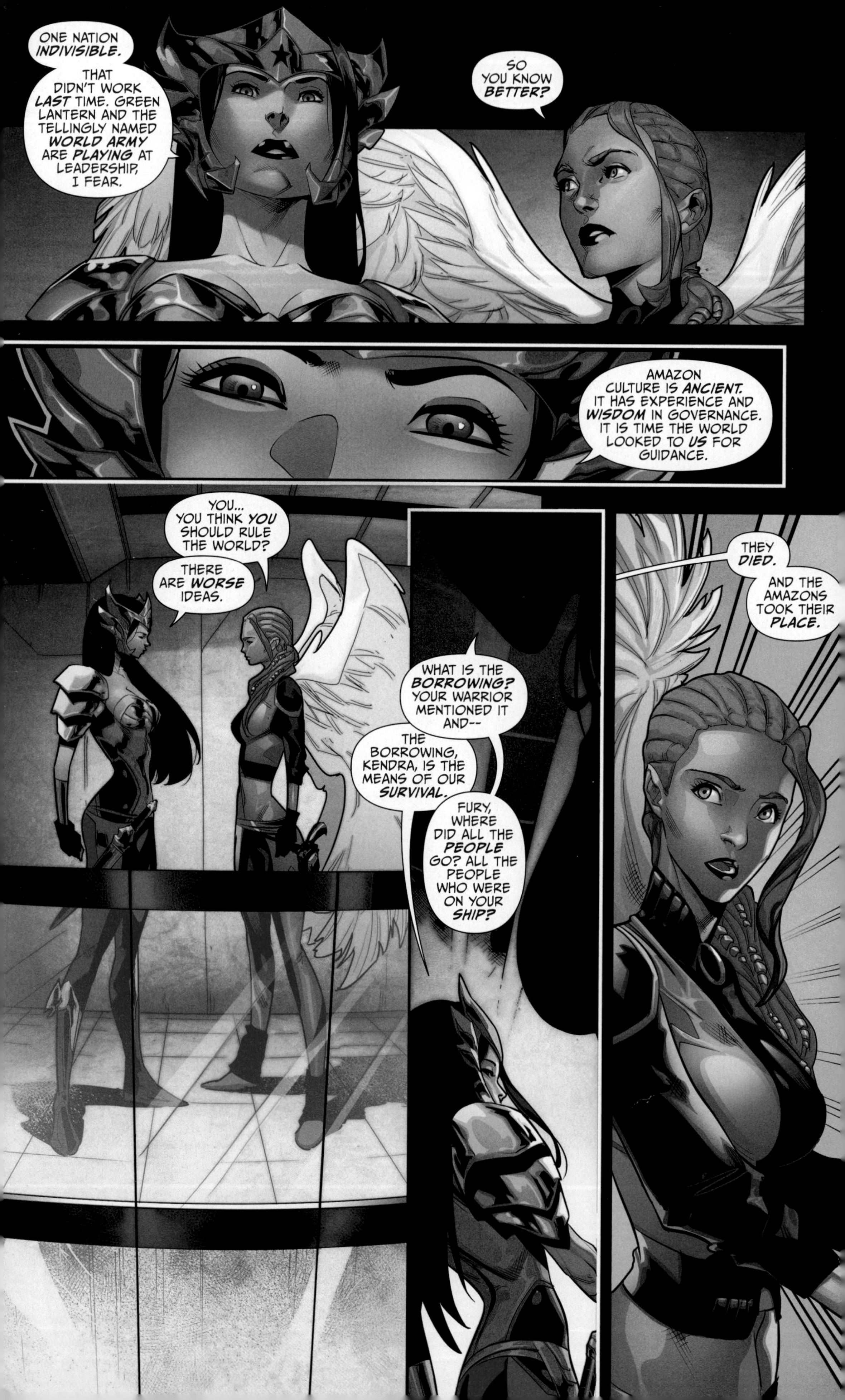
ONE NATION INDIVISIBLE.
THAT DIDN'T WORK LAST TIME. GREEN LANTERN AND THE TELLINGLY NAMED WORLD ARMY ARE PLAYING AT LEADERSHIP, I FEAR.
SO YOU KNOW BETTER?
AMAZON CULTURE IS ANCIENT. IT HAS EXPERIENCE AND WISDOM IN GOVERNANCE. IT IS TIME THE WORLD LOOKED TO US FOR GUIDANCE.
YOU... YOU THINK YOU SHOULD RULE THE WORLD?
THERE ARE WORSE IDEAS.
WHAT IS THE BORROWING? YOUR WARRIOR MENTIONED IT AND--
THE BORROWING, KENDRA, IS THE MEANS OF OUR SURVIVAL.
FURY, WHERE DID ALL THE PEOPLE GO? ALL THE PEOPLE WHO WERE ON YOUR SHIP?
THEY DIED.
AND THE AMAZONS TOOK THEIR PLACE.

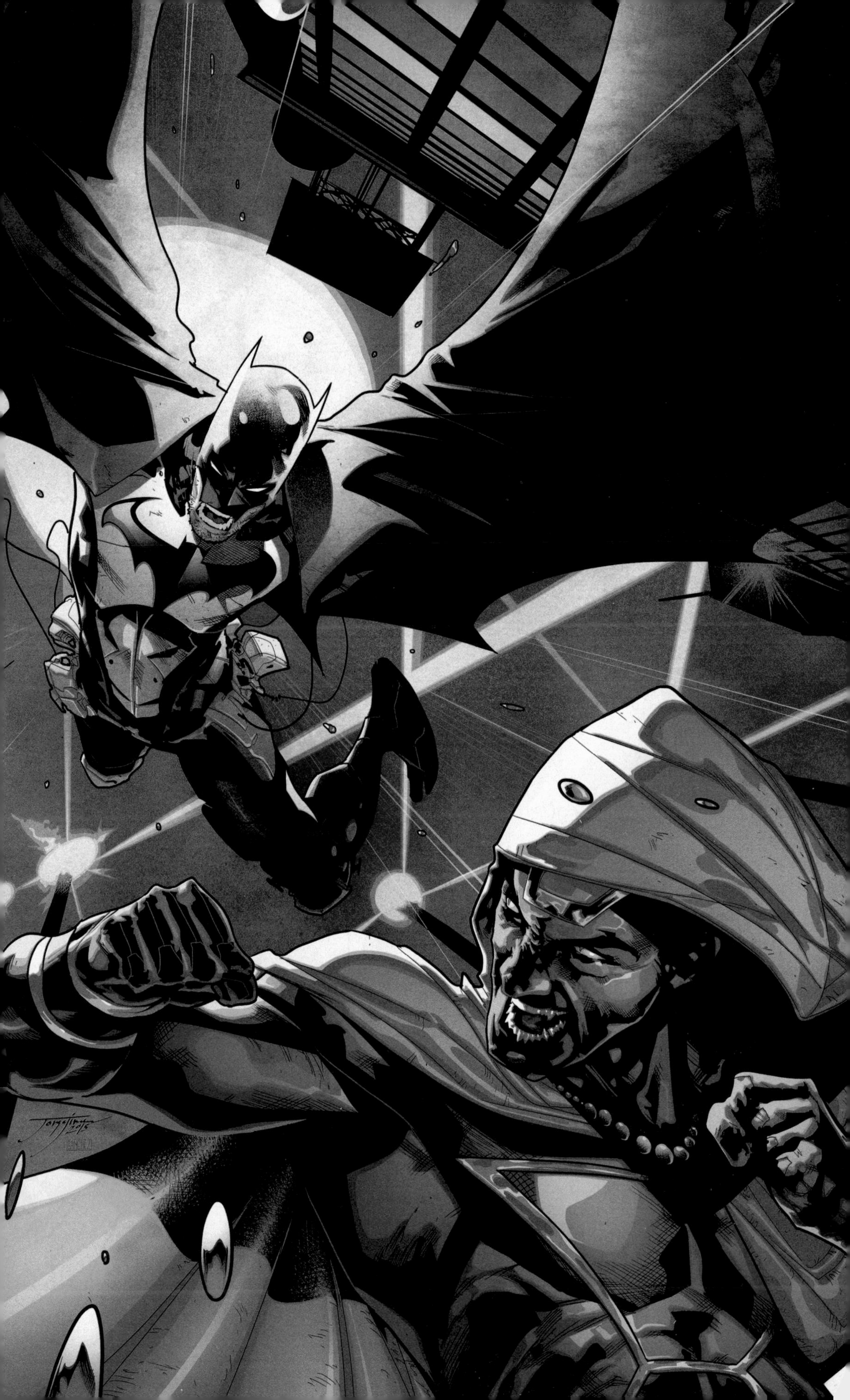

ONE NATION, INDIVISIBLE CHAPTER THREE: RUNNING ON EMPTY

DAN ABNETT writer JORGE JIMÉNEZ artist ALEJANDRO SANCHEZ colorist TRAVIS LANHAM letterer cover by JIMÉNEZ & SANCHEZ

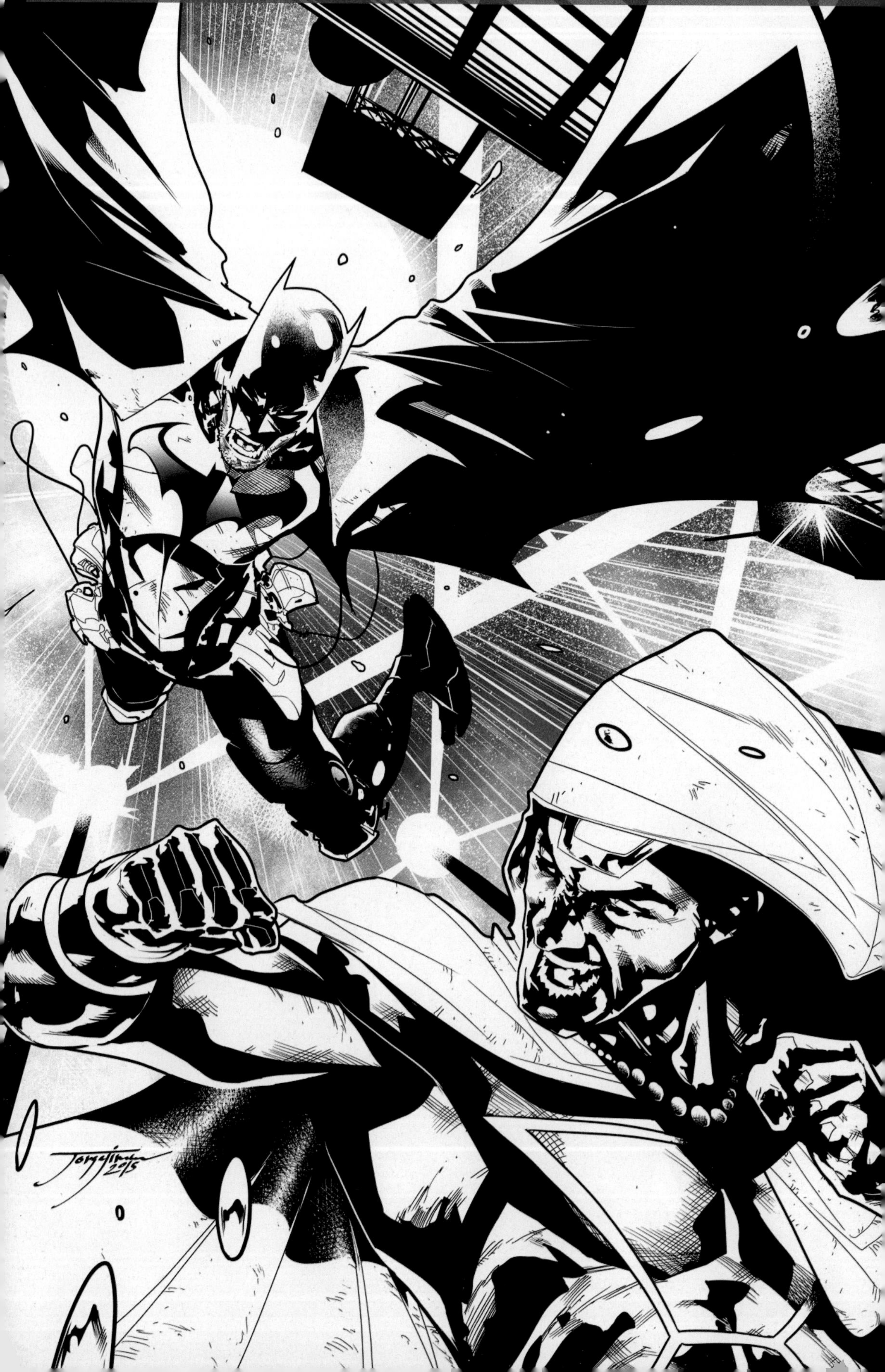

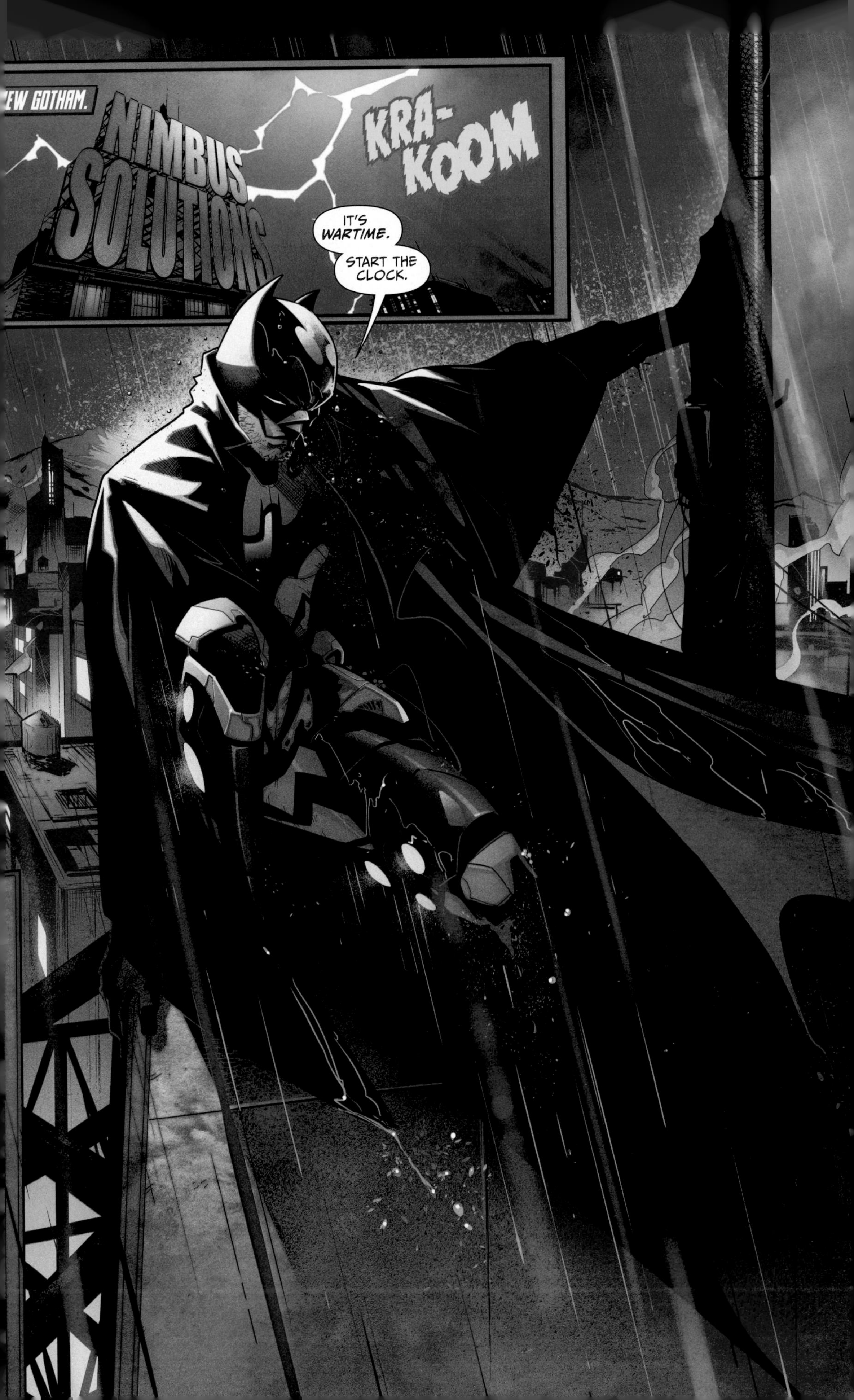

EW GOTHAM.
NIMBUS SOLUTIONS
KRA-KOOM
IT'S WARTIME.
START THE CLOCK.

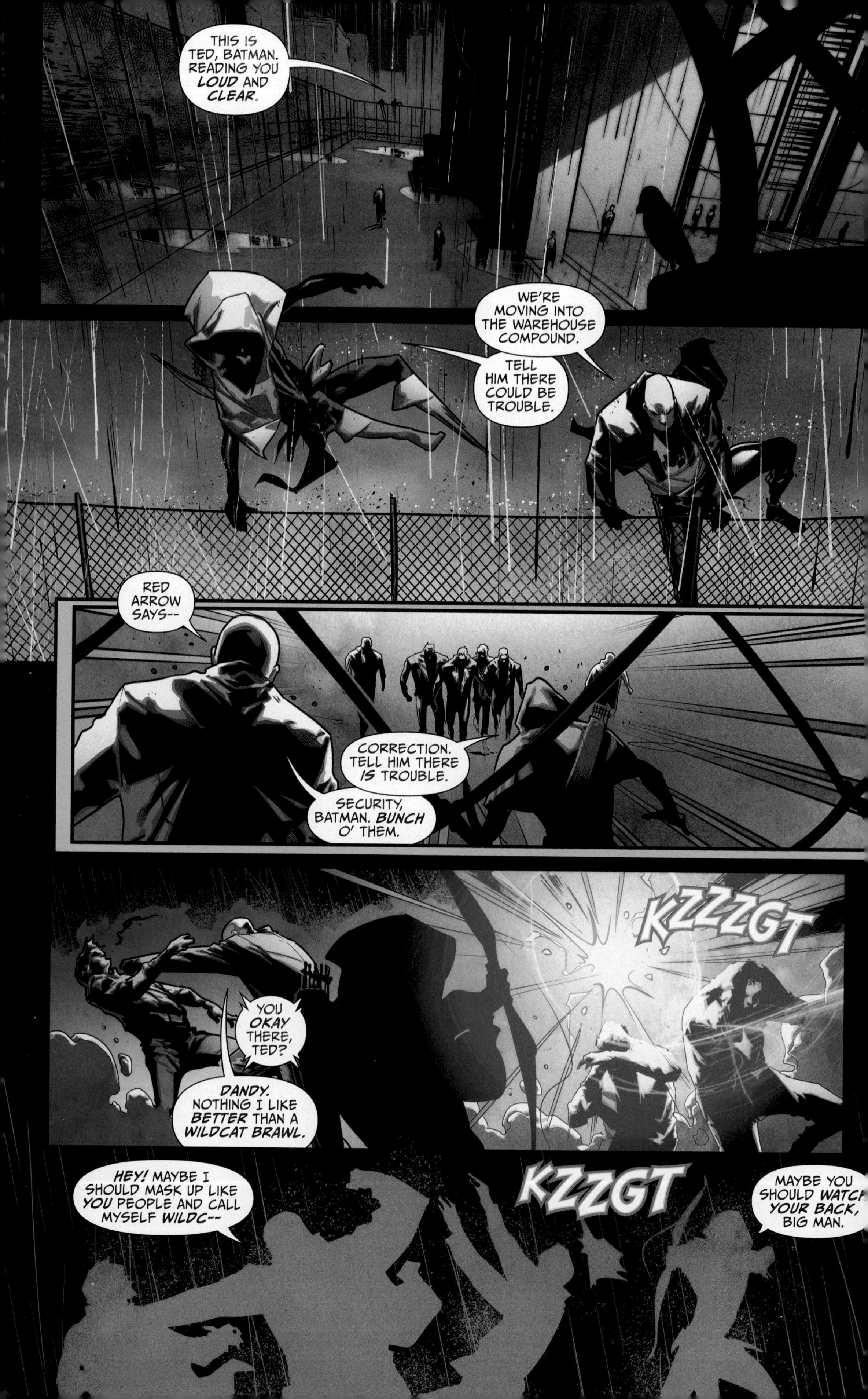
THIS IS TED, BATMAN. READING YOU LOUD AND CLEAR.
WE'RE MOVING INTO THE WAREHOUSE COMPOUND.
TELL HIM THERE COULD BE TROUBLE.
RED ARROW SAYS--
CORRECTION. TELL HIM THERE IS TROUBLE.
SECURITY, BATMAN. BUNCH O' THEM.
KZZZGT
YOU OKAY THERE, TED?
DANDY. NOTHING I LIKE BETTER THAN A WILDCAT BRAWL.
HEY! MAYBE I SHOULD MASK UP LIKE YOU PEOPLE AND CALL MYSELF WILDC--
KZZGT
MAYBE YOU SHOULD WATCH YOUR BACK, BIG MAN.

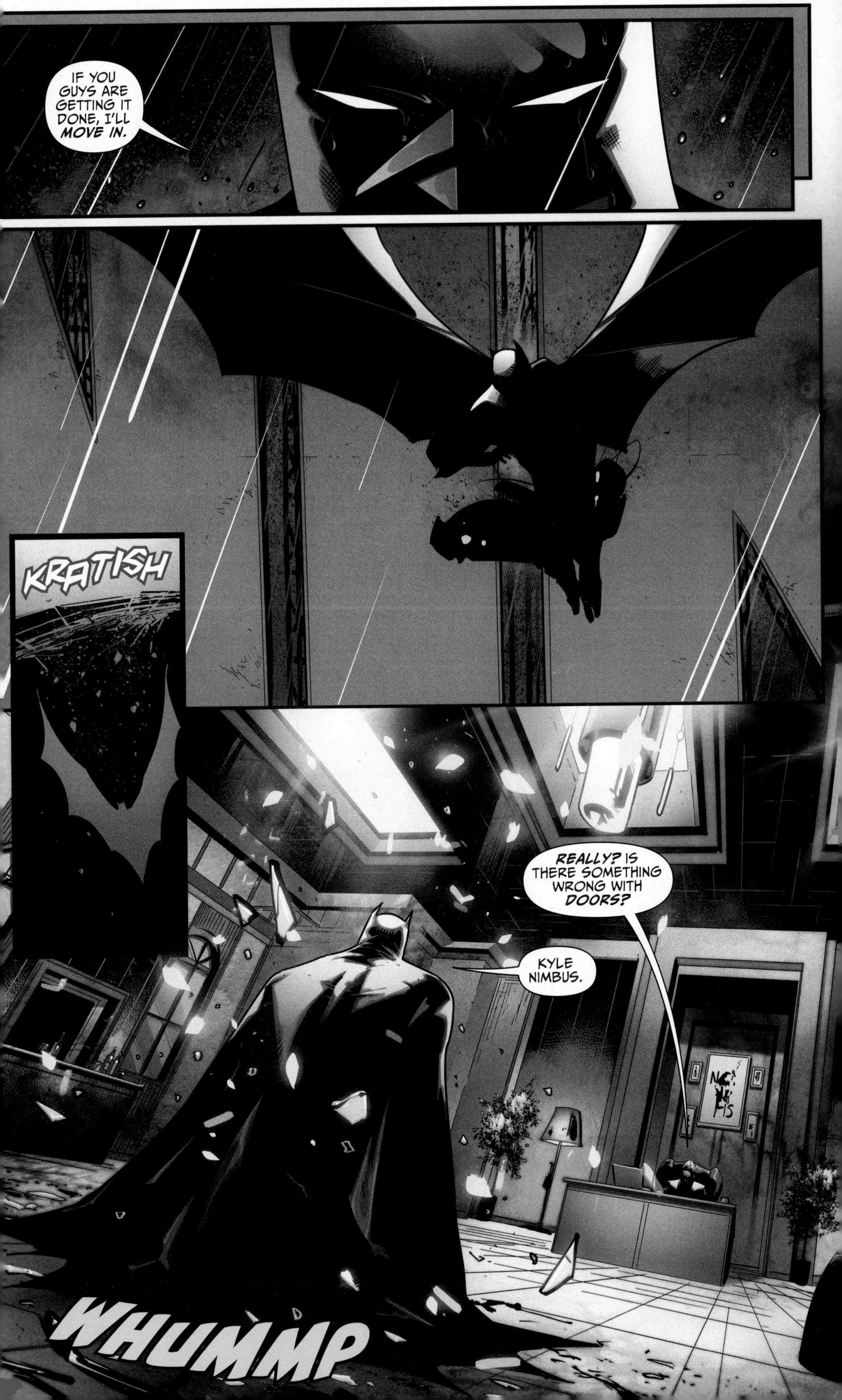
IF YOU GUYS ARE GETTING IT DONE, I'LL MOVE IN.
KRATISH
REALLY? IS THERE SOMETHING WRONG WITH DOORS?
KYLE NIMBUS.
WHUMMP

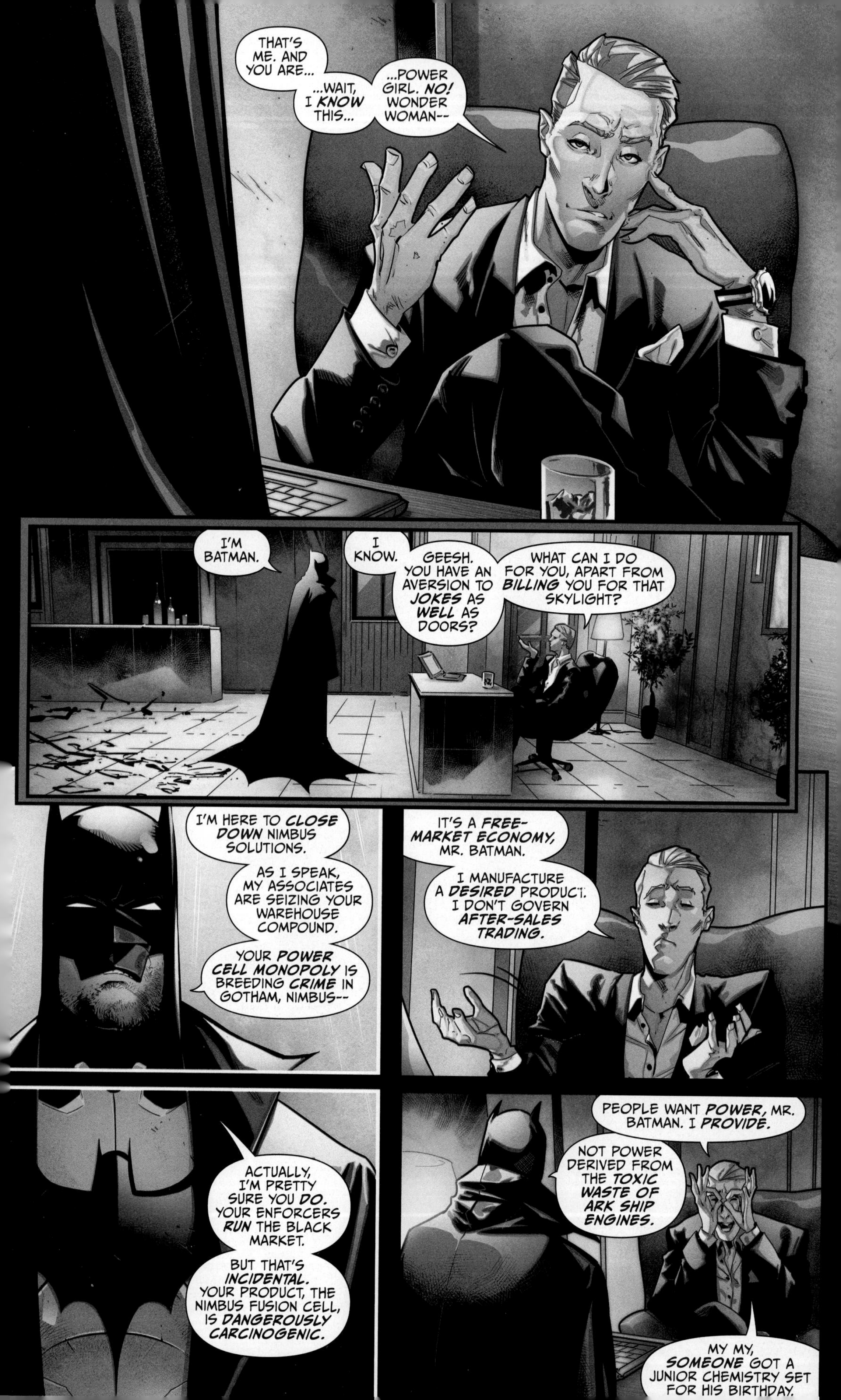
THAT'S ME. AND YOU ARE...
...WAIT, I **KNOW** THIS...
...POWER GIRL. **NO!** WONDER WOMAN--
I'M BATMAN.
I KNOW.
GEESH. YOU HAVE AN AVERSION TO **JOKES** AS **WELL** AS DOORS?
WHAT CAN I DO FOR YOU, APART FROM **BILLING** YOU FOR THAT SKYLIGHT?
I'M HERE TO **CLOSE DOWN** NIMBUS SOLUTIONS.
AS I SPEAK, MY ASSOCIATES ARE SEIZING YOUR WAREHOUSE COMPOUND.
YOUR **POWER CELL MONOPOLY** IS BREEDING **CRIME** IN GOTHAM, NIMBUS--
IT'S A **FREE-MARKET ECONOMY,** MR. BATMAN.
I MANUFACTURE A **DESIRED** PRODUCT. I DON'T GOVERN **AFTER-SALES TRADING.**
ACTUALLY, I'M PRETTY SURE YOU **DO.** YOUR ENFORCERS **RUN** THE BLACK MARKET.
BUT THAT'S **INCIDENTAL.** YOUR PRODUCT, THE NIMBUS FUSION CELL, IS **DANGEROUSLY CARCINOGENIC.**
PEOPLE WANT **POWER,** MR. BATMAN. I **PROVIDE.**
NOT POWER DERIVED FROM THE **TOXIC WASTE OF ARK SHIP ENGINES.**
MY MY, **SOMEONE** GOT A JUNIOR CHEMISTRY SET FOR HIS BIRTHDAY.

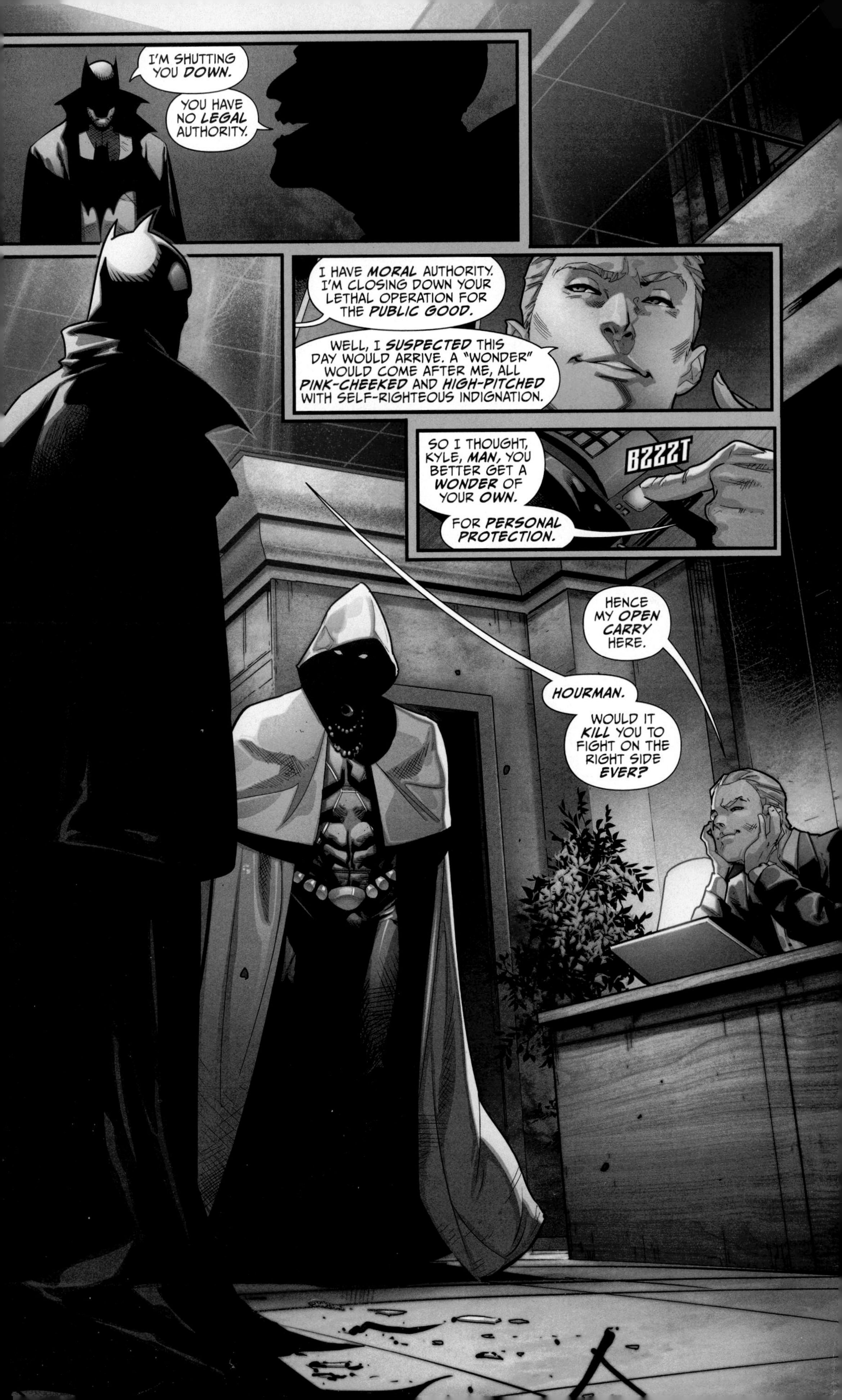

I'M SHUTTING YOU DOWN.
YOU HAVE NO LEGAL AUTHORITY.
I HAVE MORAL AUTHORITY. I'M CLOSING DOWN YOUR LETHAL OPERATION FOR THE PUBLIC GOOD.
WELL, I SUSPECTED THIS DAY WOULD ARRIVE. A "WONDER" WOULD COME AFTER ME, ALL PINK-CHEEKED AND HIGH-PITCHED WITH SELF-RIGHTEOUS INDIGNATION.
SO I THOUGHT, KYLE, MAN, YOU BETTER GET A WONDER OF YOUR OWN.
BZZZT
FOR PERSONAL PROTECTION.
HENCE MY OPEN CARRY HERE.
HOURMAN.
WOULD IT KILL YOU TO FIGHT ON THE RIGHT SIDE EVER?

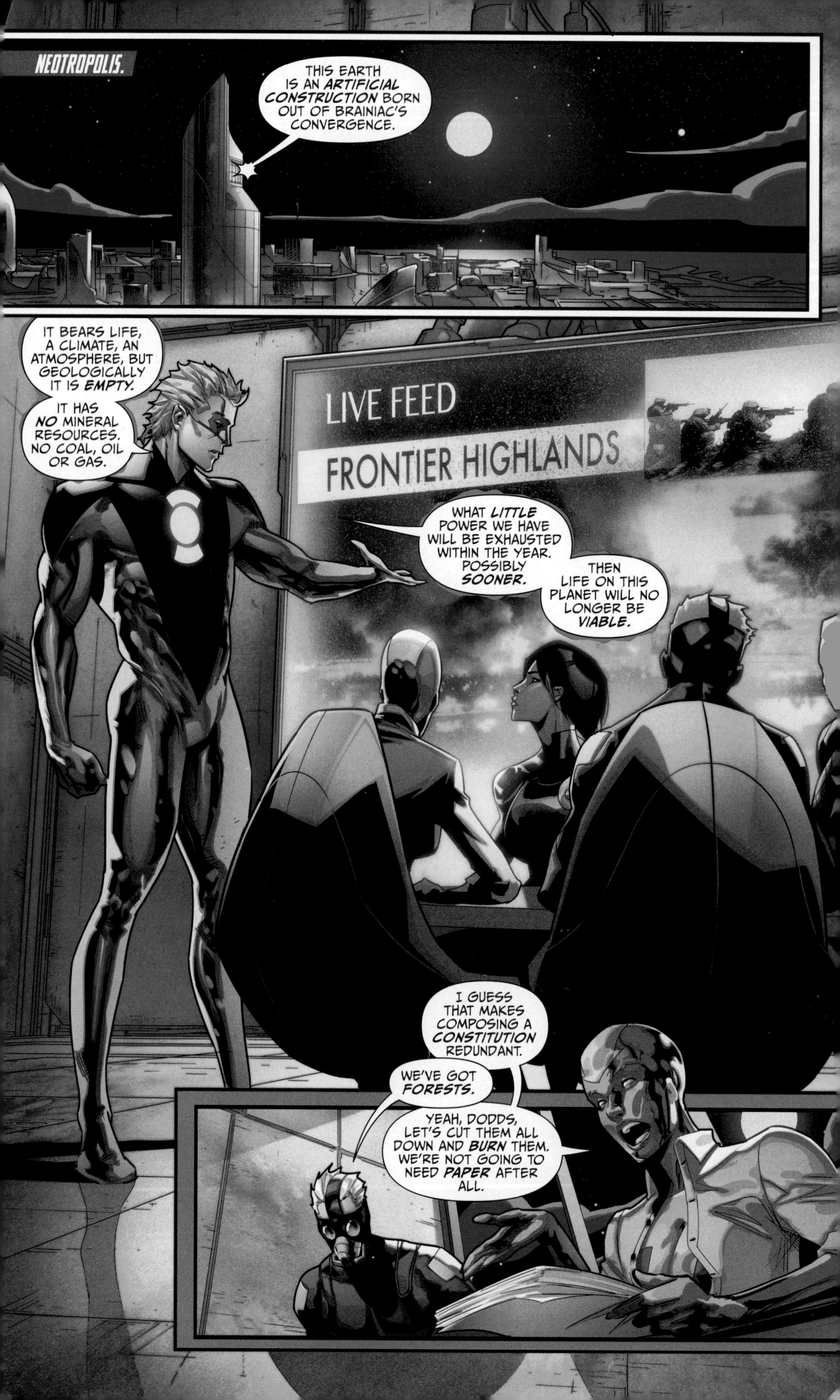
NEOTROPOLIS.
THIS EARTH IS AN ARTIFICIAL CONSTRUCTION BORN OUT OF BRAINIAC'S CONVERGENCE.
IT BEARS LIFE, A CLIMATE, AN ATMOSPHERE, BUT GEOLOGICALLY IT IS EMPTY.
IT HAS NO MINERAL RESOURCES. NO COAL, OIL OR GAS.
LIVE FEED
FRONTIER HIGHLANDS
WHAT LITTLE POWER WE HAVE WILL BE EXHAUSTED WITHIN THE YEAR. POSSIBLY SOONER.
THEN LIFE ON THIS PLANET WILL NO LONGER BE VIABLE.
I GUESS THAT MAKES COMPOSING A CONSTITUTION REDUNDANT.
WE'VE GOT FORESTS.
YEAH, DODDS, LET'S CUT THEM ALL DOWN AND BURN THEM. WE'RE NOT GOING TO NEED PAPER AFTER ALL.

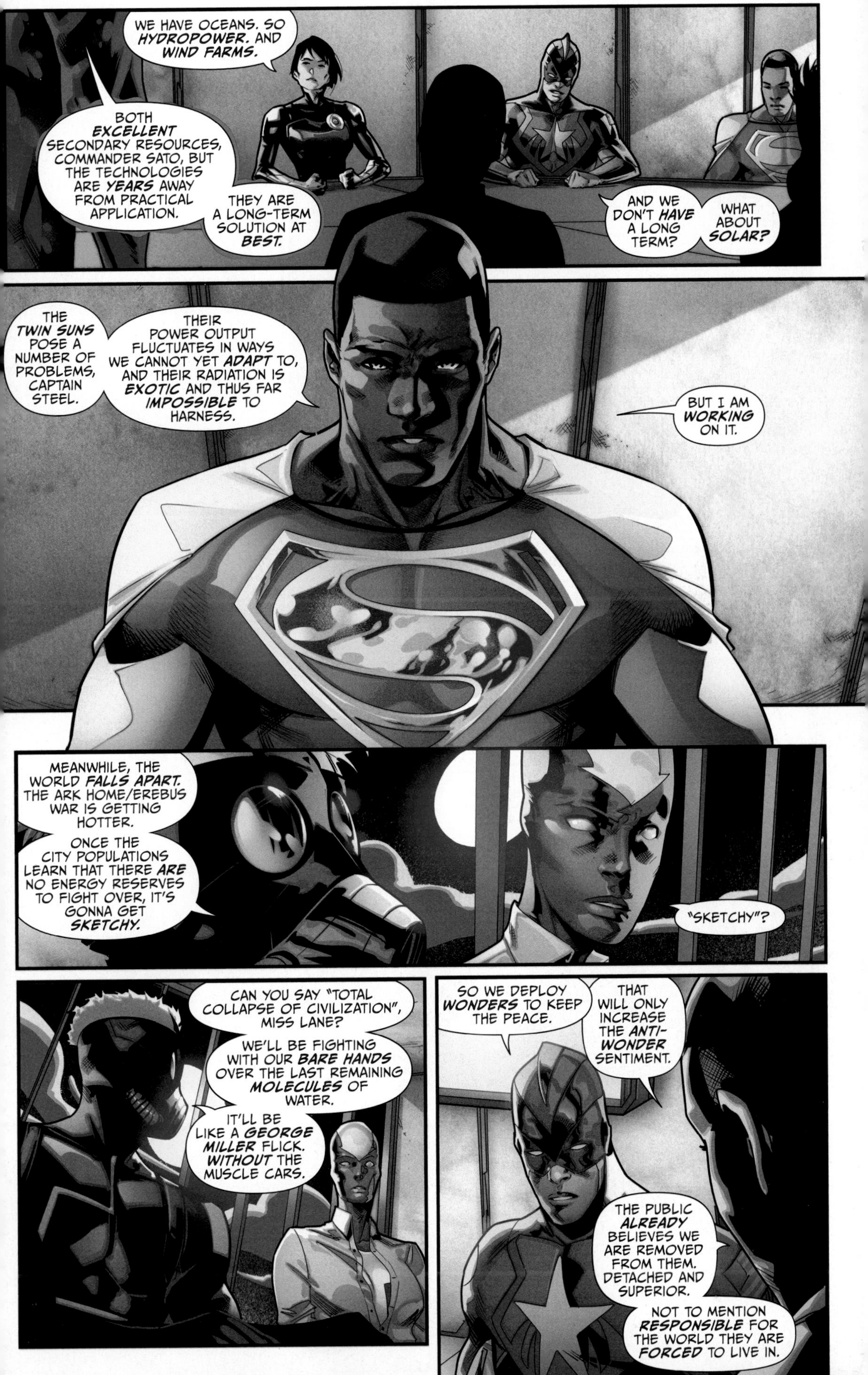
WE HAVE OCEANS. SO HYDROPOWER. AND WIND FARMS.
BOTH EXCELLENT SECONDARY RESOURCES, COMMANDER SATO, BUT THE TECHNOLOGIES ARE YEARS AWAY FROM PRACTICAL APPLICATION.
THEY ARE A LONG-TERM SOLUTION AT BEST.
AND WE DON'T HAVE A LONG TERM?
WHAT ABOUT SOLAR?
THE TWIN SUNS POSE A NUMBER OF PROBLEMS, CAPTAIN STEEL.
THEIR POWER OUTPUT FLUCTUATES IN WAYS WE CANNOT YET ADAPT TO, AND THEIR RADIATION IS EXOTIC AND THUS FAR IMPOSSIBLE TO HARNESS.
BUT I AM WORKING ON IT.
MEANWHILE, THE WORLD FALLS APART. THE ARK HOME/EREBUS WAR IS GETTING HOTTER.
ONCE THE CITY POPULATIONS LEARN THAT THERE ARE NO ENERGY RESERVES TO FIGHT OVER, IT'S GONNA GET SKETCHY.
"SKETCHY"?
CAN YOU SAY "TOTAL COLLAPSE OF CIVILIZATION", MISS LANE?
WE'LL BE FIGHTING WITH OUR BARE HANDS OVER THE LAST REMAINING MOLECULES OF WATER.
IT'LL BE LIKE A GEORGE MILLER FLICK. WITHOUT THE MUSCLE CARS.
SO WE DEPLOY WONDERS TO KEEP THE PEACE.
THAT WILL ONLY INCREASE THE ANTI-WONDER SENTIMENT.
THE PUBLIC ALREADY BELIEVES WE ARE REMOVED FROM THEM. DETACHED AND SUPERIOR.
NOT TO MENTION RESPONSIBLE FOR THE WORLD THEY ARE FORCED TO LIVE IN.

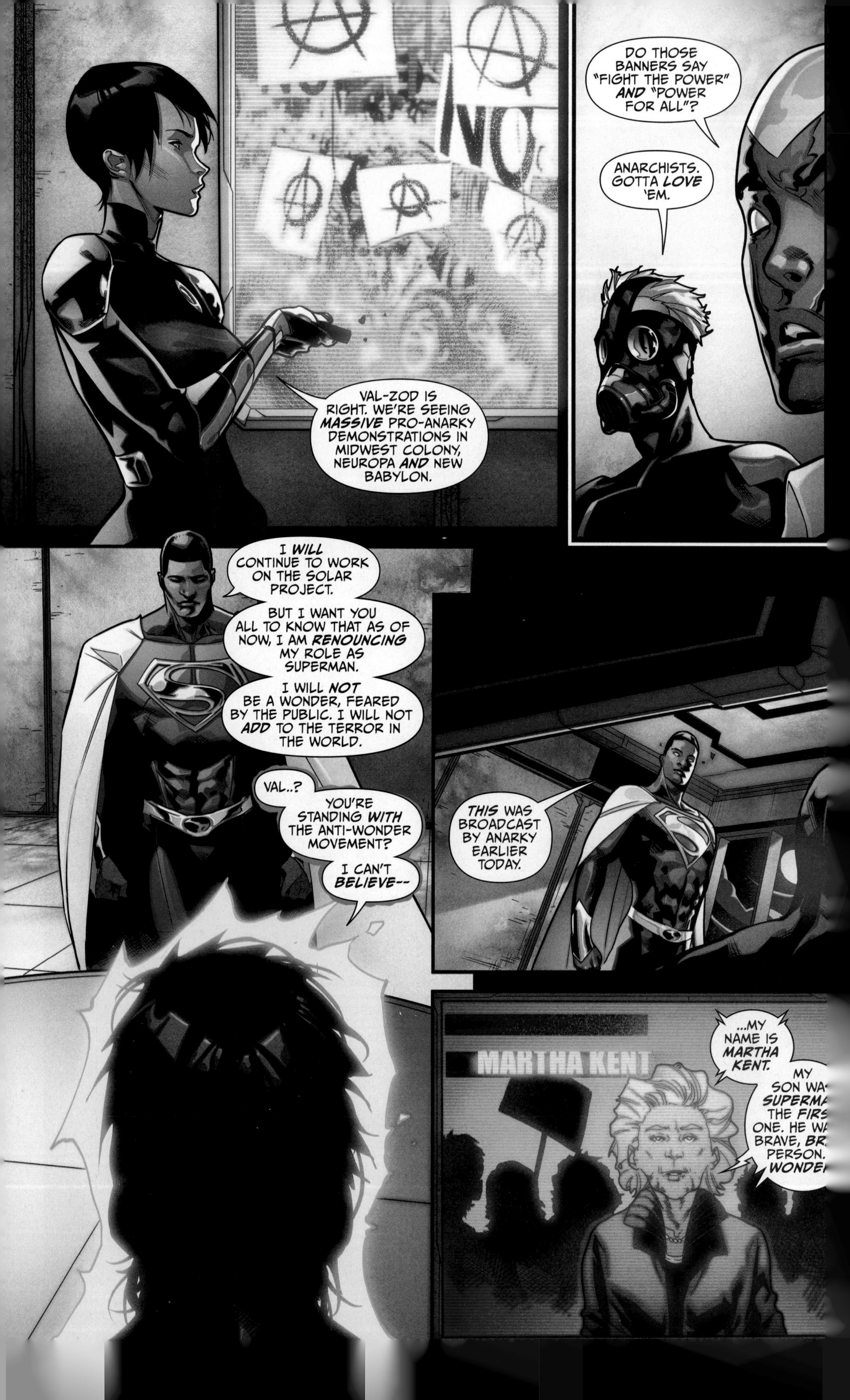
DO THOSE BANNERS SAY "FIGHT THE POWER" AND "POWER FOR ALL"?
ANARCHISTS. GOTTA LOVE 'EM.
VAL-ZOD IS RIGHT. WE'RE SEEING MASSIVE PRO-ANARKY DEMONSTRATIONS IN MIDWEST COLONY, NEUROPA AND NEW BABYLON.
I WILL CONTINUE TO WORK ON THE SOLAR PROJECT.
BUT I WANT YOU ALL TO KNOW THAT AS OF NOW, I AM RENOUNCING MY ROLE AS SUPERMAN.
I WILL NOT BE A WONDER, FEARED BY THE PUBLIC. I WILL NOT ADD TO THE TERROR IN THE WORLD.
VAL..?
YOU'RE STANDING WITH THE ANTI-WONDER MOVEMENT?
I CAN'T BELIEVE--
THIS WAS BROADCAST BY ANARKY EARLIER TODAY.
MARTHA KENT
...MY NAME IS MARTHA KENT.

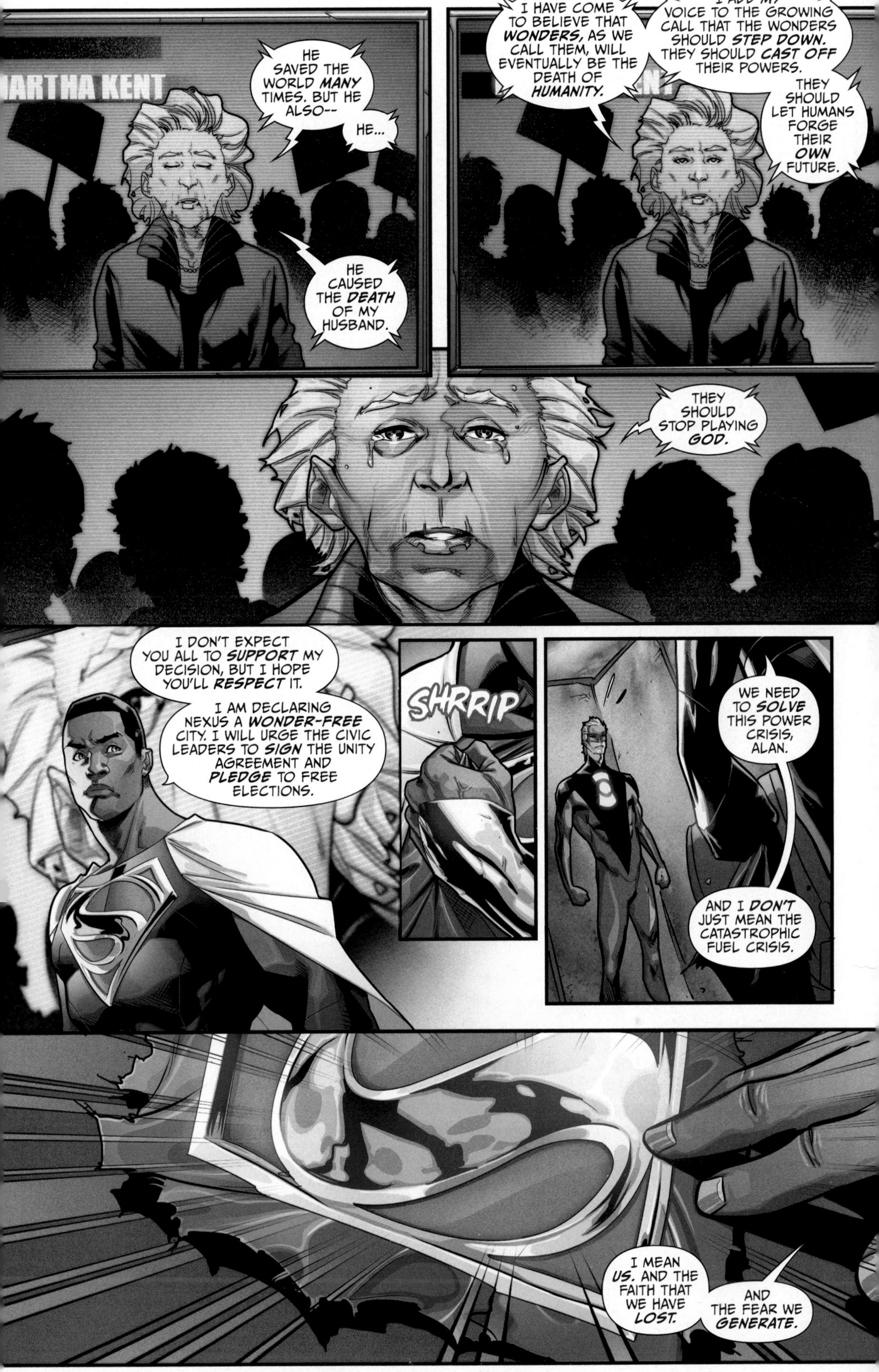
ARTHA KENT
HE SAVED THE WORLD MANY TIMES. BUT HE ALSO--
HE...
HE CAUSED THE DEATH OF MY HUSBAND.
I HAVE COME TO BELIEVE THAT WONDERS, AS WE CALL THEM, WILL EVENTUALLY BE THE DEATH OF HUMANITY.
I ADD MY VOICE TO THE GROWING CALL THAT THE WONDERS SHOULD STEP DOWN. THEY SHOULD CAST OFF THEIR POWERS.
THEY SHOULD LET HUMANS FORGE THEIR OWN FUTURE.
THEY SHOULD STOP PLAYING GOD.
I DON'T EXPECT YOU ALL TO SUPPORT MY DECISION, BUT I HOPE YOU'LL RESPECT IT.
I AM DECLARING NEXUS A WONDER-FREE CITY. I WILL URGE THE CIVIC LEADERS TO SIGN THE UNITY AGREEMENT AND PLEDGE TO FREE ELECTIONS.
SHRRIP
WE NEED TO SOLVE THIS POWER CRISIS, ALAN.
AND I DON'T JUST MEAN THE CATASTROPHIC FUEL CRISIS.
I MEAN US. AND THE FAITH THAT WE HAVE LOST.
AND THE FEAR WE GENERATE.

I SEE THE NATIVES ARE STILL *RESTLESS*.

KHALID? *BUDDY?* I SAID--

SORRY, JAY.

I HAD A DREAM LAST NIGHT. ABOUT *HAWKGIRL*.

WHOA. OKAY. THANKS FOR *SHARING*.

IDIOT.

I DREAMT SHE WAS IN *TROUBLE*. IT WAS A *PREMONITION*.

YOU *THINK?*

I *KNOW*.

I AM *NOT* DOCTOR FATE ANYMORE, BUT I CARRY A FEW *SHARDS* OF THE HELMET OF FATE WITH ME.

THEY *RESONATE*.

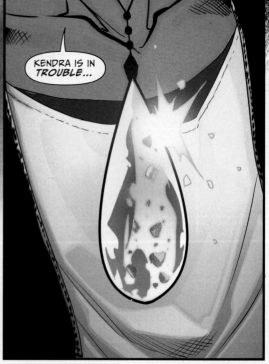

KENDRA IS IN *TROUBLE*...

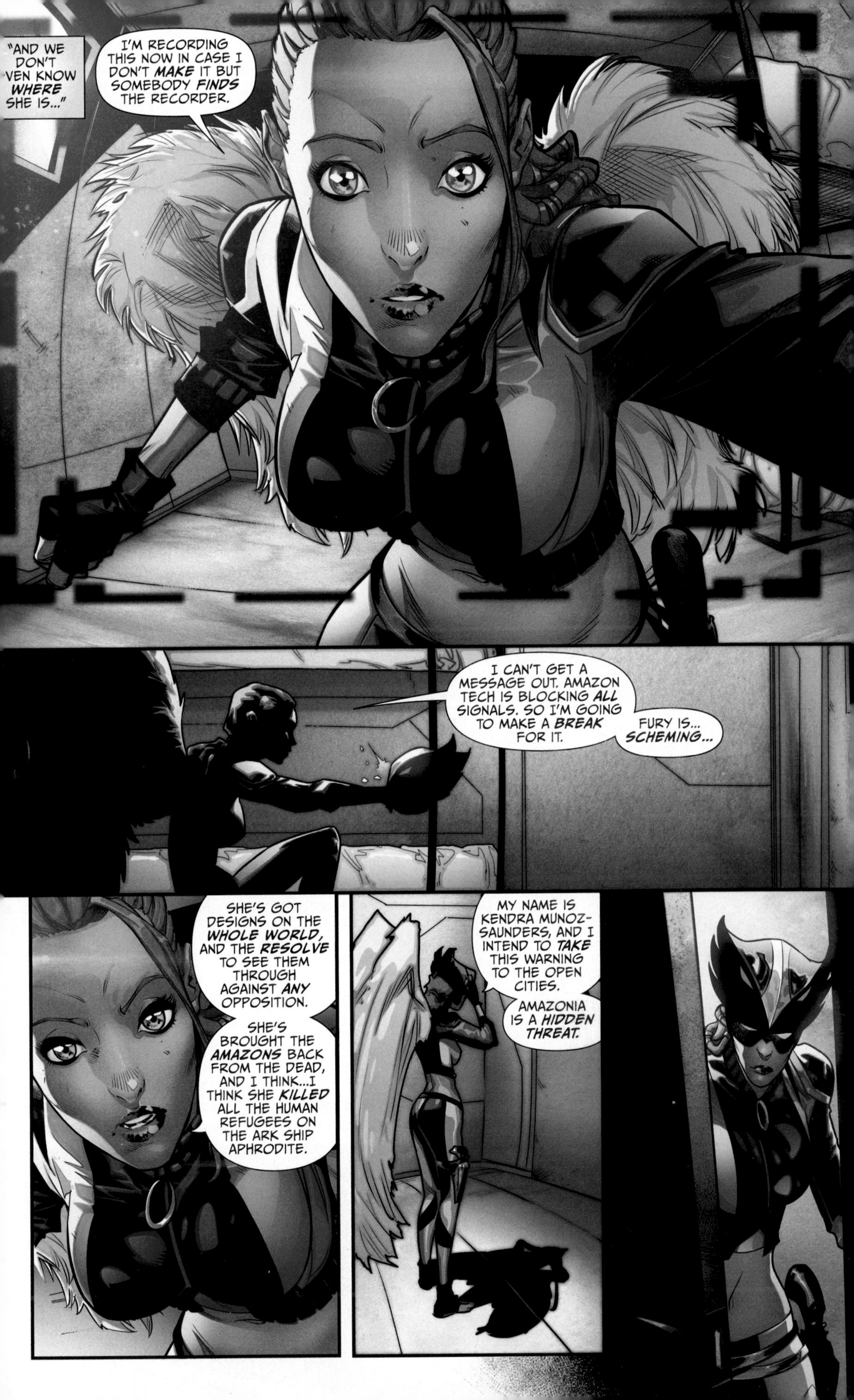
"AND WE DON'T VEN KNOW WHERE SHE IS..."
I'M RECORDING THIS NOW IN CASE I DON'T MAKE IT BUT SOMEBODY FINDS THE RECORDER.
I CAN'T GET A MESSAGE OUT. AMAZON TECH IS BLOCKING ALL SIGNALS. SO I'M GOING TO MAKE A BREAK FOR IT.
FURY IS... SCHEMING...
SHE'S GOT DESIGNS ON THE WHOLE WORLD, AND THE RESOLVE TO SEE THEM THROUGH AGAINST ANY OPPOSITION.
SHE'S BROUGHT THE AMAZONS BACK FROM THE DEAD, AND I THINK...I THINK SHE KILLED ALL THE HUMAN REFUGEES ON THE ARK SHIP APHRODITE.
MY NAME IS KENDRA MUNOZ-SAUNDERS, AND I INTEND TO TAKE THIS WARNING TO THE OPEN CITIES.
AMAZONIA IS A HIDDEN THREAT.

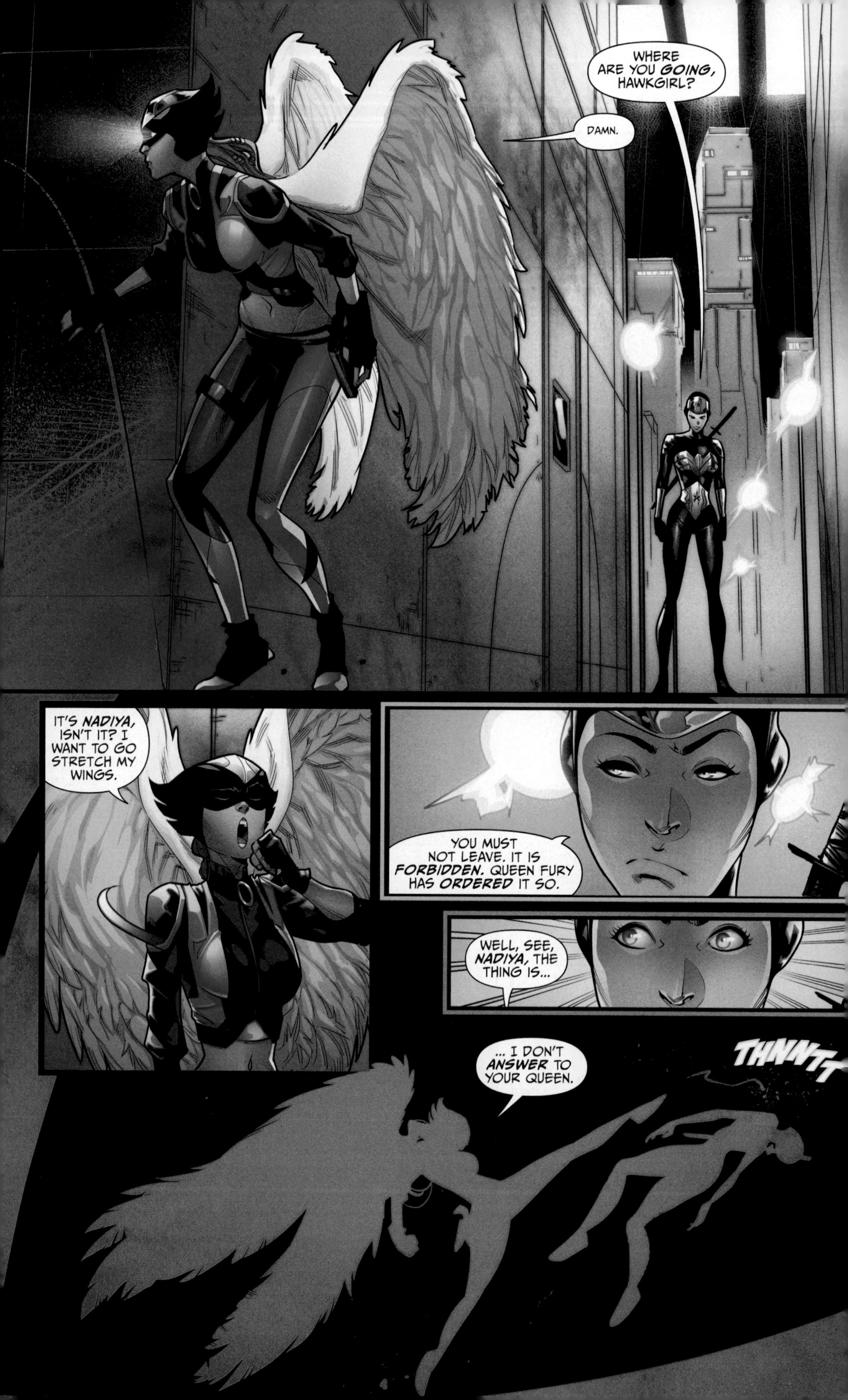
WHERE ARE YOU GOING, HAWKGIRL?
DAMN.
IT'S NADIYA, ISN'T IT? I WANT TO GO STRETCH MY WINGS.
YOU MUST NOT LEAVE. IT IS FORBIDDEN. QUEEN FURY HAS ORDERED IT SO.
WELL, SEE, NADIYA, THE THING IS...
... I DON'T ANSWER TO YOUR QUEEN.
THNNTT

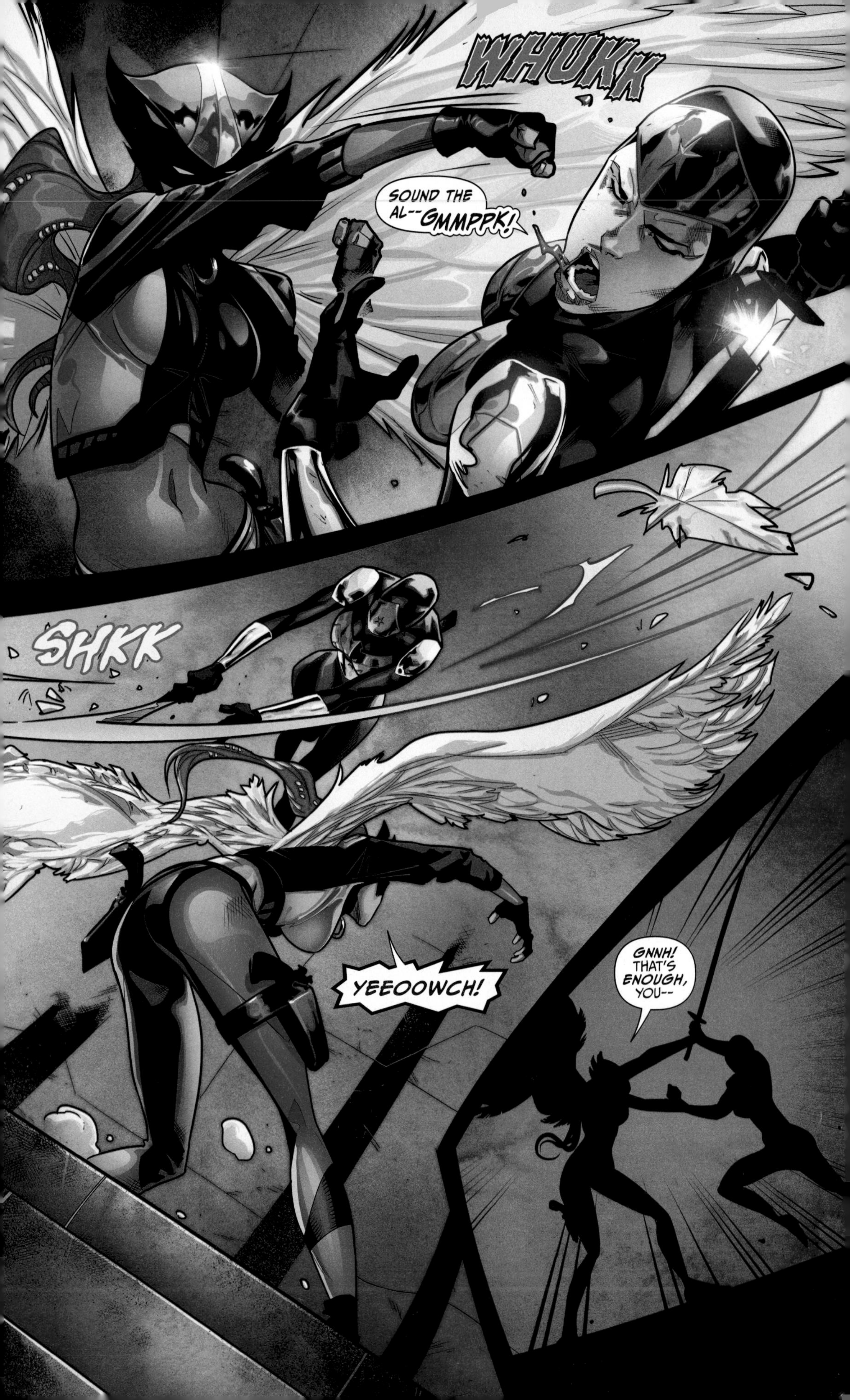
WHUKK
SOUND THE AL-- GMMPPK!
SHKK
YEEOOWCH!
GNNH! THAT'S ENOUGH, YOU--

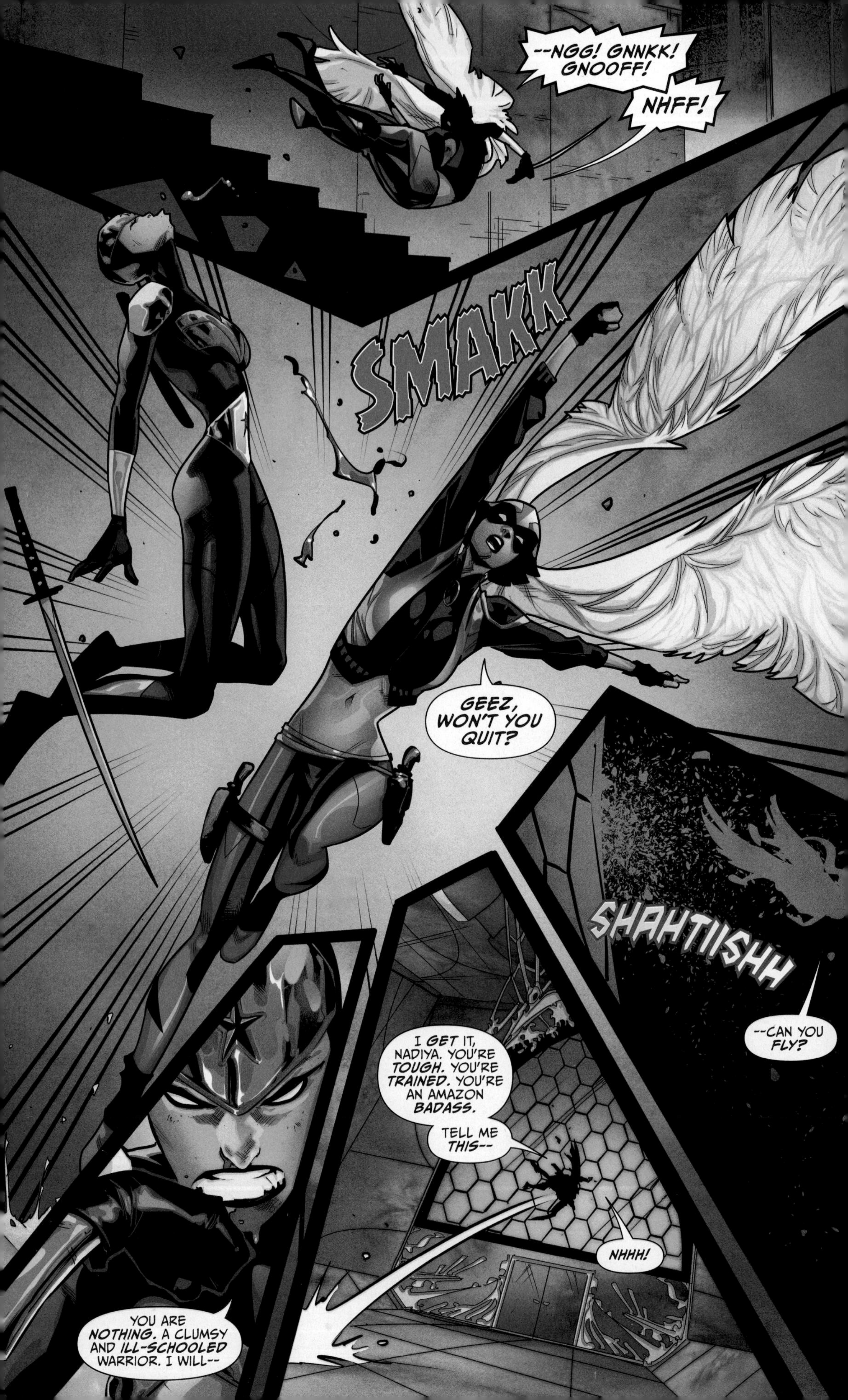
--NGG! GNNKK! GNOOFF!
NHFF!
SMAKK
GEEZ, WON'T YOU QUIT?
SHAHTIISHH
--CAN YOU FLY?
I GET IT, NADIYA. YOU'RE TOUGH. YOU'RE TRAINED. YOU'RE AN AMAZON BADASS.
TELL ME THIS--
NHHH!
YOU ARE NOTHING. A CLUMSY AND ILL-SCHOOLED WARRIOR. I WILL--

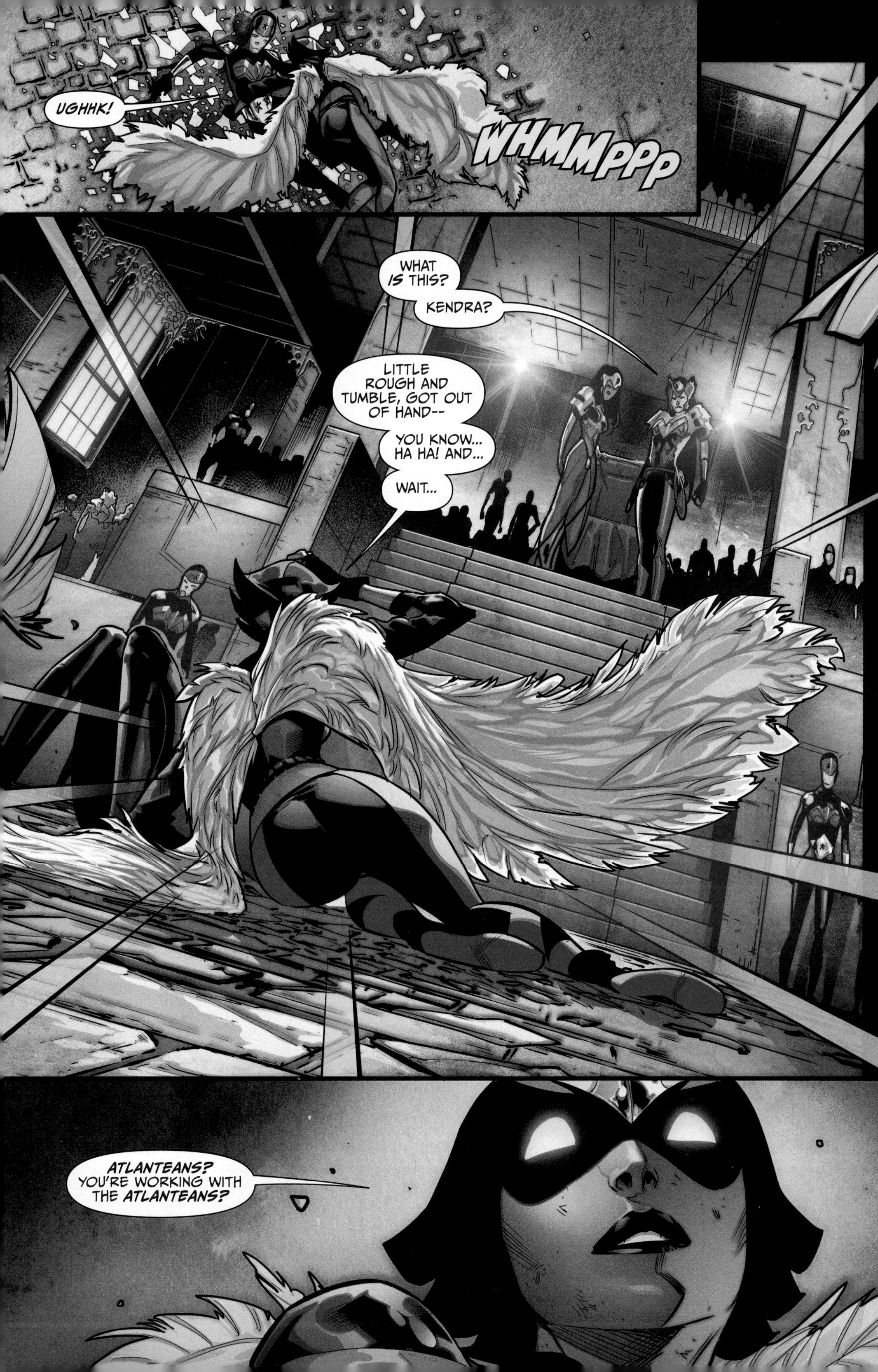
UGHHK!
WHMMPPP
WHAT IS THIS?
KENDRA?
LITTLE ROUGH AND TUMBLE, GOT OUT OF HAND--
YOU KNOW... HA HA! AND...
WAIT...
ATLANTEANS? YOU'RE WORKING WITH THE ATLANTEANS?

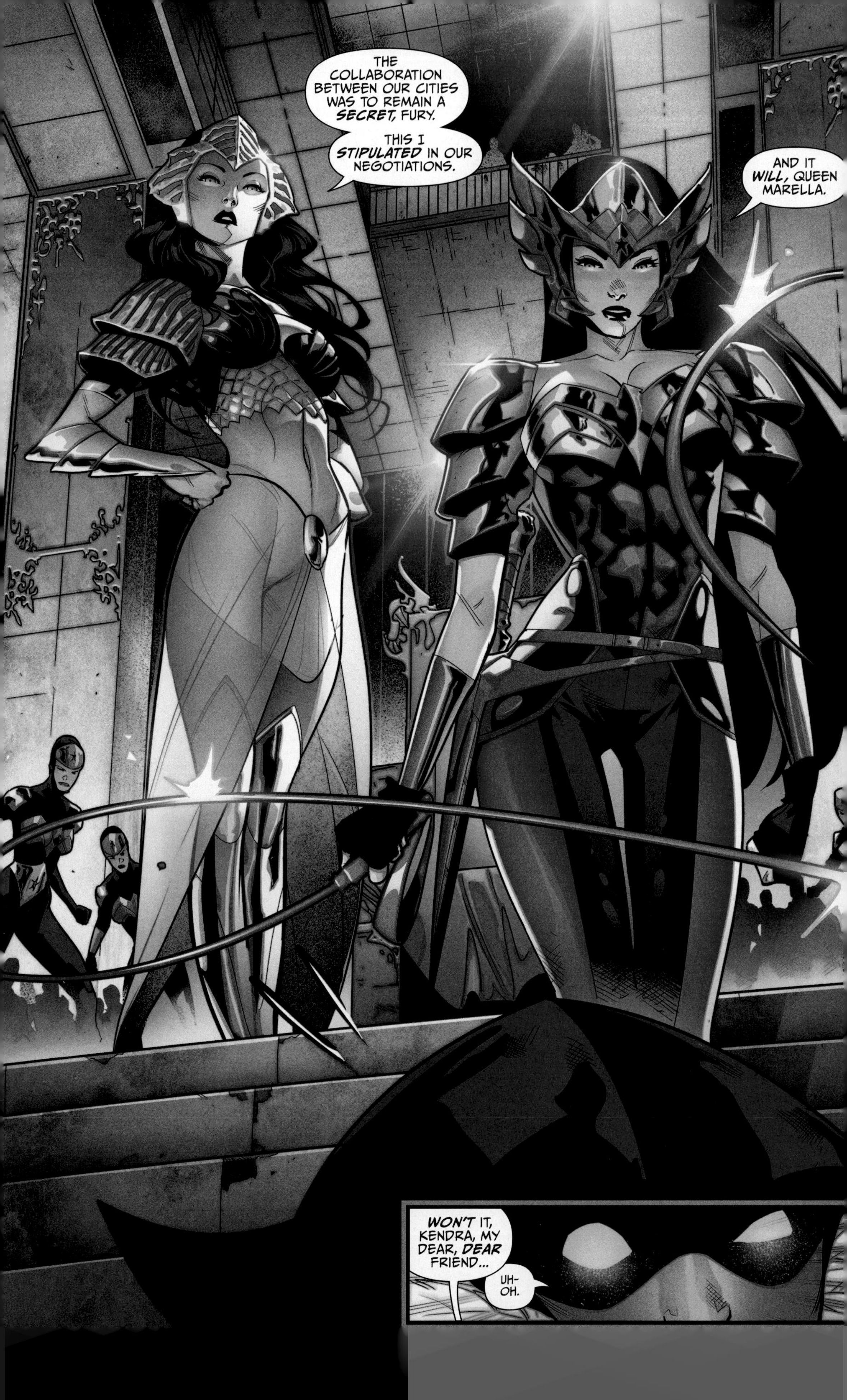
THE COLLABORATION BETWEEN OUR CITIES WAS TO REMAIN A SECRET, FURY.
THIS I STIPULATED IN OUR NEGOTIATIONS.
AND IT WILL, QUEEN MARELLA.
WON'T IT, KENDRA, MY DEAR, DEAR FRIEND...
UH-OH.

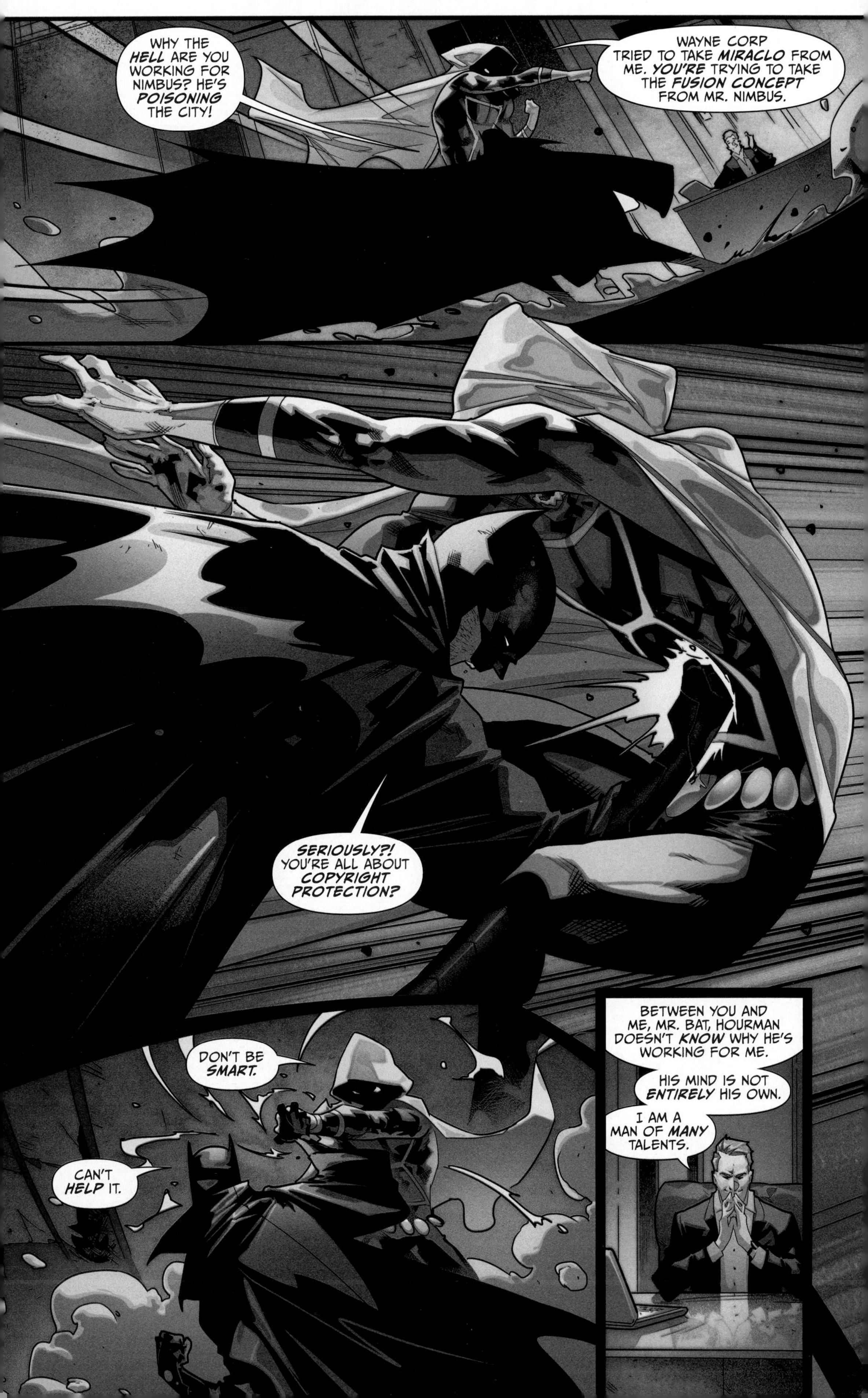
WHY THE HELL ARE YOU WORKING FOR NIMBUS? HE'S POISONING THE CITY!
WAYNE CORP TRIED TO TAKE MIRACLO FROM ME. YOU'RE TRYING TO TAKE THE FUSION CONCEPT FROM MR. NIMBUS.
SERIOUSLY?! YOU'RE ALL ABOUT COPYRIGHT PROTECTION?
DON'T BE SMART.
CAN'T HELP IT.
BETWEEN YOU AND ME, MR. BAT, HOURMAN DOESN'T KNOW WHY HE'S WORKING FOR ME.
HIS MIND IS NOT ENTIRELY HIS OWN.
I AM A MAN OF MANY TALENTS.

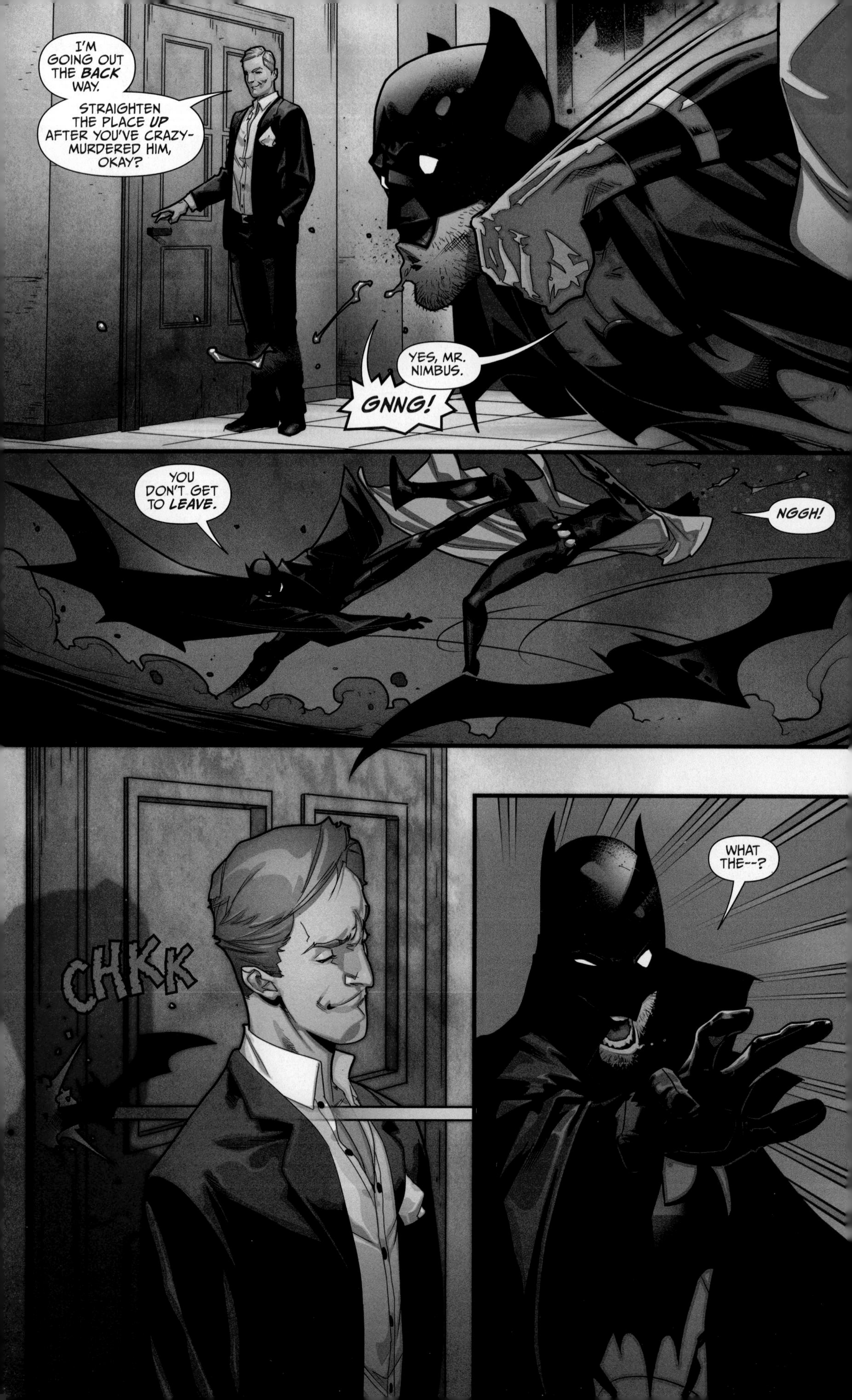
I'M GOING OUT THE BACK WAY.
STRAIGHTEN THE PLACE UP AFTER YOU'VE CRAZY-MURDERED HIM, OKAY?
YES, MR. NIMBUS.
GNNG!
YOU DON'T GET TO LEAVE.
NGGH!
CHKK
WHAT THE--?

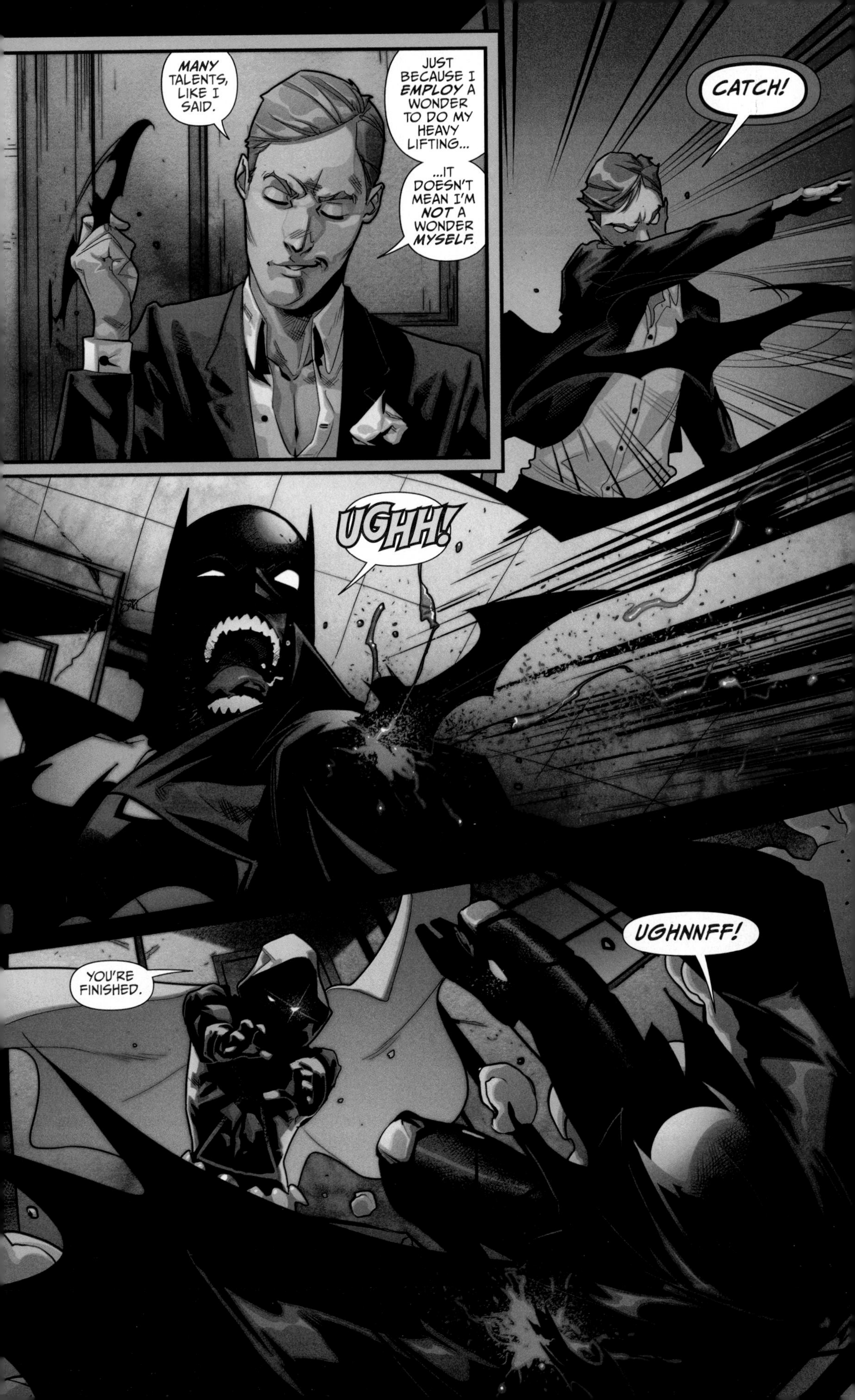
MANY TALENTS, LIKE I SAID.
JUST BECAUSE I EMPLOY A WONDER TO DO MY HEAVY LIFTING...
...IT DOESN'T MEAN I'M NOT A WONDER MYSELF.
CATCH!
UGHH!
UGHNNFF!
YOU'RE FINISHED.

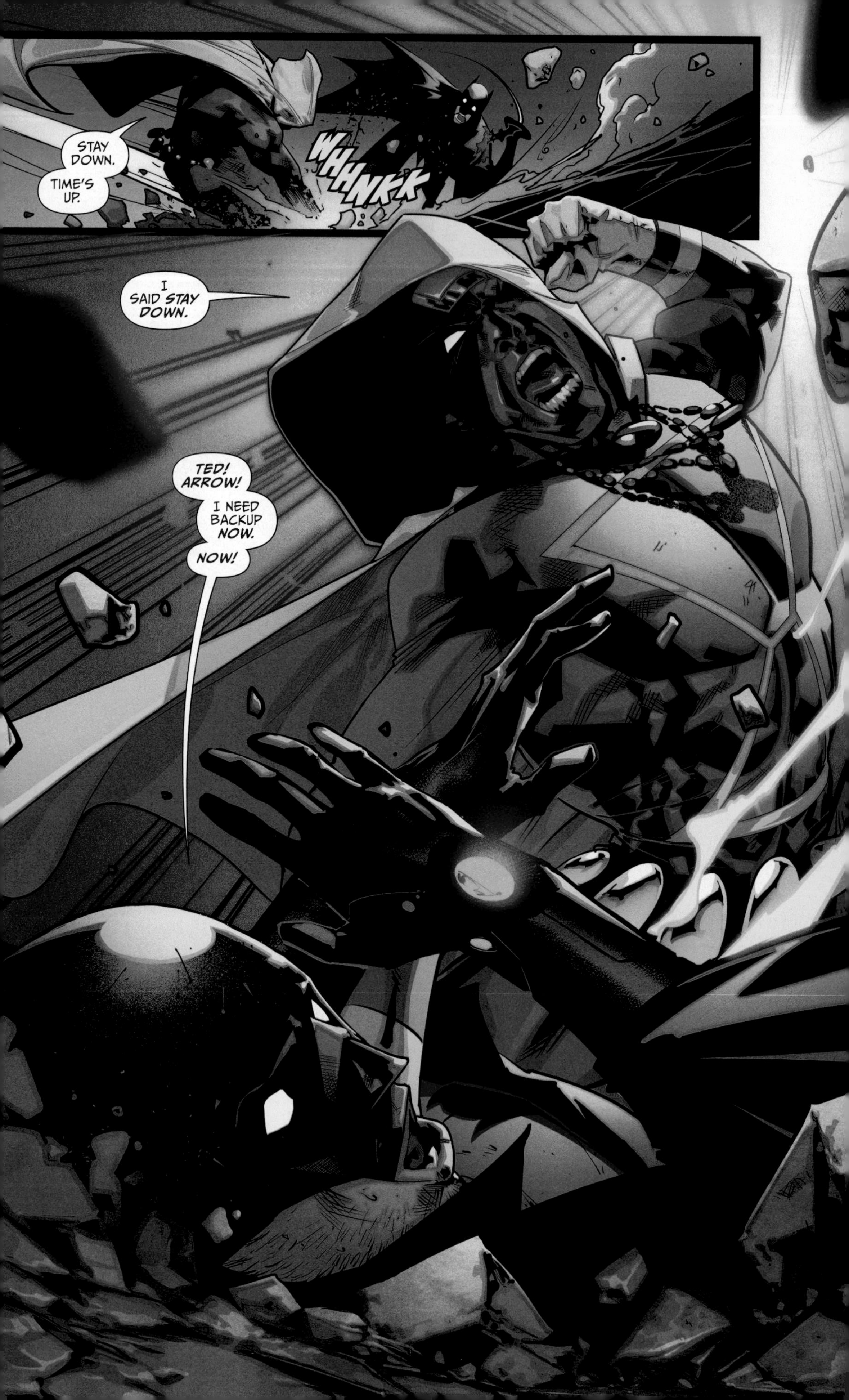
STAY DOWN.
TIME'S UP.
WHHNKK
I SAID STAY DOWN.
TED! ARROW!
I NEED BACKUP NOW.
NOW!

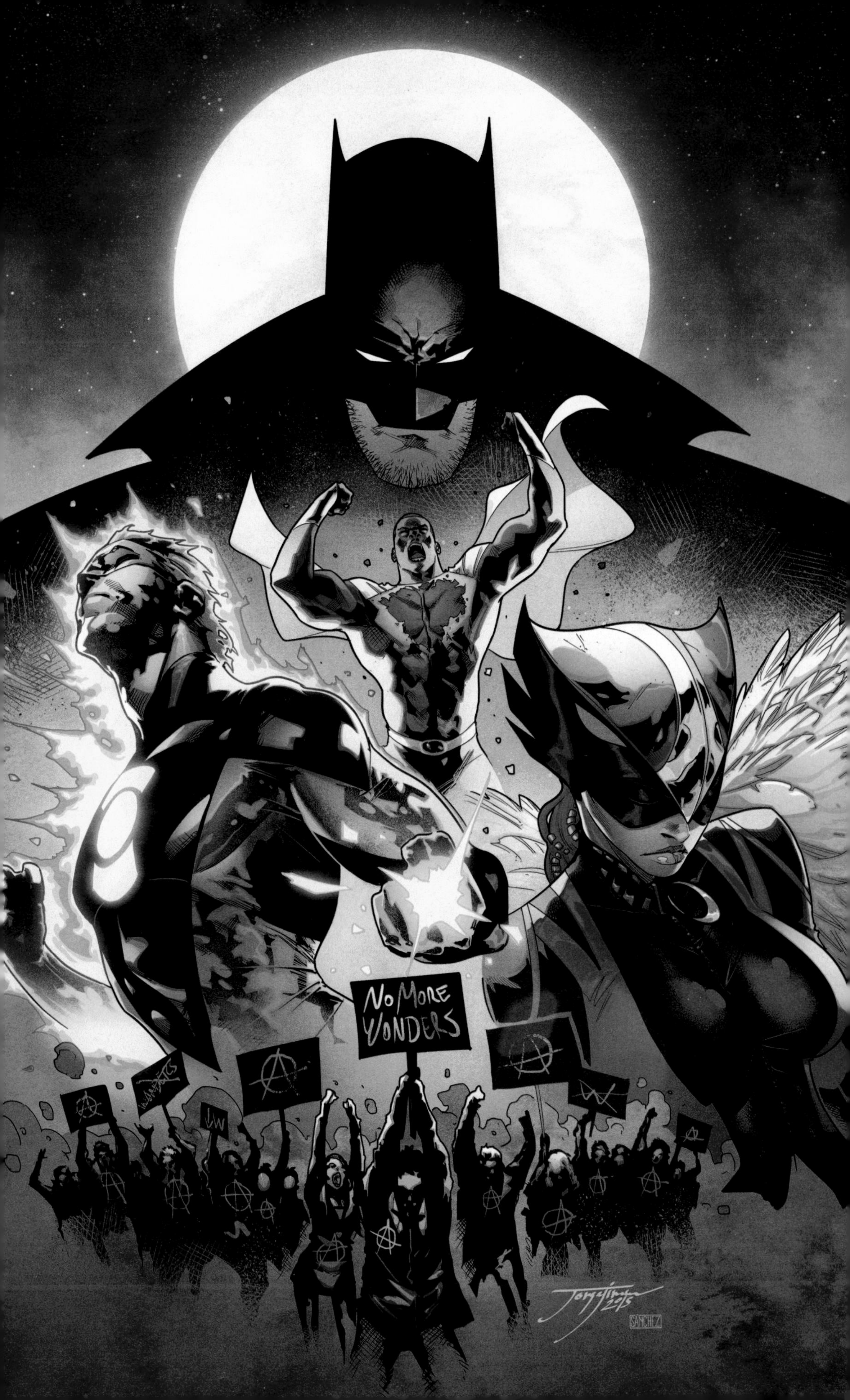
NO MORE
WONDERS
SANCHEZ

ONE NATION, INDIVISIBLE CHAPTER FOUR: TOGETHER, ALONE

DAN ABNETT writer **FEDERICO DALLOCCHIO** artist **DAVID CALDERON OF IKARI STUDIO** colorist **TRAVIS LANHAM** letterer cover by **JIMÉNEZ & SANCHEZ**

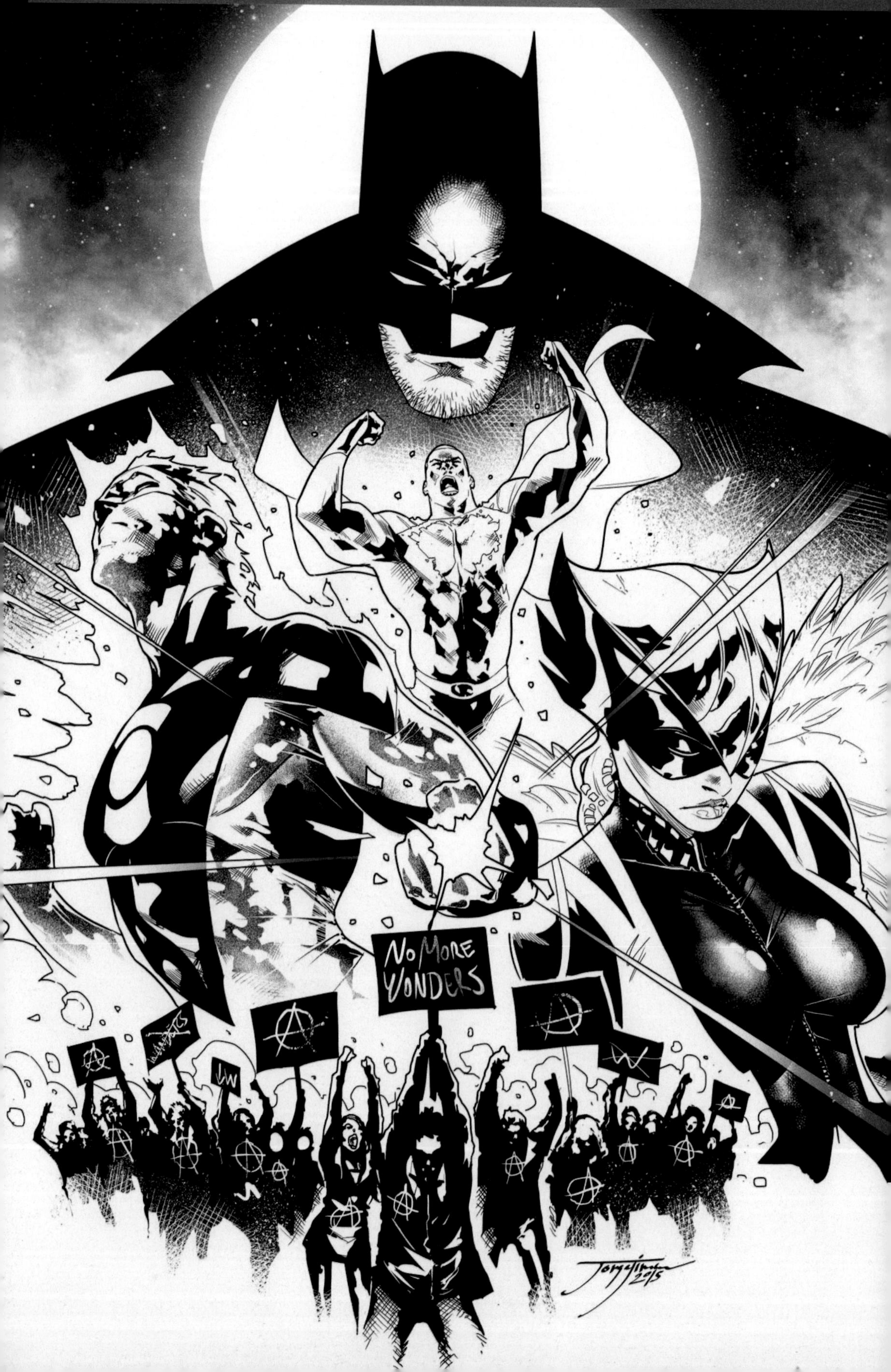

NO MORE WONDERS

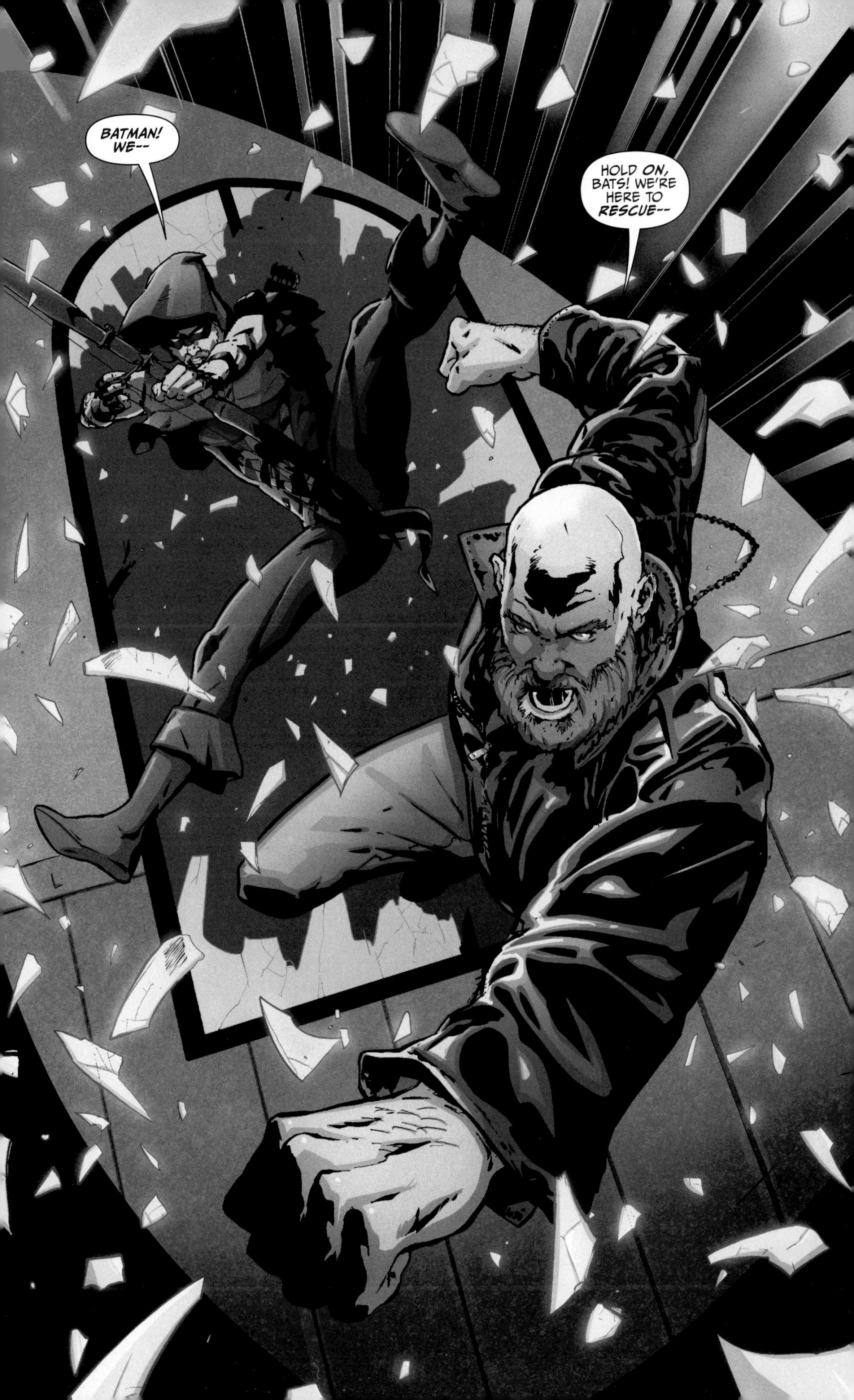
BATMAN! WE--
HOLD ON, BATS! WE'RE HERE TO RESCUE--

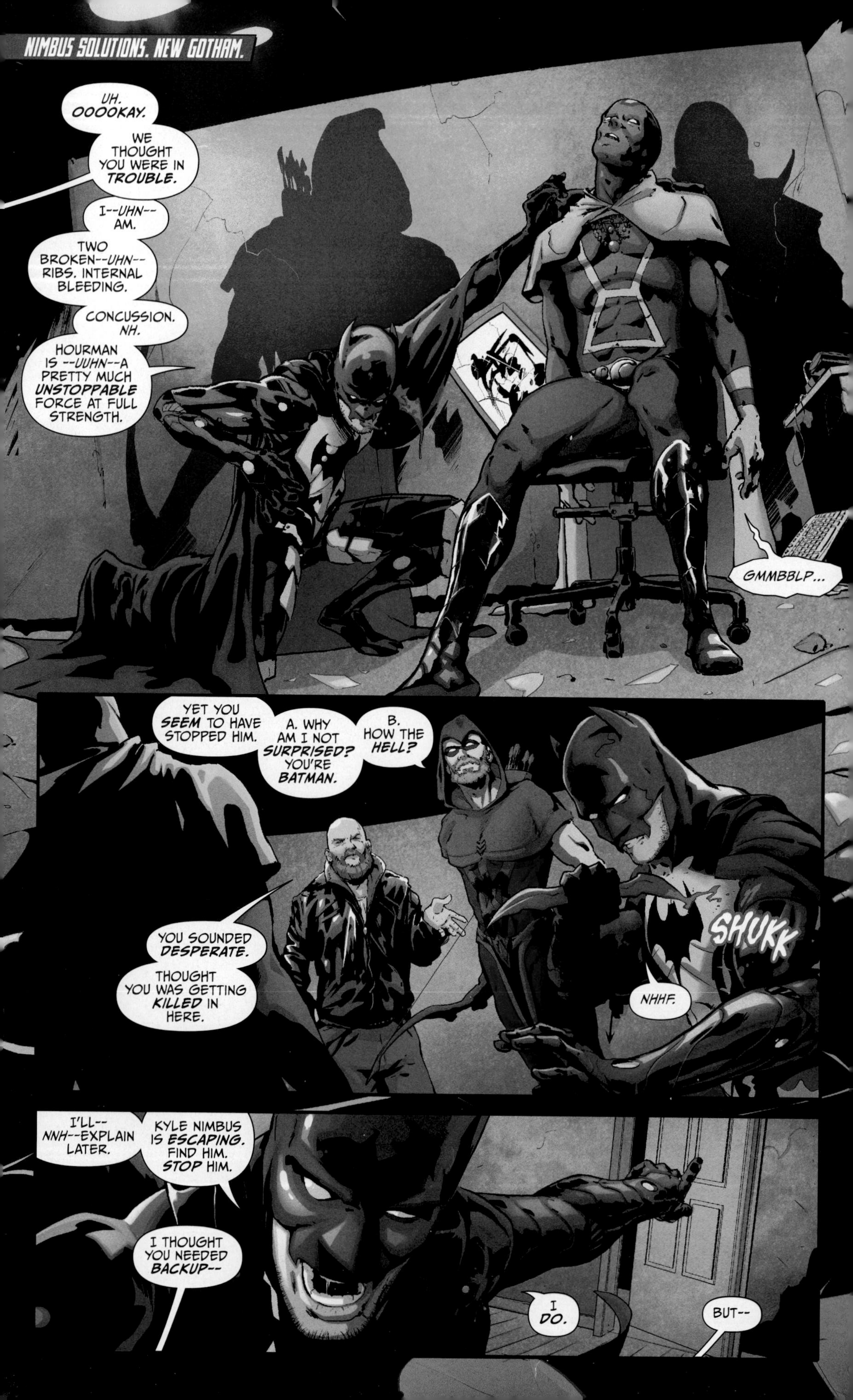
NIMBUS SOLUTIONS. NEW GOTHAM.
UH. OOOOKAY.
WE THOUGHT YOU WERE IN TROUBLE.
I--UHN--AM.
TWO BROKEN--UHN--RIBS. INTERNAL BLEEDING.
CONCUSSION. NH.
HOURMAN IS --UUHN--A PRETTY MUCH UNSTOPPABLE FORCE AT FULL STRENGTH.
GMMBBLP...
YET YOU SEEM TO HAVE STOPPED HIM.
A. WHY AM I NOT SURPRISED? YOU'RE BATMAN.
B. HOW THE HELL?
YOU SOUNDED DESPERATE.
THOUGHT YOU WAS GETTING KILLED IN HERE.
SHUKK
NHHF.
I'LL--NNH--EXPLAIN LATER.
KYLE NIMBUS IS ESCAPING. FIND HIM. STOP HIM.
I THOUGHT YOU NEEDED BACKUP--
I DO.
BUT--

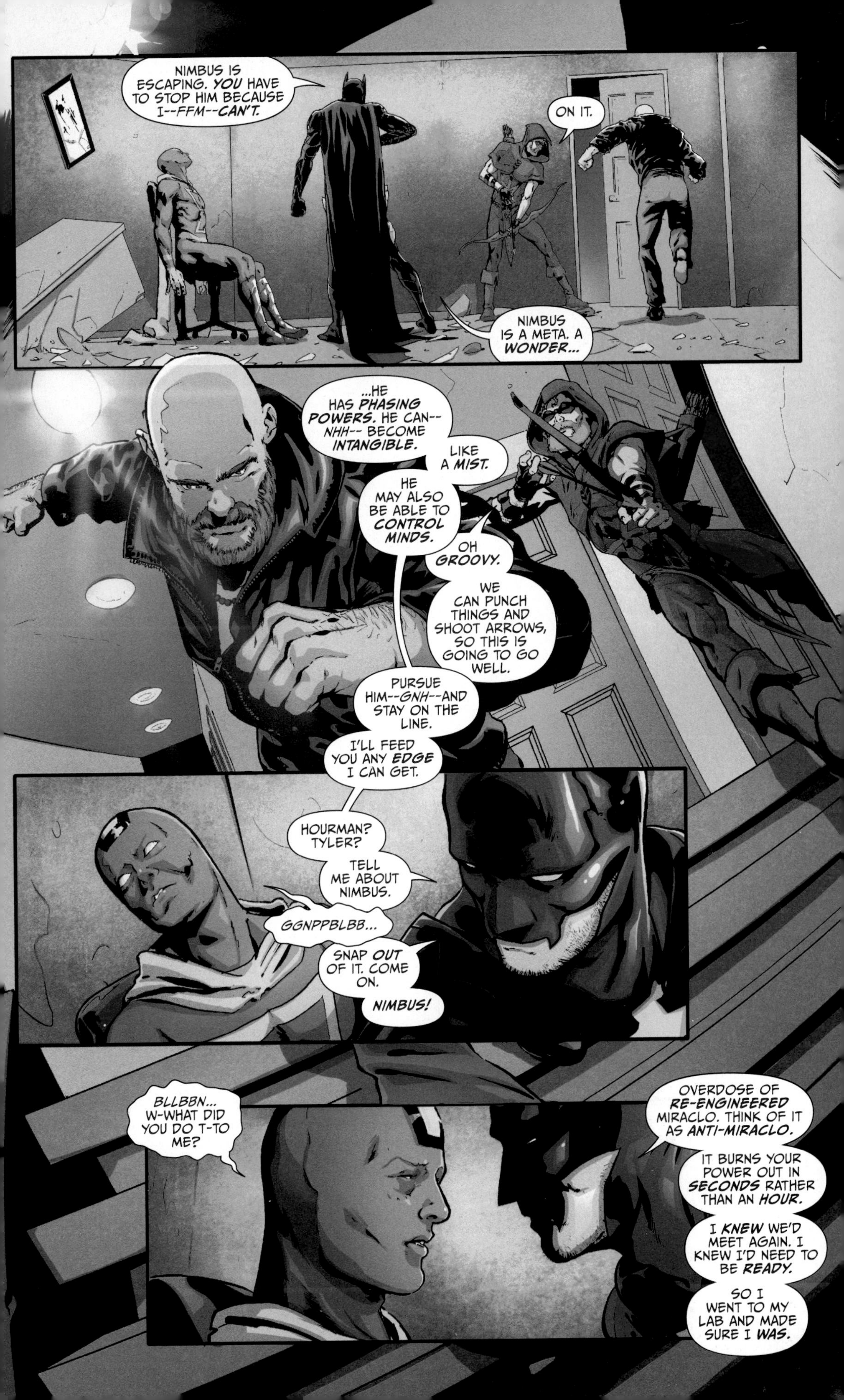
NIMBUS IS ESCAPING. YOU HAVE TO STOP HIM BECAUSE I--FFM--CAN'T.
ON IT.
NIMBUS IS A META. A WONDER...
...HE HAS PHASING POWERS. HE CAN--NHH-- BECOME INTANGIBLE.
LIKE A MIST.
HE MAY ALSO BE ABLE TO CONTROL MINDS.
OH GROOVY.
WE CAN PUNCH THINGS AND SHOOT ARROWS, SO THIS IS GOING TO GO WELL.
PURSUE HIM--GNH--AND STAY ON THE LINE.
I'LL FEED YOU ANY EDGE I CAN GET.
HOURMAN? TYLER?
TELL ME ABOUT NIMBUS.
GGNPPBLBB...
SNAP OUT OF IT. COME ON.
NIMBUS!
BLLBBN... W-WHAT DID YOU DO T-TO ME?
OVERDOSE OF RE-ENGINEERED MIRACLO. THINK OF IT AS ANTI-MIRACLO.
IT BURNS YOUR POWER OUT IN SECONDS RATHER THAN AN HOUR.
I KNEW WE'D MEET AGAIN. I KNEW I'D NEED TO BE READY.
SO I WENT TO MY LAB AND MADE SURE I WAS.

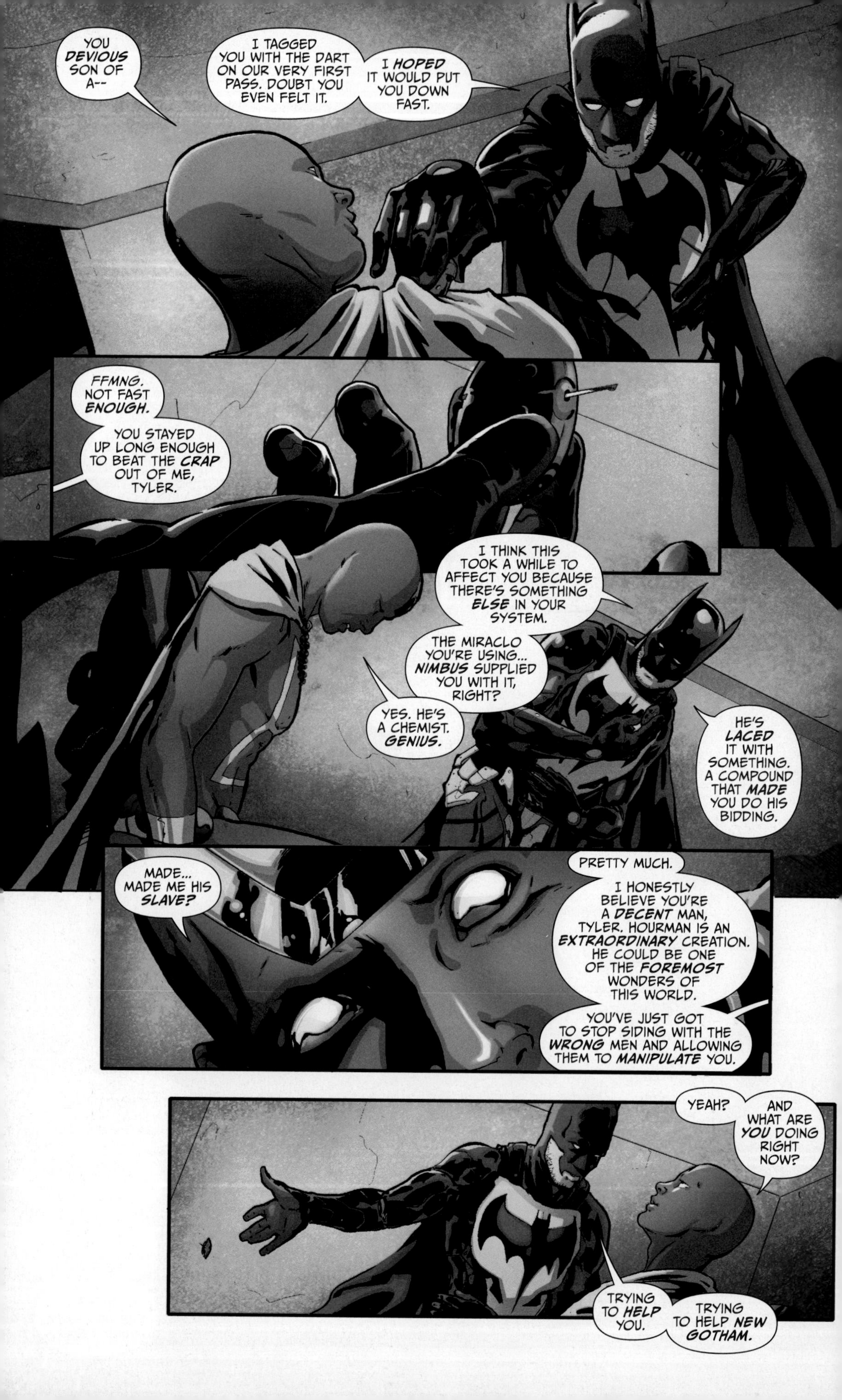

YOU DEVIOUS SON OF A--
I TAGGED YOU WITH THE DART ON OUR VERY FIRST PASS. DOUBT YOU EVEN FELT IT.
I HOPED IT WOULD PUT YOU DOWN FAST.
FFMNG. NOT FAST ENOUGH.
YOU STAYED UP LONG ENOUGH TO BEAT THE CRAP OUT OF ME, TYLER.
I THINK THIS TOOK A WHILE TO AFFECT YOU BECAUSE THERE'S SOMETHING ELSE IN YOUR SYSTEM.
THE MIRACLO YOU'RE USING... NIMBUS SUPPLIED YOU WITH IT, RIGHT?
YES. HE'S A CHEMIST. GENIUS.
HE'S LACED IT WITH SOMETHING. A COMPOUND THAT MADE YOU DO HIS BIDDING.
MADE... MADE ME HIS SLAVE?
PRETTY MUCH.
I HONESTLY BELIEVE YOU'RE A DECENT MAN, TYLER. HOURMAN IS AN EXTRAORDINARY CREATION. HE COULD BE ONE OF THE FOREMOST WONDERS OF THIS WORLD.
YOU'VE JUST GOT TO STOP SIDING WITH THE WRONG MEN AND ALLOWING THEM TO MANIPULATE YOU.
YEAH?
AND WHAT ARE YOU DOING RIGHT NOW?
TRYING TO HELP YOU.
TRYING TO HELP NEW GOTHAM.

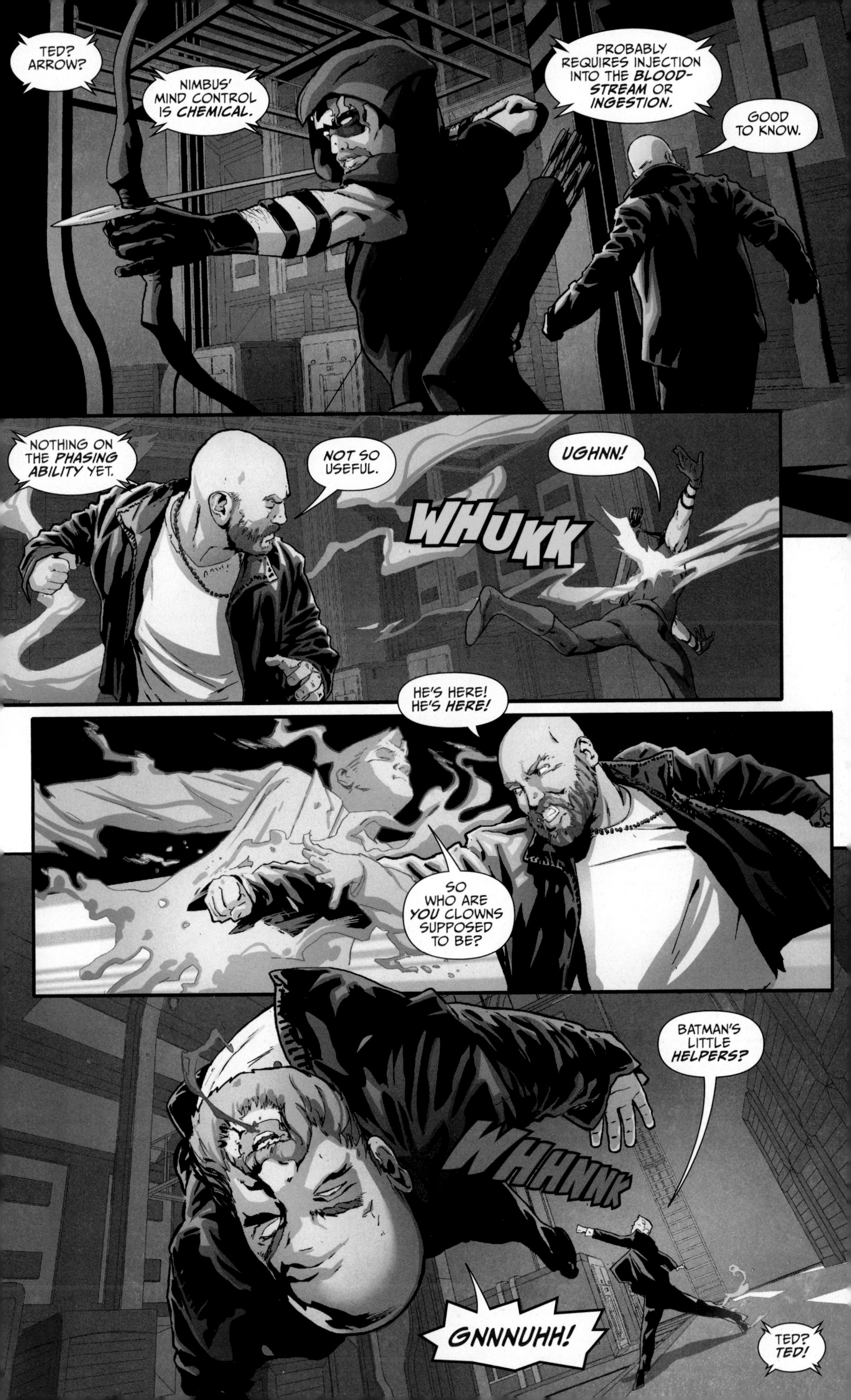
TED? ARROW?
NIMBUS' MIND CONTROL IS CHEMICAL.
PROBABLY REQUIRES INJECTION INTO THE BLOOD-STREAM OR INGESTION.
GOOD TO KNOW.
NOTHING ON THE PHASING ABILITY YET.
NOT SO USEFUL.
WHUKK
UGHNN!
HE'S HERE! HE'S HERE!
SO WHO ARE YOU CLOWNS SUPPOSED TO BE?
BATMAN'S LITTLE HELPERS?
WHHNNK
GNNNUHH!
TED? TED!

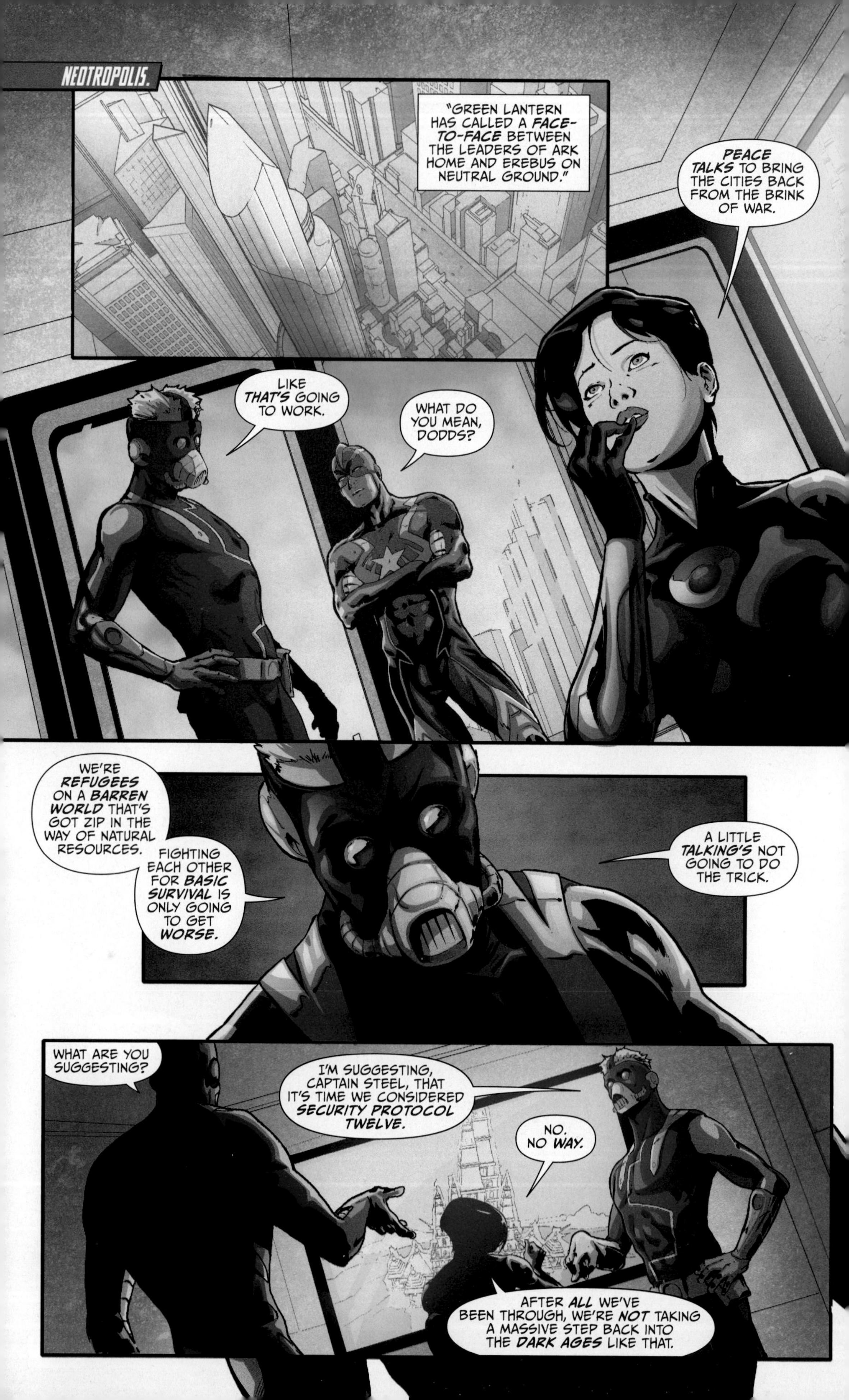
NEOTROPOLIS.
"GREEN LANTERN HAS CALLED A FACE-TO-FACE BETWEEN THE LEADERS OF ARK HOME AND EREBUS ON NEUTRAL GROUND."
PEACE TALKS TO BRING THE CITIES BACK FROM THE BRINK OF WAR.
LIKE THAT'S GOING TO WORK.
WHAT DO YOU MEAN, DODDS?
WE'RE REFUGEES ON A BARREN WORLD THAT'S GOT ZIP IN THE WAY OF NATURAL RESOURCES.
FIGHTING EACH OTHER FOR BASIC SURVIVAL IS ONLY GOING TO GET WORSE.
A LITTLE TALKING'S NOT GOING TO DO THE TRICK.
WHAT ARE YOU SUGGESTING?
I'M SUGGESTING, CAPTAIN STEEL, THAT IT'S TIME WE CONSIDERED SECURITY PROTOCOL TWELVE.
NO. NO WAY.
AFTER ALL WE'VE BEEN THROUGH, WE'RE NOT TAKING A MASSIVE STEP BACK INTO THE DARK AGES LIKE THAT.

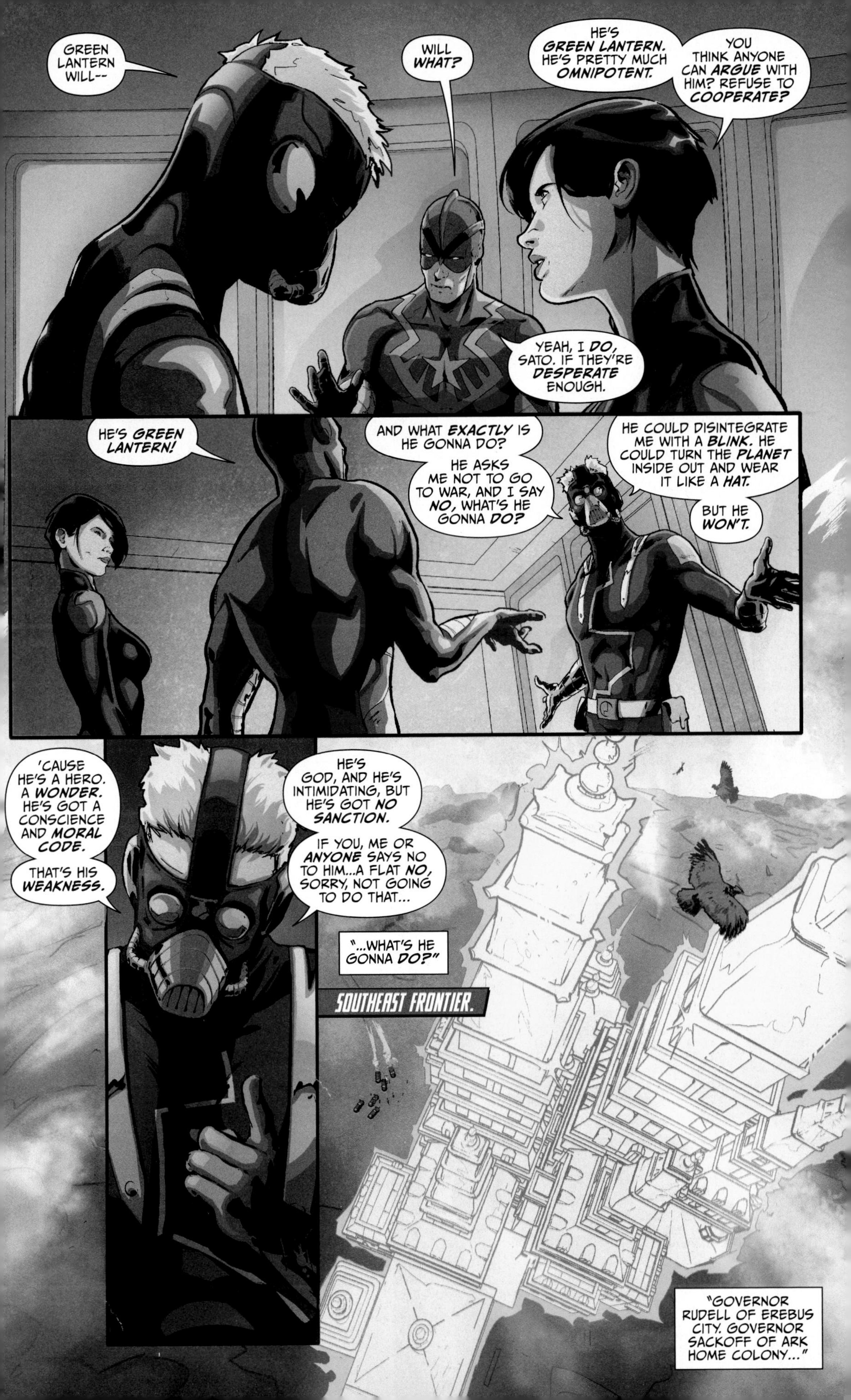
GREEN LANTERN WILL--
WILL WHAT?
HE'S GREEN LANTERN. HE'S PRETTY MUCH OMNIPOTENT.
YOU THINK ANYONE CAN ARGUE WITH HIM? REFUSE TO COOPERATE?
YEAH, I DO, SATO. IF THEY'RE DESPERATE ENOUGH.
HE'S GREEN LANTERN!
AND WHAT EXACTLY IS HE GONNA DO?
HE ASKS ME NOT TO GO TO WAR, AND I SAY NO, WHAT'S HE GONNA DO?
HE COULD DISINTEGRATE ME WITH A BLINK. HE COULD TURN THE PLANET INSIDE OUT AND WEAR IT LIKE A HAT.
BUT HE WON'T.
'CAUSE HE'S A HERO. A WONDER. HE'S GOT A CONSCIENCE AND MORAL CODE.
THAT'S HIS WEAKNESS.
HE'S GOD, AND HE'S INTIMIDATING, BUT HE'S GOT NO SANCTION.
IF YOU, ME OR ANYONE SAYS NO TO HIM...A FLAT NO, SORRY, NOT GOING TO DO THAT...
"...WHAT'S HE GONNA DO?"
SOUTHEAST FRONTIER.
"GOVERNOR RUDELL OF EREBUS CITY. GOVERNOR SACKOFF OF ARK HOME COLONY..."

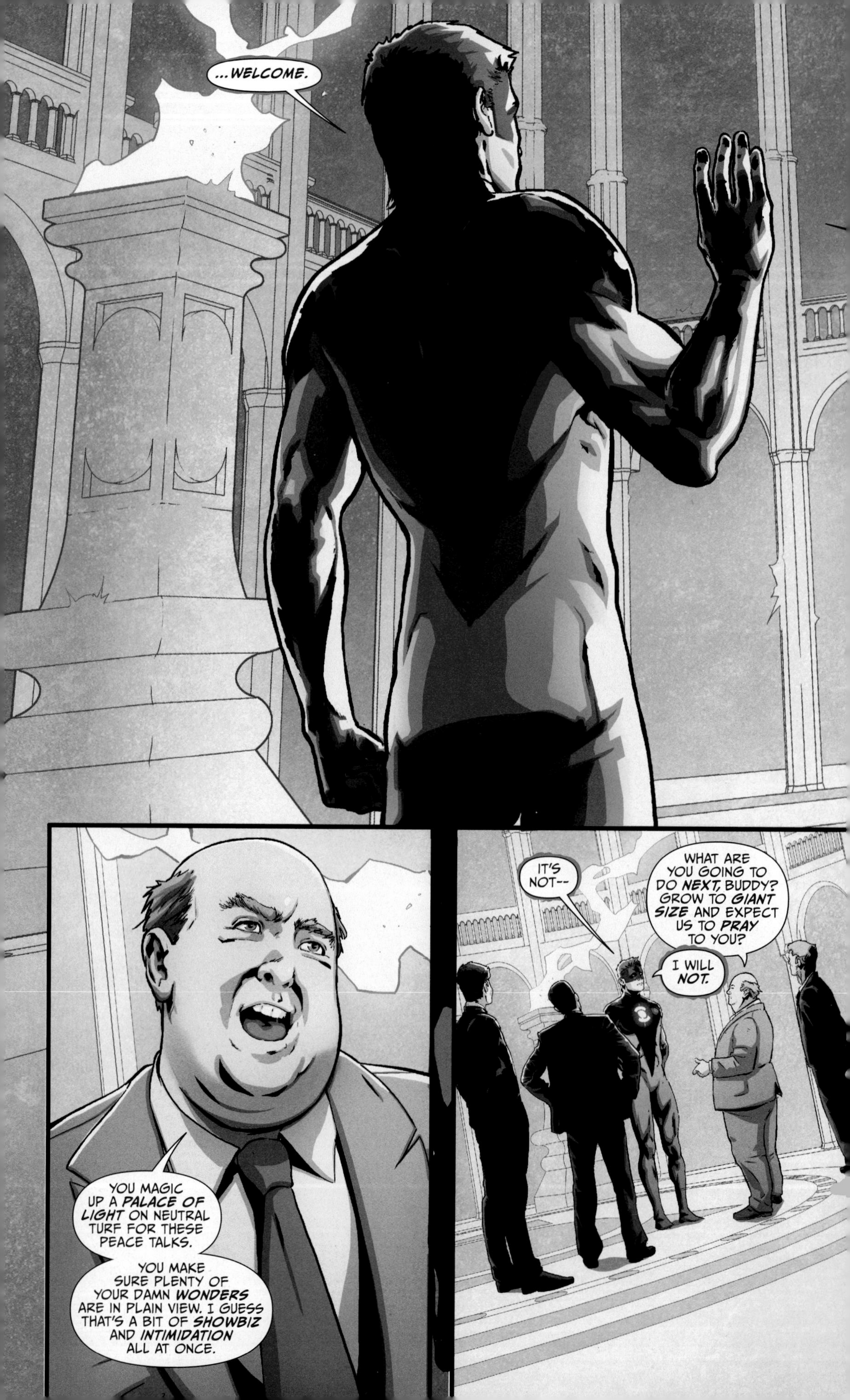
...WELCOME.
YOU MAGIC UP A PALACE OF LIGHT ON NEUTRAL TURF FOR THESE PEACE TALKS.
YOU MAKE SURE PLENTY OF YOUR DAMN WONDERS ARE IN PLAIN VIEW. I GUESS THAT'S A BIT OF SHOWBIZ AND INTIMIDATION ALL AT ONCE.
IT'S NOT--
WHAT ARE YOU GOING TO DO NEXT, BUDDY? GROW TO GIANT SIZE AND EXPECT US TO PRAY TO YOU?
I WILL NOT.

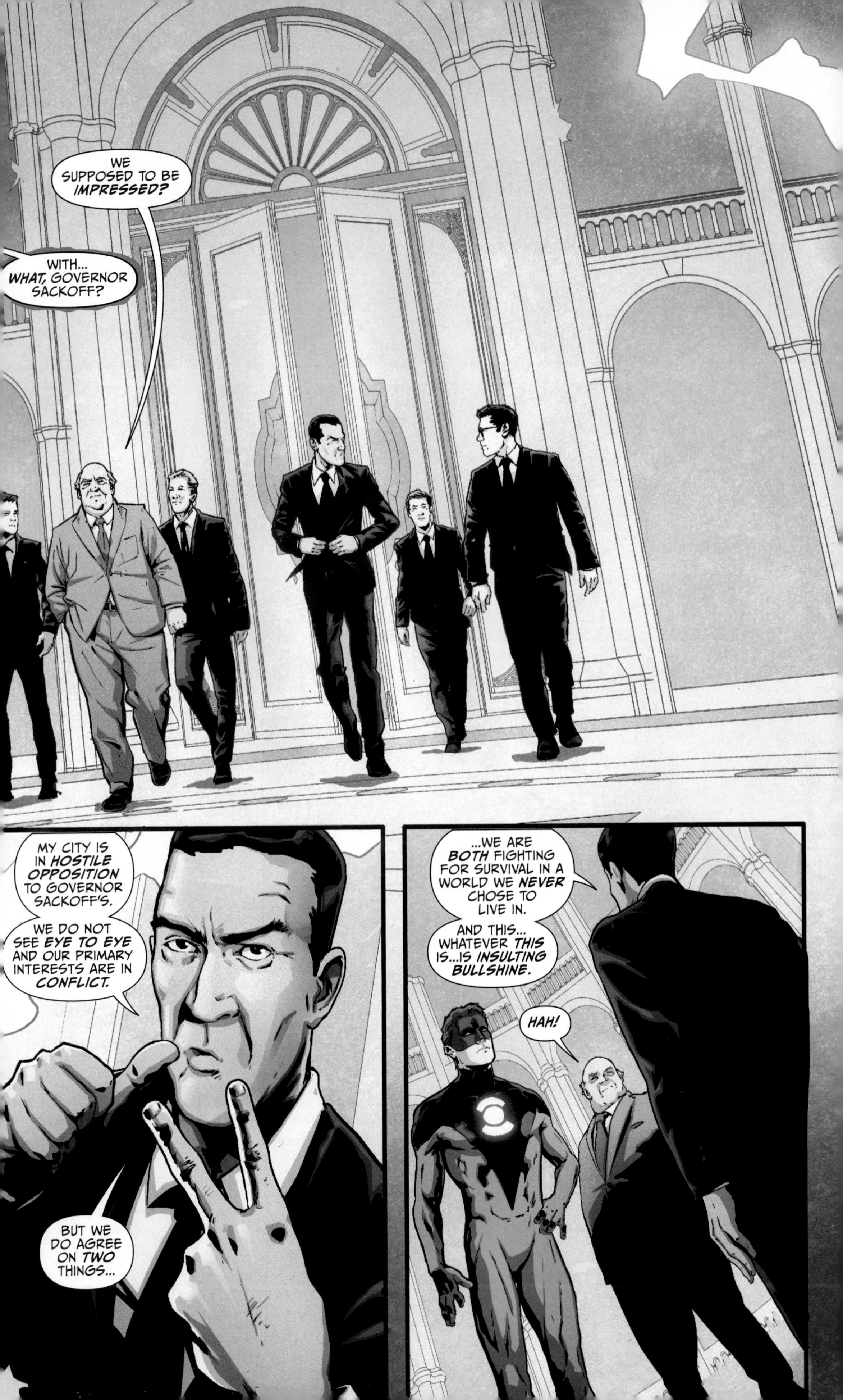

WE SUPPOSED TO BE IMPRESSED?
WITH... WHAT, GOVERNOR SACKOFF?
MY CITY IS IN HOSTILE OPPOSITION TO GOVERNOR SACKOFF'S.
WE DO NOT SEE EYE TO EYE AND OUR PRIMARY INTERESTS ARE IN CONFLICT.
BUT WE DO AGREE ON TWO THINGS...
...WE ARE BOTH FIGHTING FOR SURVIVAL IN A WORLD WE NEVER CHOSE TO LIVE IN.
AND THIS... WHATEVER THIS IS...IS INSULTING BULLSHINE.
HAH!

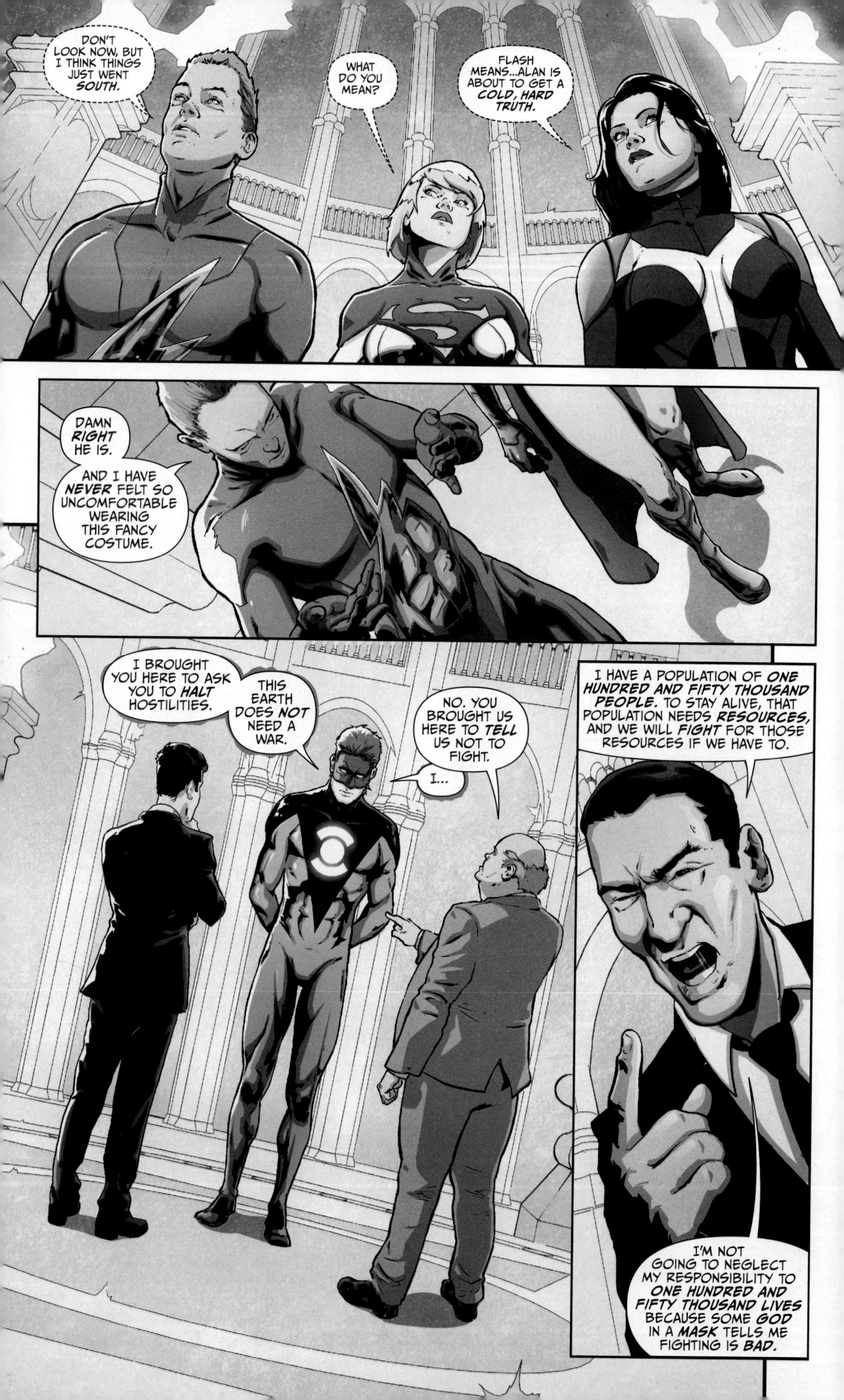
DON'T LOOK NOW, BUT I THINK THINGS JUST WENT SOUTH.
WHAT DO YOU MEAN?
FLASH MEANS...ALAN IS ABOUT TO GET A COLD, HARD TRUTH.
DAMN RIGHT HE IS.
AND I HAVE NEVER FELT SO UNCOMFORTABLE WEARING THIS FANCY COSTUME.
I BROUGHT YOU HERE TO ASK YOU TO HALT HOSTILITIES.
THIS EARTH DOES NOT NEED A WAR.
NO. YOU BROUGHT US HERE TO TELL US NOT TO FIGHT.
I...
I HAVE A POPULATION OF ONE HUNDRED AND FIFTY THOUSAND PEOPLE. TO STAY ALIVE, THAT POPULATION NEEDS RESOURCES, AND WE WILL FIGHT FOR THOSE RESOURCES IF WE HAVE TO.
I'M NOT GOING TO NEGLECT MY RESPONSIBILITY TO ONE HUNDRED AND FIFTY THOUSAND LIVES BECAUSE SOME GOD IN A MASK TELLS ME FIGHTING IS BAD.

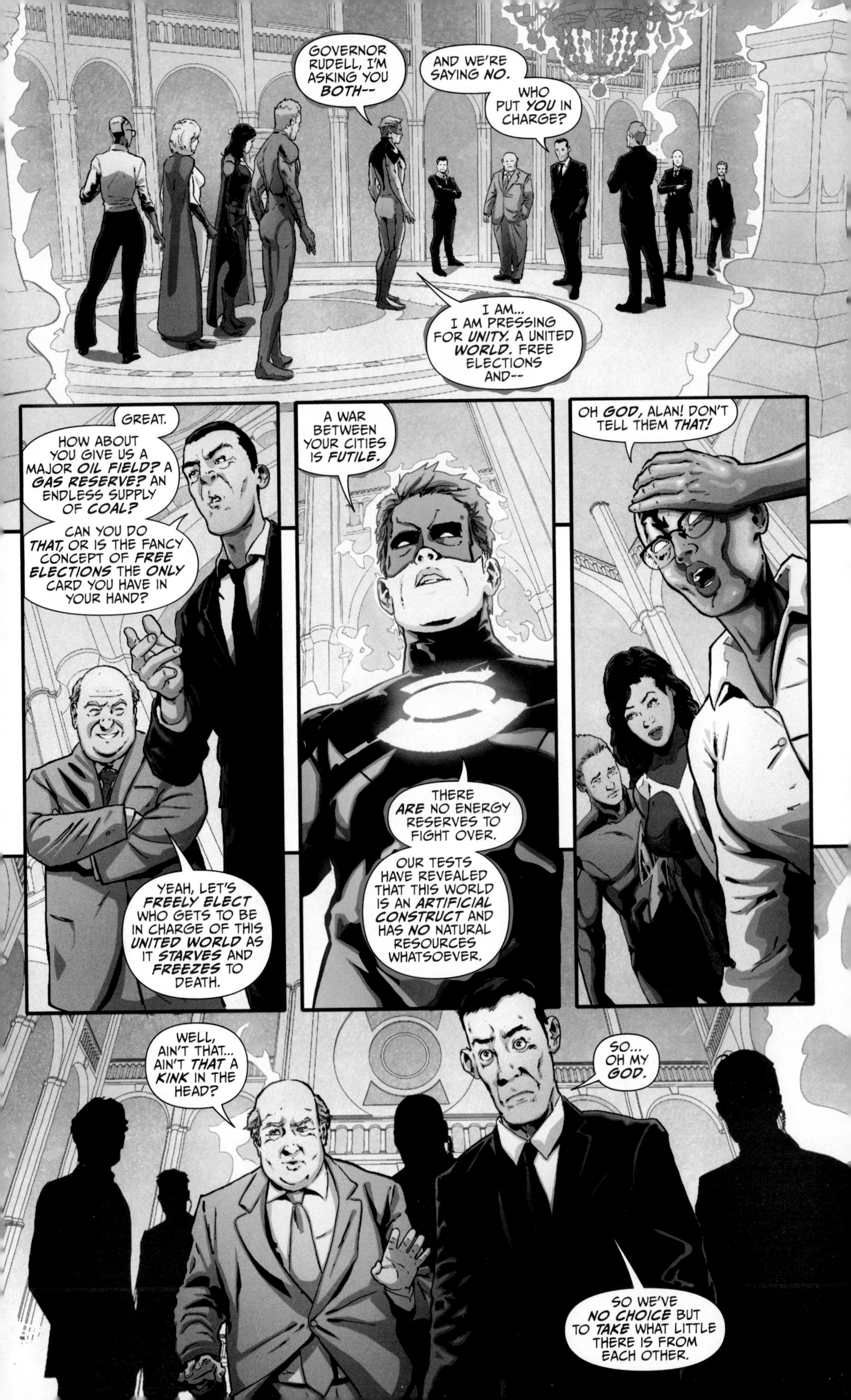
GOVERNOR RUDELL, I'M ASKING YOU BOTH--
AND WE'RE SAYING NO.
WHO PUT YOU IN CHARGE?
I AM... I AM PRESSING FOR UNITY. A UNITED WORLD. FREE ELECTIONS AND--
GREAT.
HOW ABOUT YOU GIVE US A MAJOR OIL FIELD? A GAS RESERVE? AN ENDLESS SUPPLY OF COAL?
CAN YOU DO THAT, OR IS THE FANCY CONCEPT OF FREE ELECTIONS THE ONLY CARD YOU HAVE IN YOUR HAND?
YEAH, LET'S FREELY ELECT WHO GETS TO BE IN CHARGE OF THIS UNITED WORLD AS IT STARVES AND FREEZES TO DEATH.
A WAR BETWEEN YOUR CITIES IS FUTILE.
THERE ARE NO ENERGY RESERVES TO FIGHT OVER.
OUR TESTS HAVE REVEALED THAT THIS WORLD IS AN ARTIFICIAL CONSTRUCT AND HAS NO NATURAL RESOURCES WHATSOEVER.
OH GOD, ALAN! DON'T TELL THEM THAT!
WELL, AIN'T THAT... AIN'T THAT A KINK IN THE HEAD?
SO... OH MY GOD.
SO WE'VE NO CHOICE BUT TO TAKE WHAT LITTLE THERE IS FROM EACH OTHER.

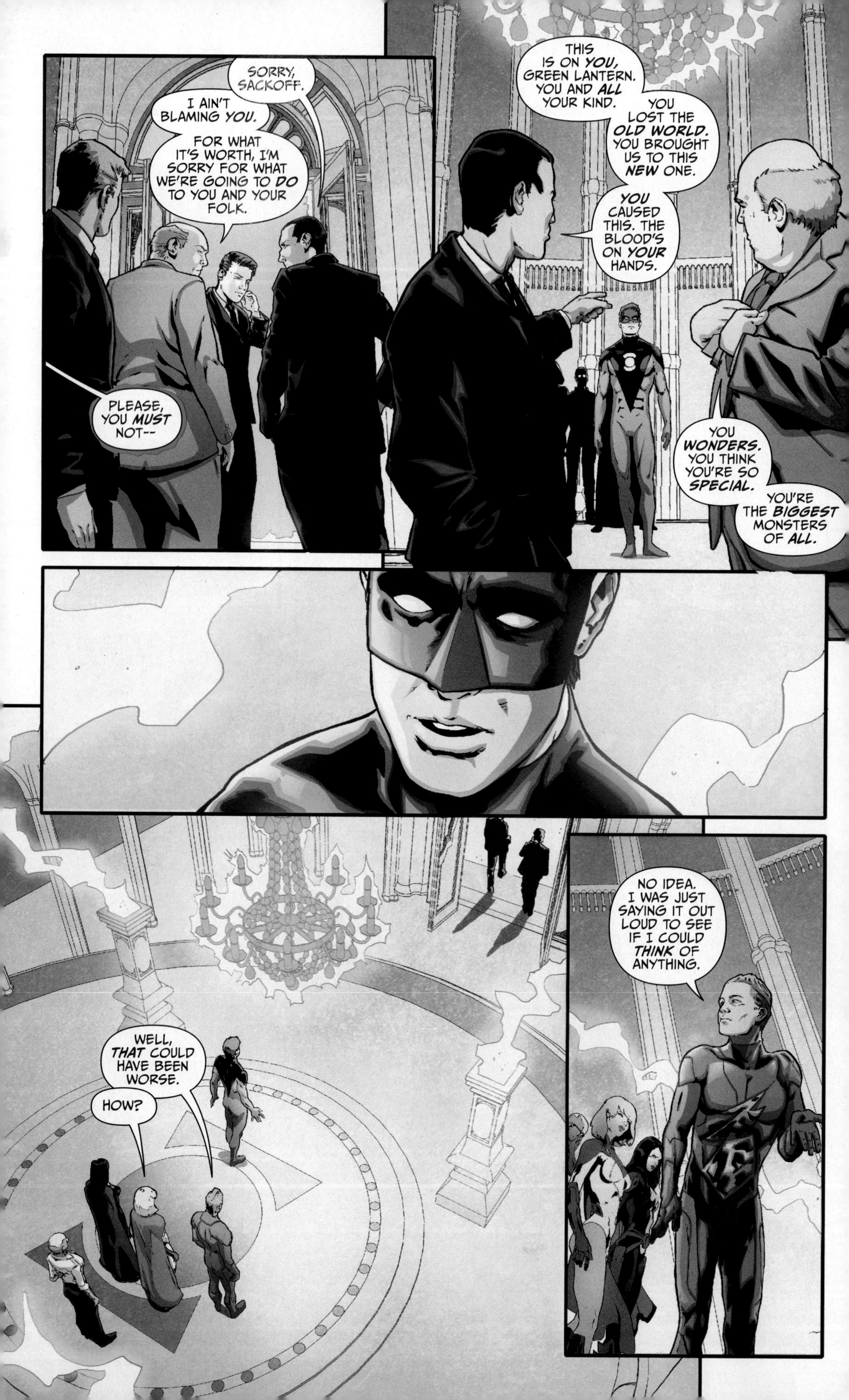
SORRY, SACKOFF.
I AIN'T BLAMING YOU.
FOR WHAT IT'S WORTH, I'M SORRY FOR WHAT WE'RE GOING TO DO TO YOU AND YOUR FOLK.
PLEASE, YOU MUST NOT--
THIS IS ON YOU, GREEN LANTERN. YOU AND ALL YOUR KIND.
YOU LOST THE OLD WORLD. YOU BROUGHT US TO THIS NEW ONE.
YOU CAUSED THIS. THE BLOOD'S ON YOUR HANDS.
YOU WONDERS. YOU THINK YOU'RE SO SPECIAL.
YOU'RE THE BIGGEST MONSTERS OF ALL.
WELL, THAT COULD HAVE BEEN WORSE.
HOW?
NO IDEA. I WAS JUST SAYING IT OUT LOUD TO SEE IF I COULD THINK OF ANYTHING.

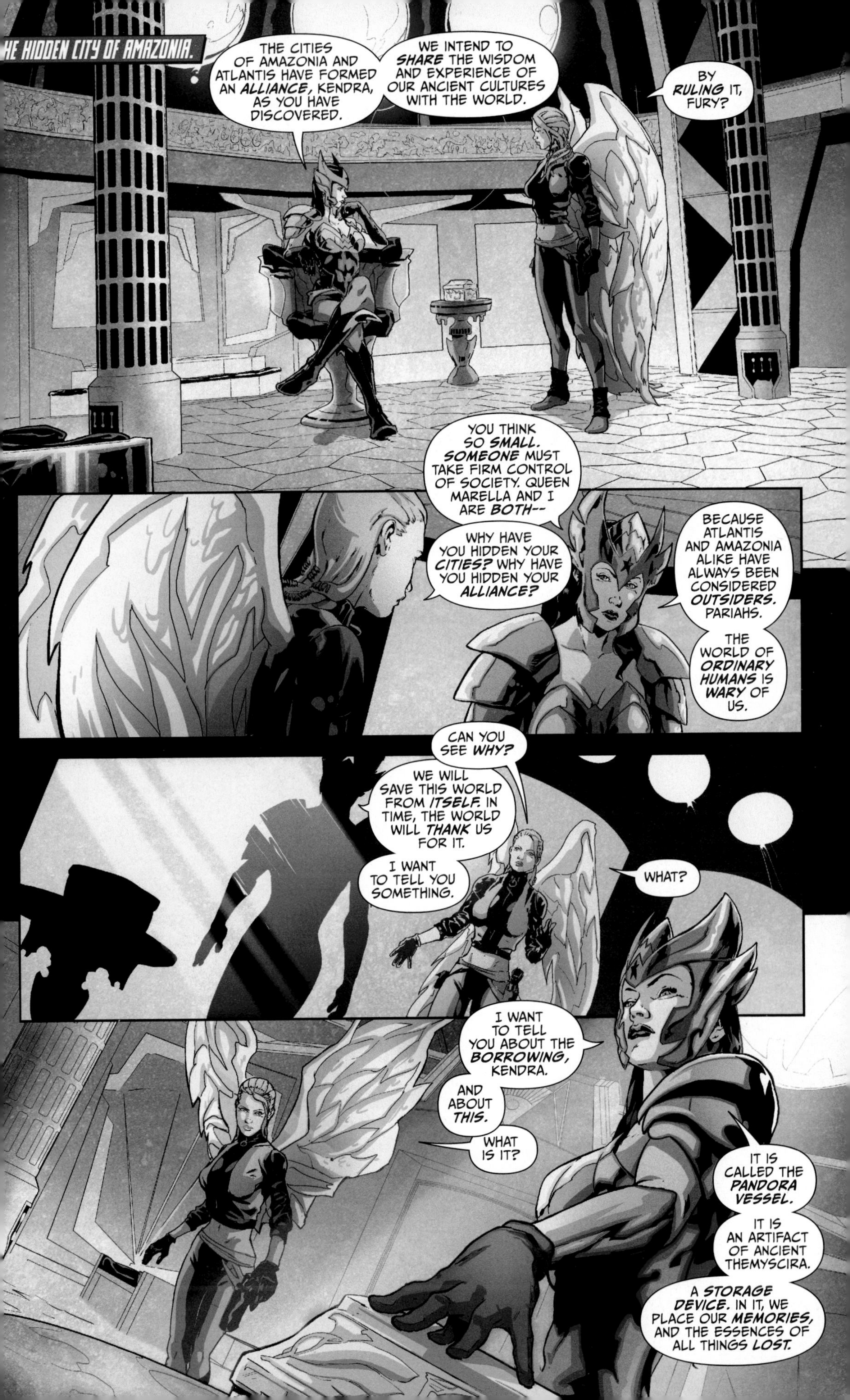

HE HIDDEN CITY OF AMAZONIA.
THE CITIES OF AMAZONIA AND ATLANTIS HAVE FORMED AN ALLIANCE, KENDRA, AS YOU HAVE DISCOVERED.
WE INTEND TO SHARE THE WISDOM AND EXPERIENCE OF OUR ANCIENT CULTURES WITH THE WORLD.
BY RULING IT, FURY?
YOU THINK SO SMALL. SOMEONE MUST TAKE FIRM CONTROL OF SOCIETY. QUEEN MARELLA AND I ARE BOTH--
WHY HAVE YOU HIDDEN YOUR CITIES? WHY HAVE YOU HIDDEN YOUR ALLIANCE?
BECAUSE ATLANTIS AND AMAZONIA ALIKE HAVE ALWAYS BEEN CONSIDERED OUTSIDERS. PARIAHS.
THE WORLD OF ORDINARY HUMANS IS WARY OF US.
CAN YOU SEE WHY?
WE WILL SAVE THIS WORLD FROM ITSELF. IN TIME, THE WORLD WILL THANK US FOR IT.
I WANT TO TELL YOU SOMETHING.
WHAT?
I WANT TO TELL YOU ABOUT THE BORROWING, KENDRA.
AND ABOUT THIS.
WHAT IS IT?
IT IS CALLED THE PANDORA VESSEL.
IT IS AN ARTIFACT OF ANCIENT THEMYSCIRA.
A STORAGE DEVICE. IN IT, WE PLACE OUR MEMORIES, AND THE ESSENCES OF ALL THINGS LOST.

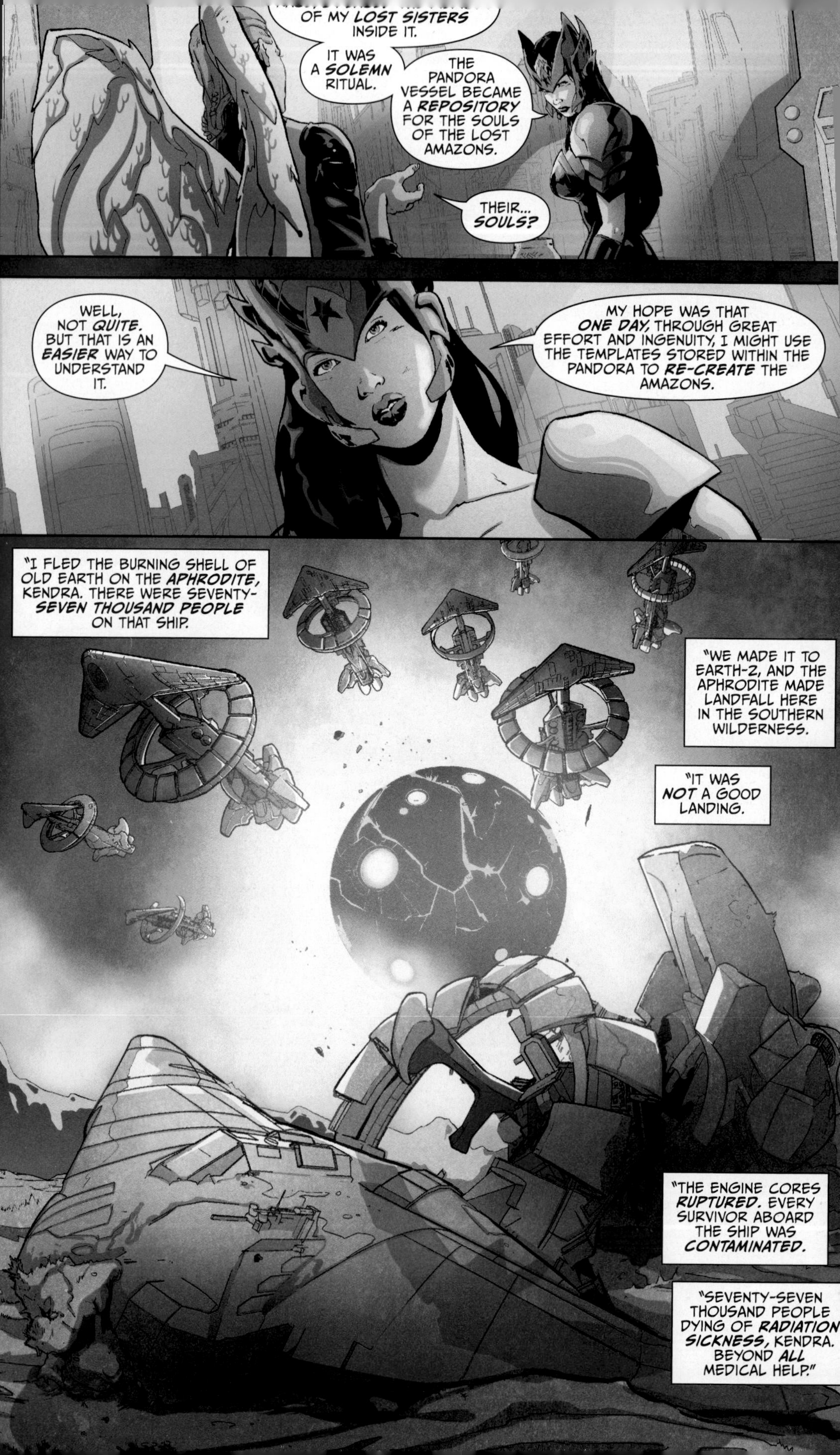
OF MY LOST SISTERS INSIDE IT.
IT WAS A SOLEMN RITUAL.
THE PANDORA VESSEL BECAME A REPOSITORY FOR THE SOULS OF THE LOST AMAZONS.
THEIR... SOULS?
WELL, NOT QUITE. BUT THAT IS AN EASIER WAY TO UNDERSTAND IT.
MY HOPE WAS THAT ONE DAY, THROUGH GREAT EFFORT AND INGENUITY, I MIGHT USE THE TEMPLATES STORED WITHIN THE PANDORA TO RE-CREATE THE AMAZONS.
"I FLED THE BURNING SHELL OF OLD EARTH ON THE APHRODITE, KENDRA. THERE WERE SEVENTY-SEVEN THOUSAND PEOPLE ON THAT SHIP.
"WE MADE IT TO EARTH-2, AND THE APHRODITE MADE LANDFALL HERE IN THE SOUTHERN WILDERNESS.
"IT WAS NOT A GOOD LANDING.
"THE ENGINE CORES RUPTURED. EVERY SURVIVOR ABOARD THE SHIP WAS CONTAMINATED.
"SEVENTY-SEVEN THOUSAND PEOPLE DYING OF RADIATION SICKNESS, KENDRA. BEYOND ALL MEDICAL HELP."

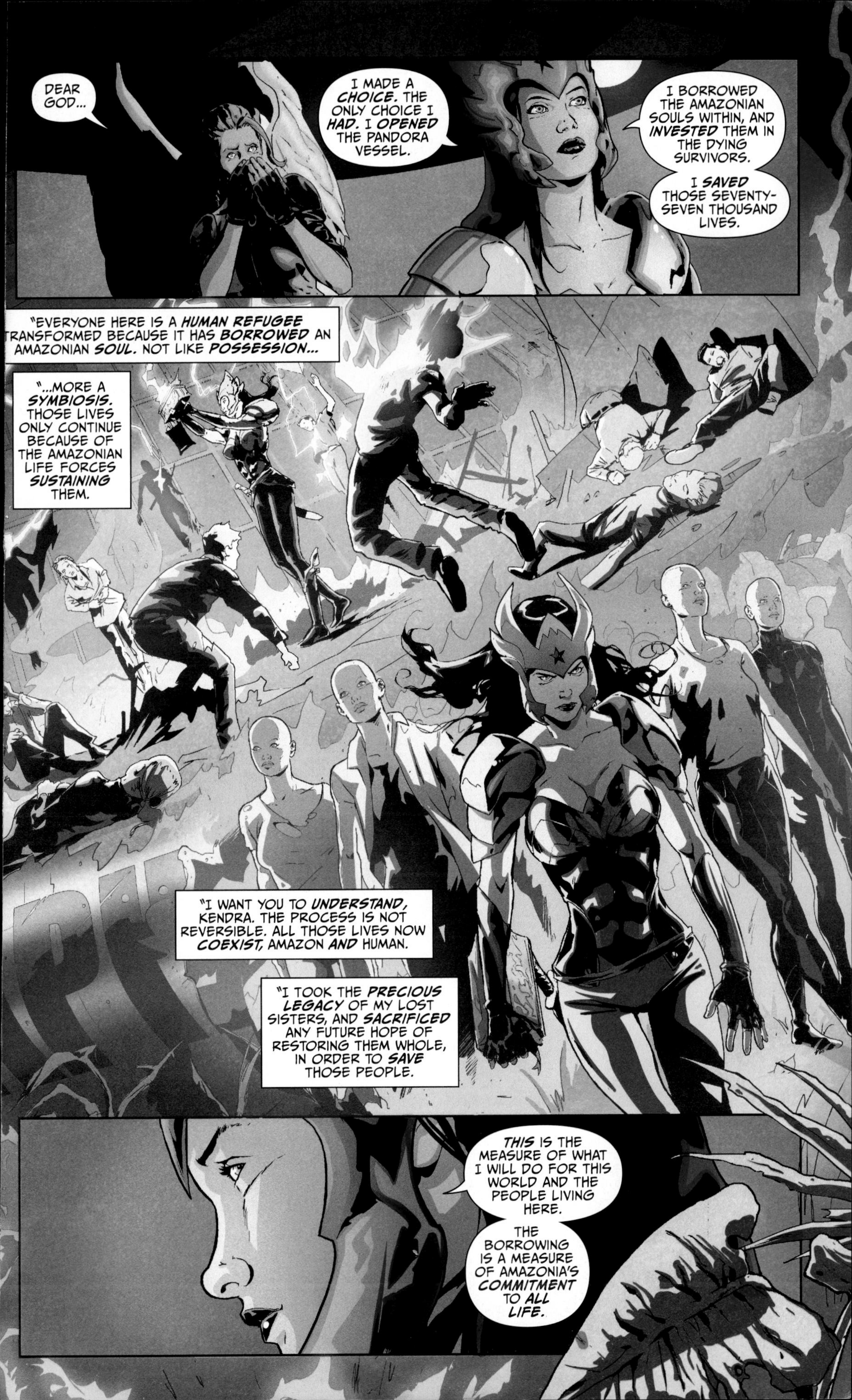
DEAR GOD...
I MADE A CHOICE. THE ONLY CHOICE I HAD. I OPENED THE PANDORA VESSEL.
I BORROWED THE AMAZONIAN SOULS WITHIN, AND INVESTED THEM IN THE DYING SURVIVORS.
I SAVED THOSE SEVENTY-SEVEN THOUSAND LIVES.
"EVERYONE HERE IS A HUMAN REFUGEE TRANSFORMED BECAUSE IT HAS BORROWED AN AMAZONIAN SOUL. NOT LIKE POSSESSION...
"...MORE A SYMBIOSIS. THOSE LIVES ONLY CONTINUE BECAUSE OF THE AMAZONIAN LIFE FORCES SUSTAINING THEM.
"I WANT YOU TO UNDERSTAND, KENDRA. THE PROCESS IS NOT REVERSIBLE. ALL THOSE LIVES NOW COEXIST, AMAZON AND HUMAN.
"I TOOK THE PRECIOUS LEGACY OF MY LOST SISTERS, AND SACRIFICED ANY FUTURE HOPE OF RESTORING THEM WHOLE, IN ORDER TO SAVE THOSE PEOPLE.
THIS IS THE MEASURE OF WHAT I WILL DO FOR THIS WORLD AND THE PEOPLE LIVING HERE.
THE BORROWING IS A MEASURE OF AMAZONIA'S COMMITMENT TO ALL LIFE.

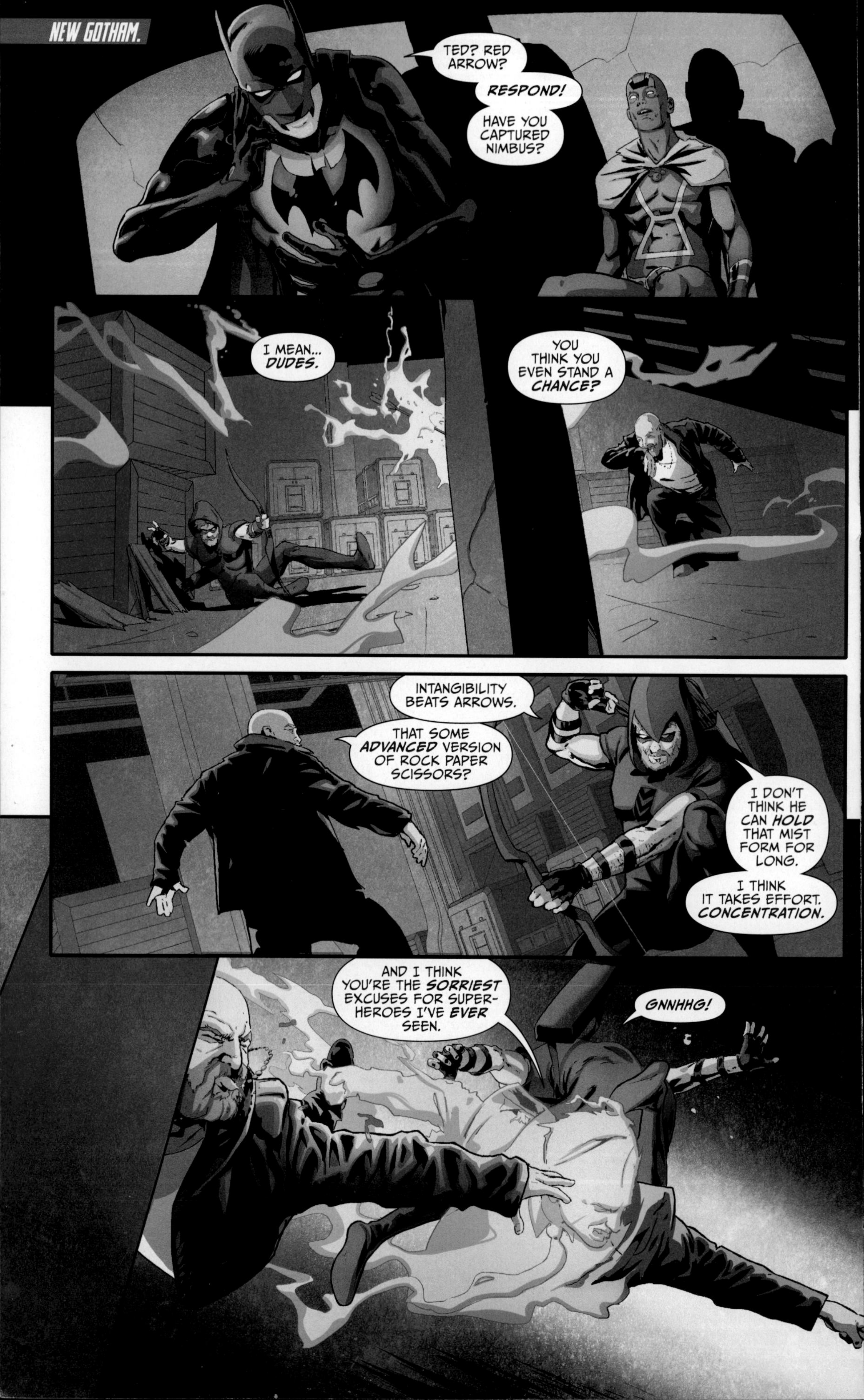
NEW GOTHAM.
TED? RED ARROW?
RESPOND!
HAVE YOU CAPTURED NIMBUS?
I MEAN... DUDES.
YOU THINK YOU EVEN STAND A CHANCE?
INTANGIBILITY BEATS ARROWS.
THAT SOME ADVANCED VERSION OF ROCK PAPER SCISSORS?
I DON'T THINK HE CAN HOLD THAT MIST FORM FOR LONG.
I THINK IT TAKES EFFORT. CONCENTRATION.
AND I THINK YOU'RE THE SORRIEST EXCUSES FOR SUPER-HEROES I'VE EVER SEEN.
GNNHHG!

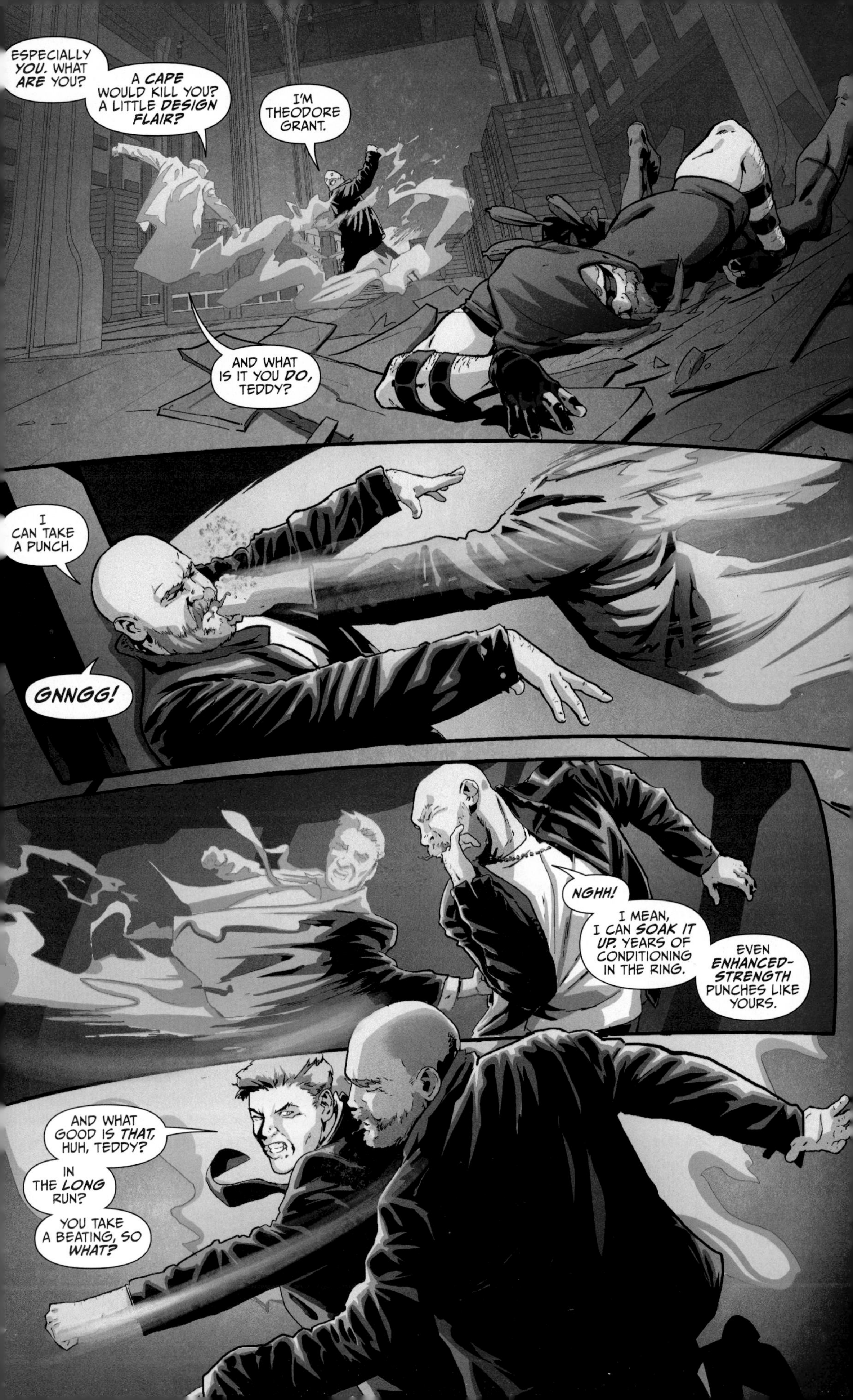
ESPECIALLY YOU. WHAT ARE YOU?
A CAPE WOULD KILL YOU? A LITTLE DESIGN FLAIR?
I'M THEODORE GRANT.
AND WHAT IS IT YOU DO, TEDDY?
I CAN TAKE A PUNCH.
GNNGG!
NGHH!
I MEAN, I CAN SOAK IT UP. YEARS OF CONDITIONING IN THE RING.
EVEN ENHANCED-STRENGTH PUNCHES LIKE YOURS.
AND WHAT GOOD IS THAT, HUH, TEDDY?
IN THE LONG RUN?
YOU TAKE A BEATING, SO WHAT?

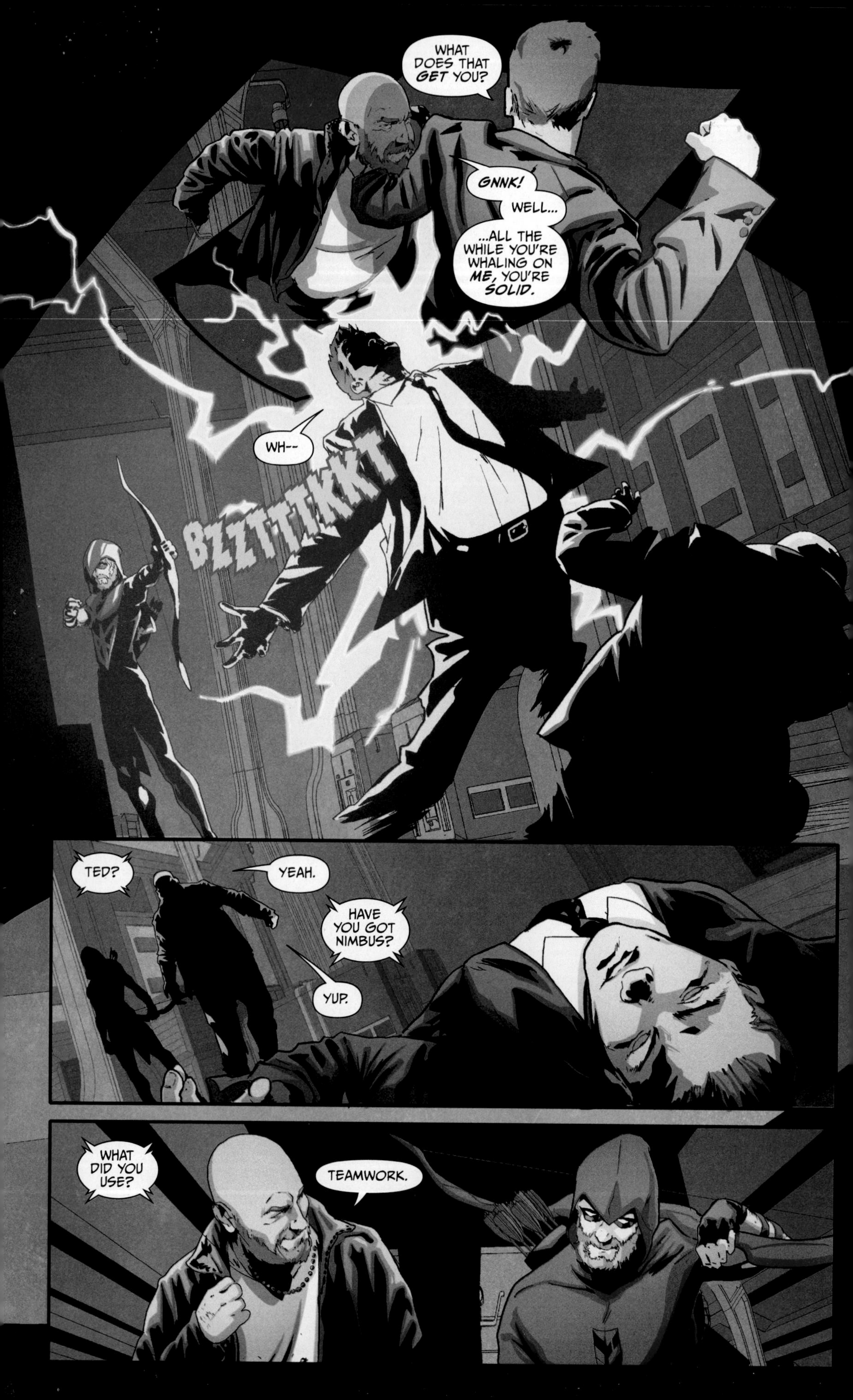
WHAT DOES THAT GET YOU?
GNNK!
WELL...
...ALL THE WHILE YOU'RE WHALING ON ME, YOU'RE SOLID.
WH--
BZZTTTTKKKT
TED?
YEAH.
HAVE YOU GOT NIMBUS?
YUP.
WHAT DID YOU USE?
TEAMWORK.

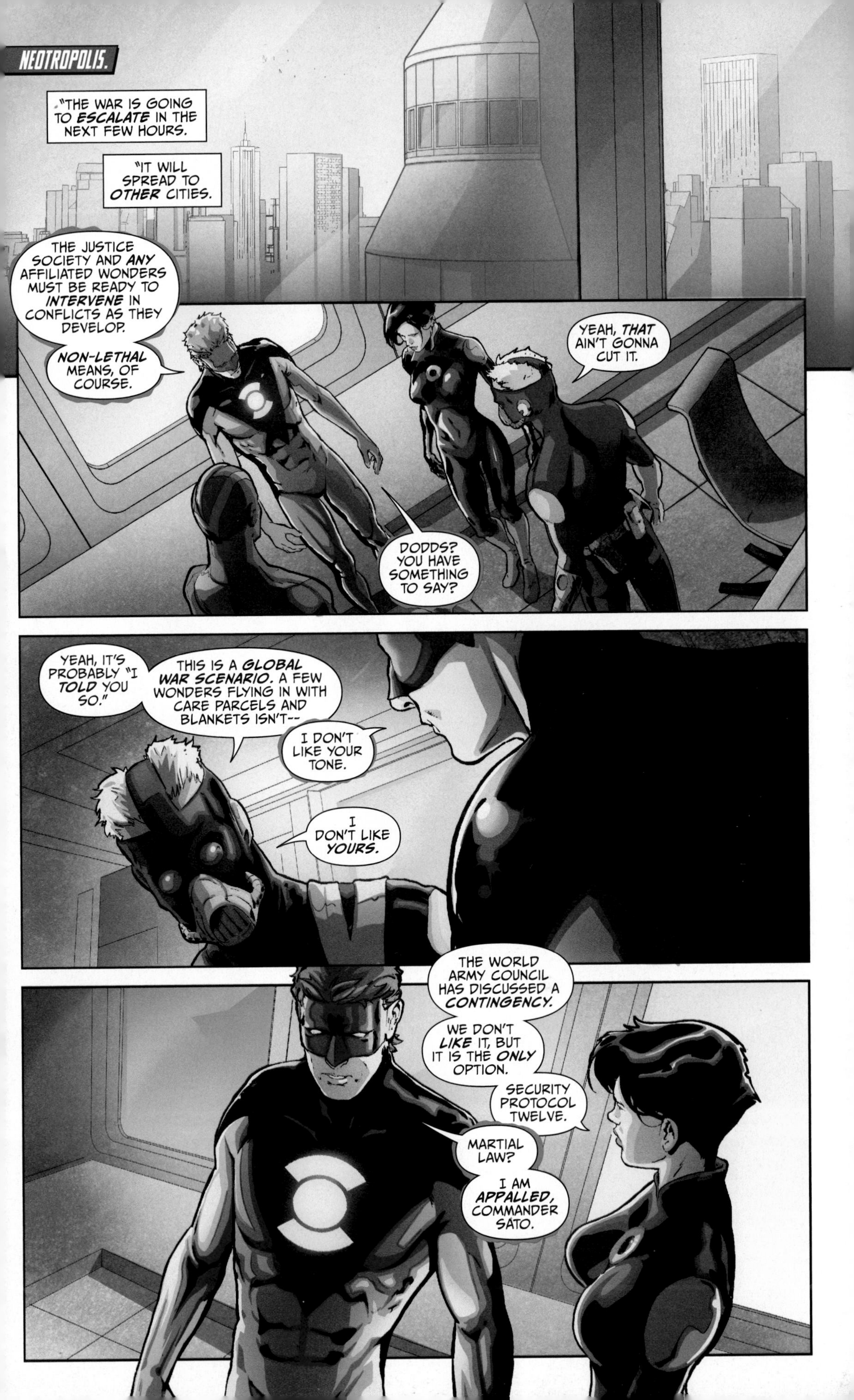
NEOTROPOLIS.
"THE WAR IS GOING TO ESCALATE IN THE NEXT FEW HOURS.
"IT WILL SPREAD TO OTHER CITIES.
THE JUSTICE SOCIETY AND ANY AFFILIATED WONDERS MUST BE READY TO INTERVENE IN CONFLICTS AS THEY DEVELOP.
NON-LETHAL MEANS, OF COURSE.
YEAH, THAT AIN'T GONNA CUT IT.
DODDS? YOU HAVE SOMETHING TO SAY?
YEAH, IT'S PROBABLY "I TOLD YOU SO."
THIS IS A GLOBAL WAR SCENARIO. A FEW WONDERS FLYING IN WITH CARE PARCELS AND BLANKETS ISN'T--
I DON'T LIKE YOUR TONE.
I DON'T LIKE YOURS.
THE WORLD ARMY COUNCIL HAS DISCUSSED A CONTINGENCY.
WE DON'T LIKE IT, BUT IT IS THE ONLY OPTION.
SECURITY PROTOCOL TWELVE.
MARTIAL LAW?
I AM APPALLED, COMMANDER SATO.

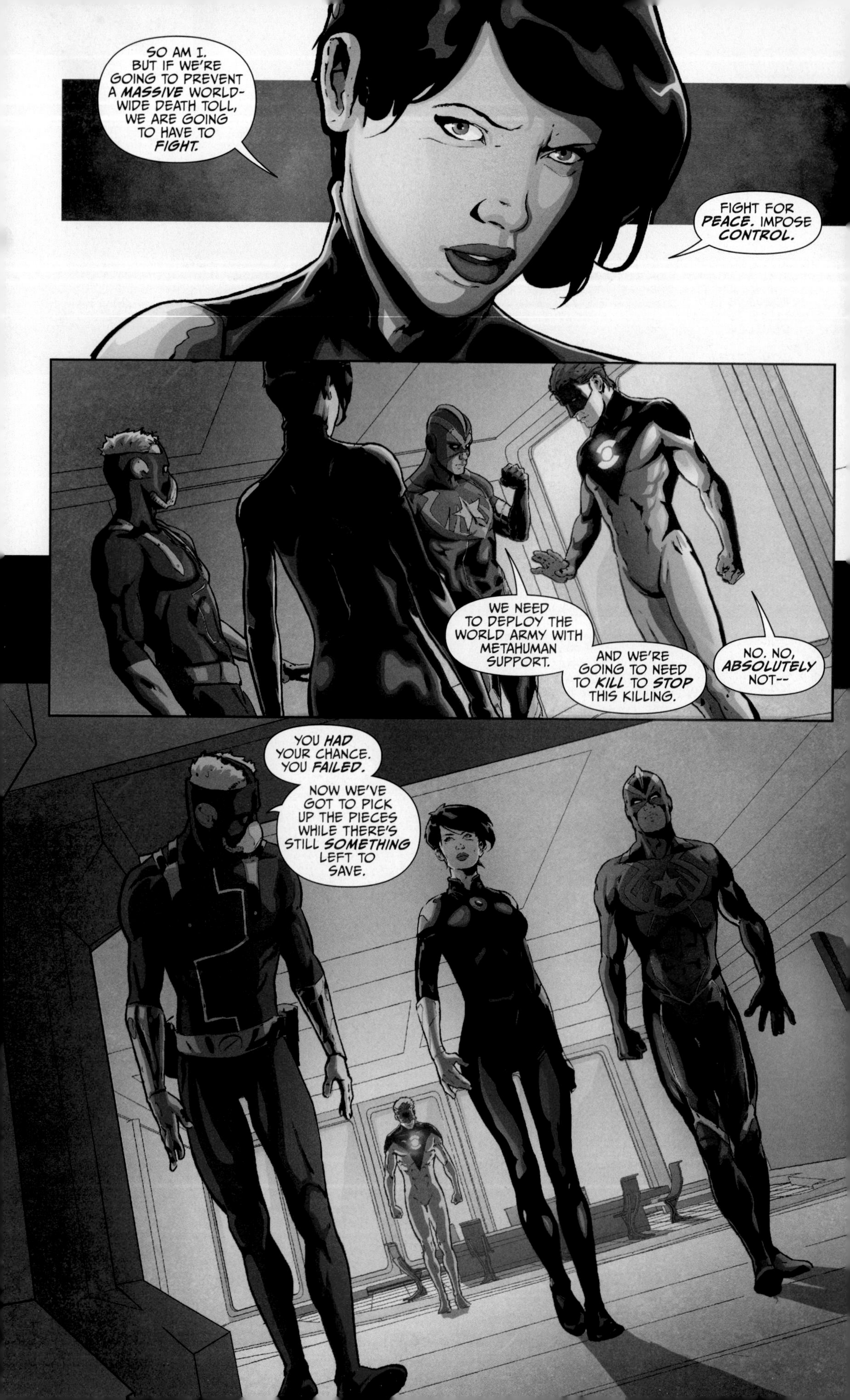
SO AM I. BUT IF WE'RE GOING TO PREVENT A MASSIVE WORLD-WIDE DEATH TOLL, WE ARE GOING TO HAVE TO FIGHT.
FIGHT FOR PEACE. IMPOSE CONTROL.
WE NEED TO DEPLOY THE WORLD ARMY WITH METAHUMAN SUPPORT.
AND WE'RE GOING TO NEED TO KILL TO STOP THIS KILLING.
NO. NO, ABSOLUTELY NOT--
YOU HAD YOUR CHANCE. YOU FAILED.
NOW WE'VE GOT TO PICK UP THE PIECES WHILE THERE'S STILL SOMETHING LEFT TO SAVE.

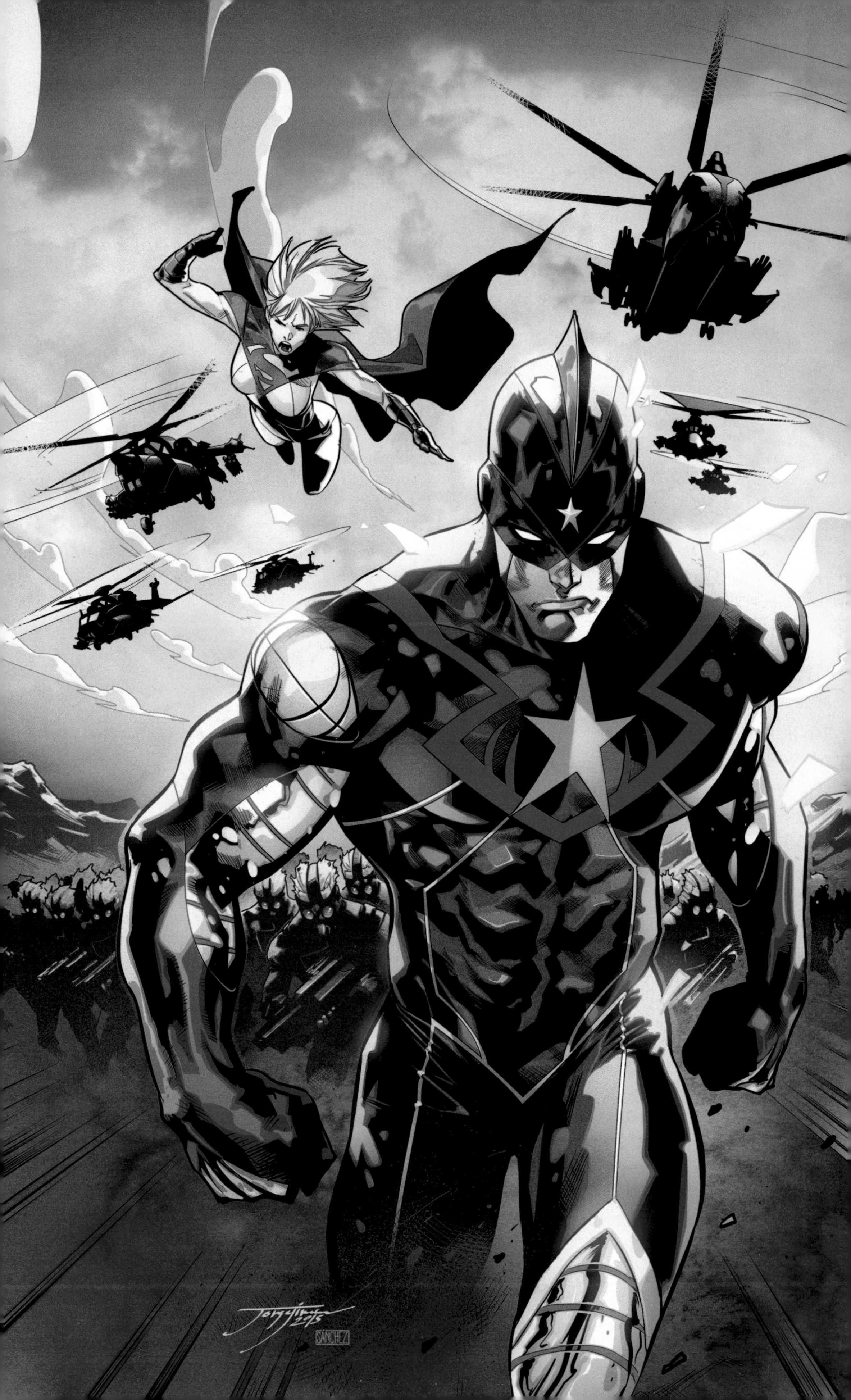
SANCHEZ

ONE NATION, INDIVISIBLE CHAPTER FIVE: AND JUSTICE FOR ALL

DAN ABNETT writer IBAN COELLO artist DAVID CALDERON OF IKARI STUDIO colorist TRAVIS LANHAM letterer cover by JIMÉNEZ & SANCHEZ

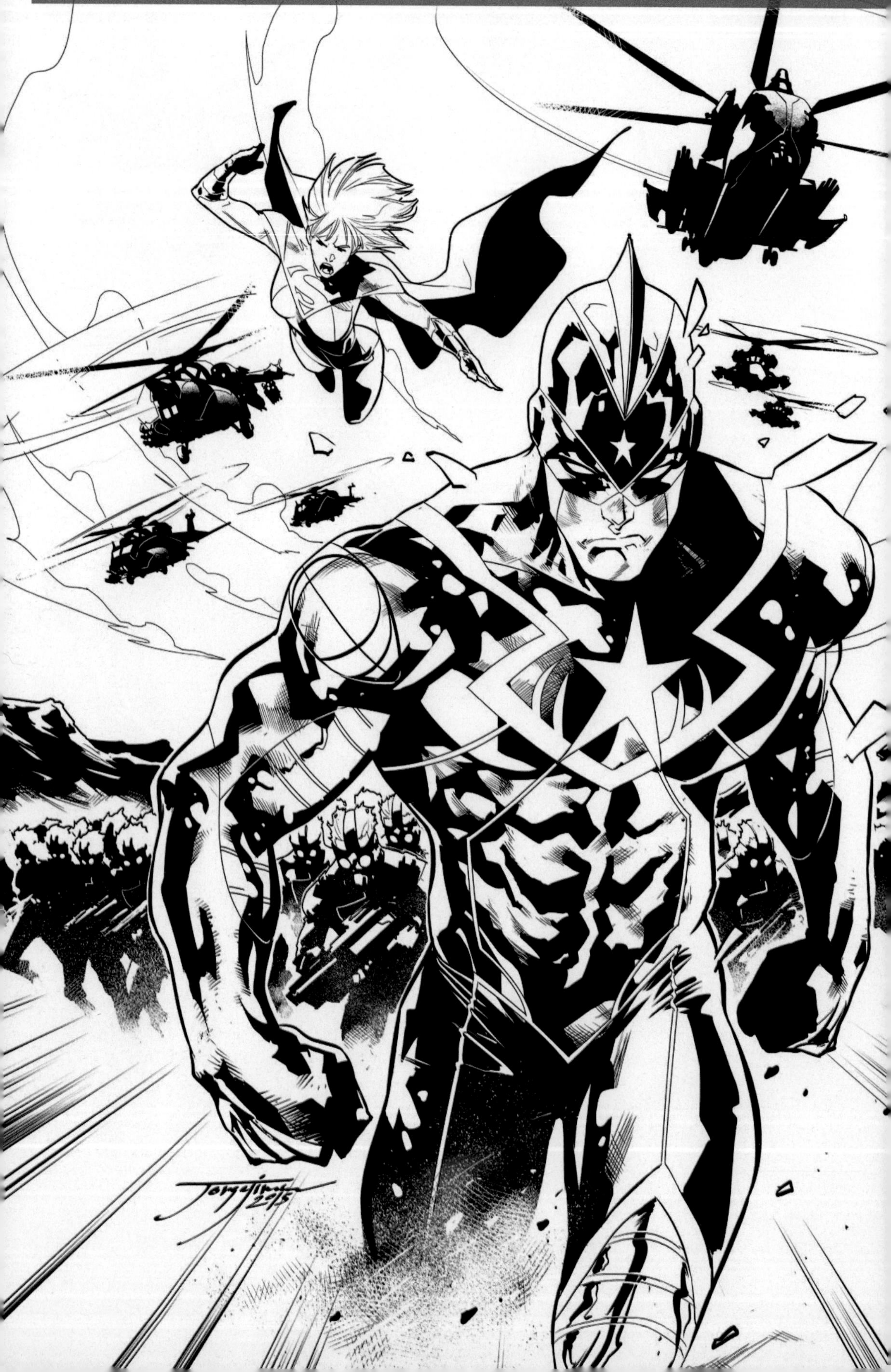

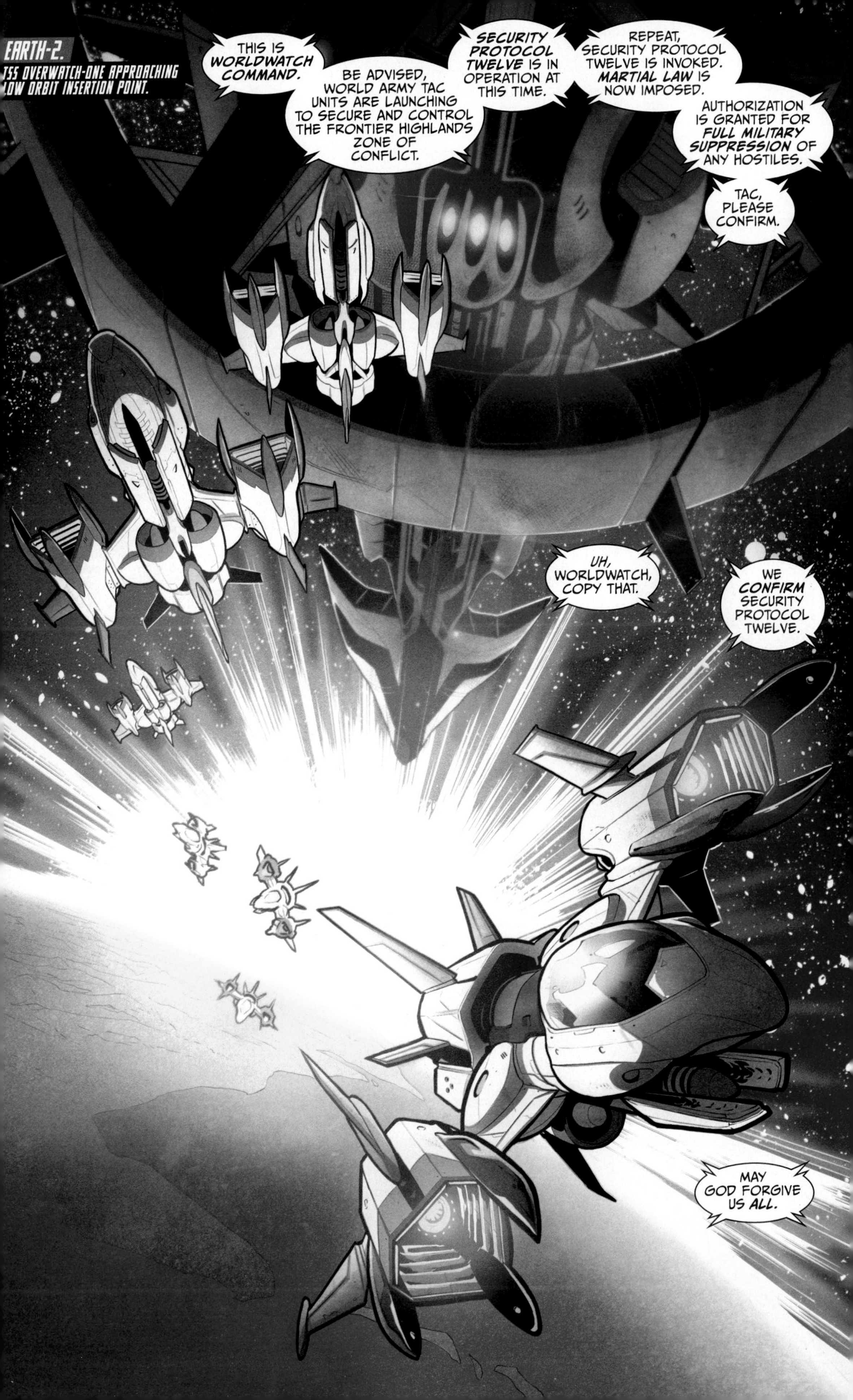
EARTH-2.
TSS OVERWATCH-ONE APPROACHING LOW ORBIT INSERTION POINT.
THIS IS WORLDWATCH COMMAND.
BE ADVISED, WORLD ARMY TAC UNITS ARE LAUNCHING TO SECURE AND CONTROL THE FRONTIER HIGHLANDS ZONE OF CONFLICT.
SECURITY PROTOCOL TWELVE IS IN OPERATION AT THIS TIME.
REPEAT, SECURITY PROTOCOL TWELVE IS INVOKED. MARTIAL LAW IS NOW IMPOSED.
AUTHORIZATION IS GRANTED FOR FULL MILITARY SUPPRESSION OF ANY HOSTILES.
TAC, PLEASE CONFIRM.
UH, WORLDWATCH, COPY THAT.
WE CONFIRM SECURITY PROTOCOL TWELVE.
MAY GOD FORGIVE US ALL.

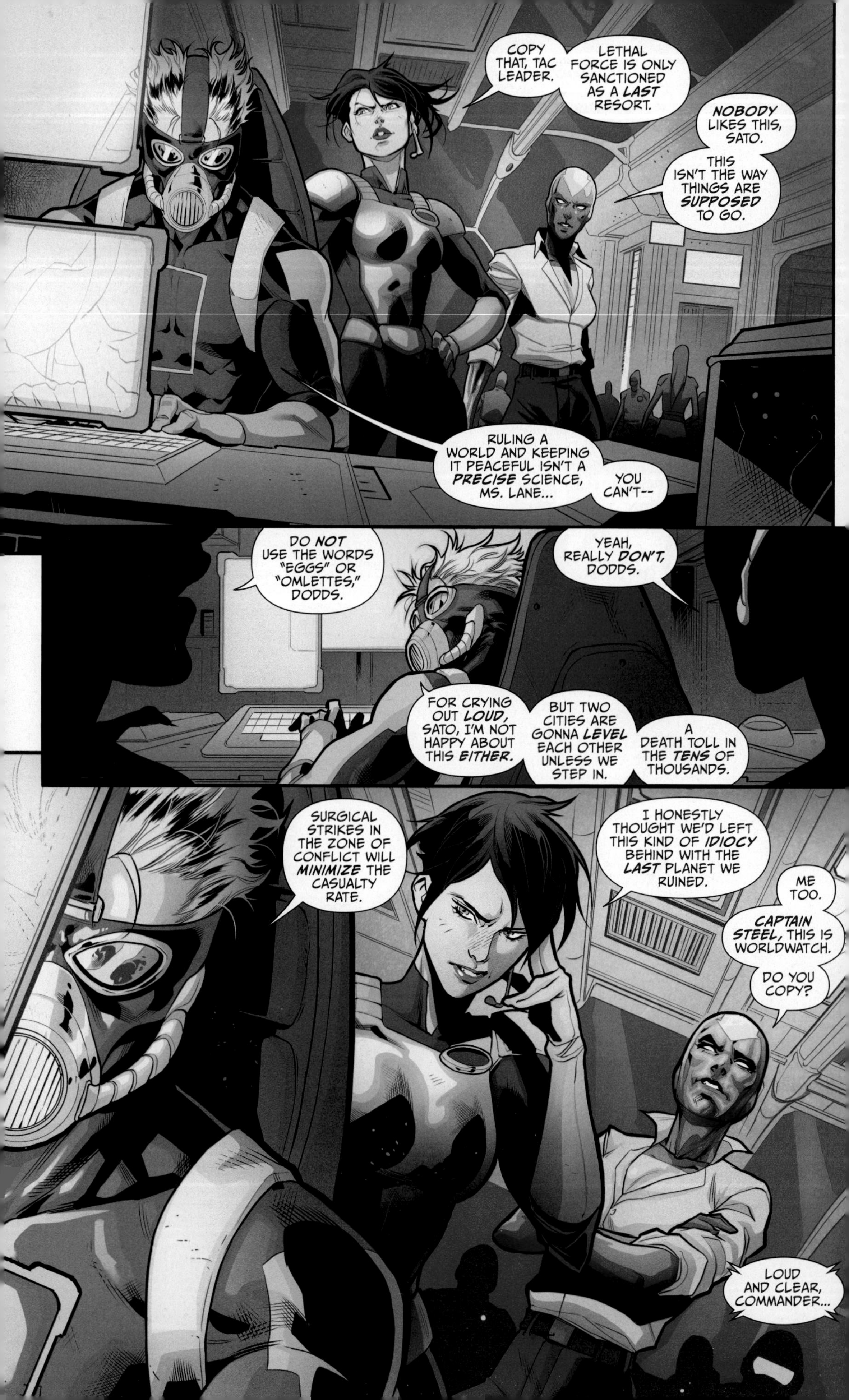
COPY THAT, TAC LEADER.
LETHAL FORCE IS ONLY SANCTIONED AS A LAST RESORT.
NOBODY LIKES THIS, SATO.
THIS ISN'T THE WAY THINGS ARE SUPPOSED TO GO.
RULING A WORLD AND KEEPING IT PEACEFUL ISN'T A PRECISE SCIENCE, MS. LANE...
YOU CAN'T--
DO NOT USE THE WORDS "EGGS" OR "OMLETTES," DODDS.
YEAH, REALLY DON'T, DODDS.
FOR CRYING OUT LOUD, SATO, I'M NOT HAPPY ABOUT THIS EITHER.
BUT TWO CITIES ARE GONNA LEVEL EACH OTHER UNLESS WE STEP IN.
A DEATH TOLL IN THE TENS OF THOUSANDS.
SURGICAL STRIKES IN THE ZONE OF CONFLICT WILL MINIMIZE THE CASUALTY RATE.
I HONESTLY THOUGHT WE'D LEFT THIS KIND OF IDIOCY BEHIND WITH THE LAST PLANET WE RUINED.
ME TOO.
CAPTAIN STEEL, THIS IS WORLDWATCH.
DO YOU COPY?
LOUD AND CLEAR, COMMANDER...

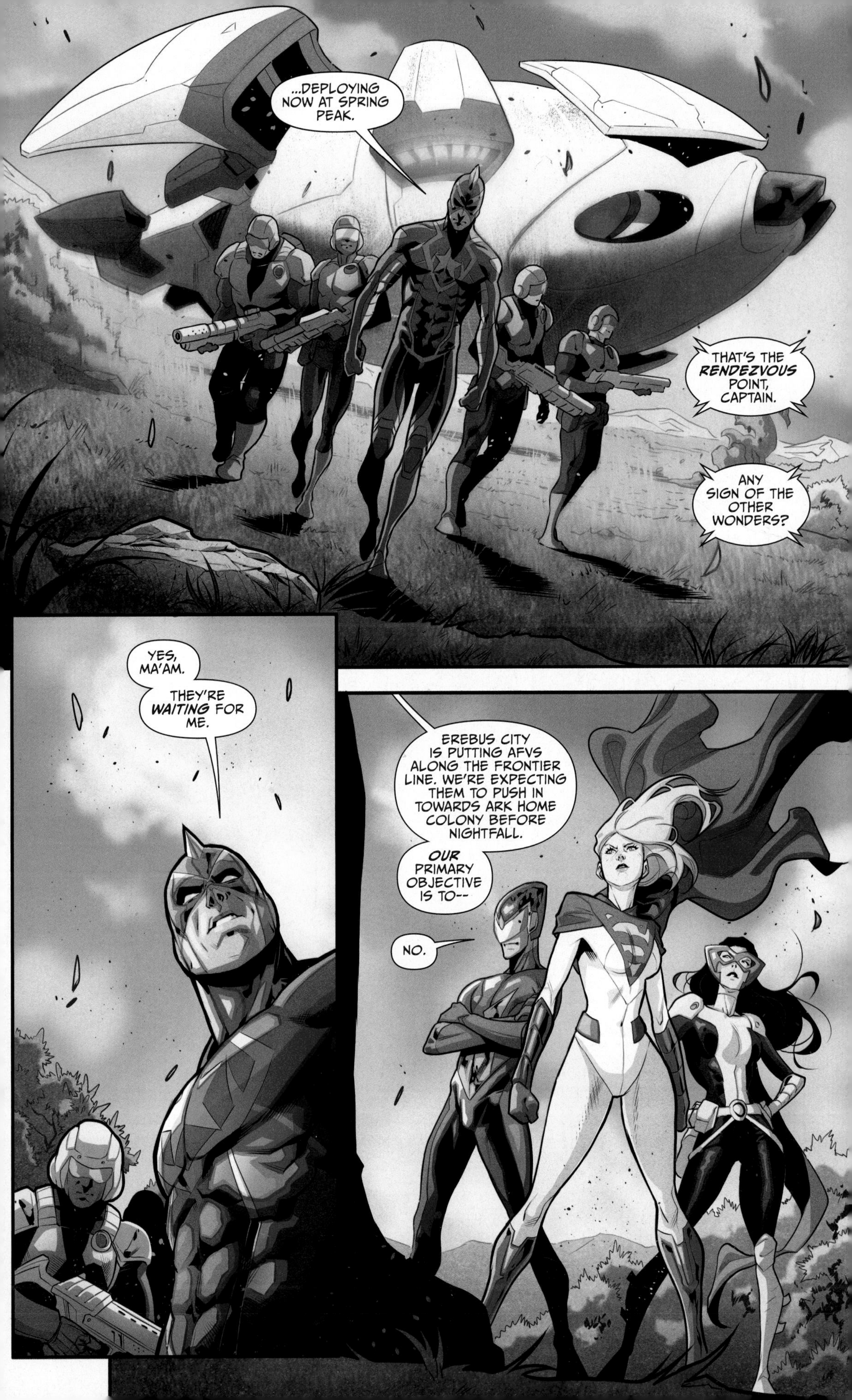
...DEPLOYING NOW AT SPRING PEAK.
THAT'S THE RENDEZVOUS POINT, CAPTAIN.
ANY SIGN OF THE OTHER WONDERS?
YES, MA'AM.
THEY'RE WAITING FOR ME.
EREBUS CITY IS PUTTING AFVS ALONG THE FRONTIER LINE. WE'RE EXPECTING THEM TO PUSH IN TOWARDS ARK HOME COLONY BEFORE NIGHTFALL.
OUR PRIMARY OBJECTIVE IS TO--
NO.

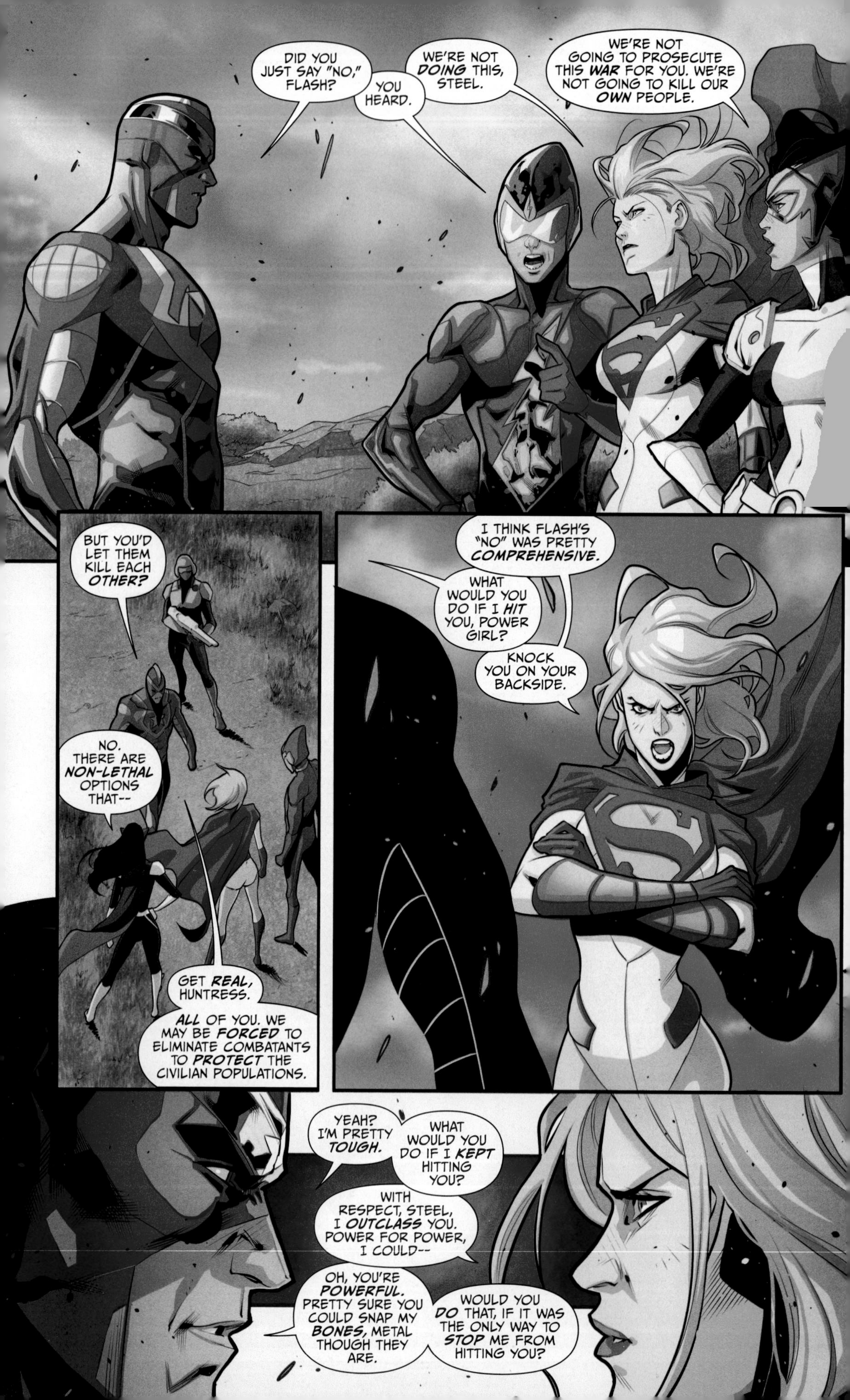
DID YOU JUST SAY "NO," FLASH?
YOU HEARD.
WE'RE NOT DOING THIS, STEEL.
WE'RE NOT GOING TO PROSECUTE THIS WAR FOR YOU. WE'RE NOT GOING TO KILL OUR OWN PEOPLE.
BUT YOU'D LET THEM KILL EACH OTHER?
NO. THERE ARE NON-LETHAL OPTIONS THAT--
GET REAL, HUNTRESS.
ALL OF YOU. WE MAY BE FORCED TO ELIMINATE COMBATANTS TO PROTECT THE CIVILIAN POPULATIONS.
I THINK FLASH'S "NO" WAS PRETTY COMPREHENSIVE.
WHAT WOULD YOU DO IF I HIT YOU, POWER GIRL?
KNOCK YOU ON YOUR BACKSIDE.
YEAH? I'M PRETTY TOUGH.
WHAT WOULD YOU DO IF I KEPT HITTING YOU?
WITH RESPECT, STEEL, I OUTCLASS YOU. POWER FOR POWER, I COULD--
OH, YOU'RE POWERFUL. PRETTY SURE YOU COULD SNAP MY BONES, METAL THOUGH THEY ARE.
WOULD YOU DO THAT, IF IT WAS THE ONLY WAY TO STOP ME FROM HITTING YOU?

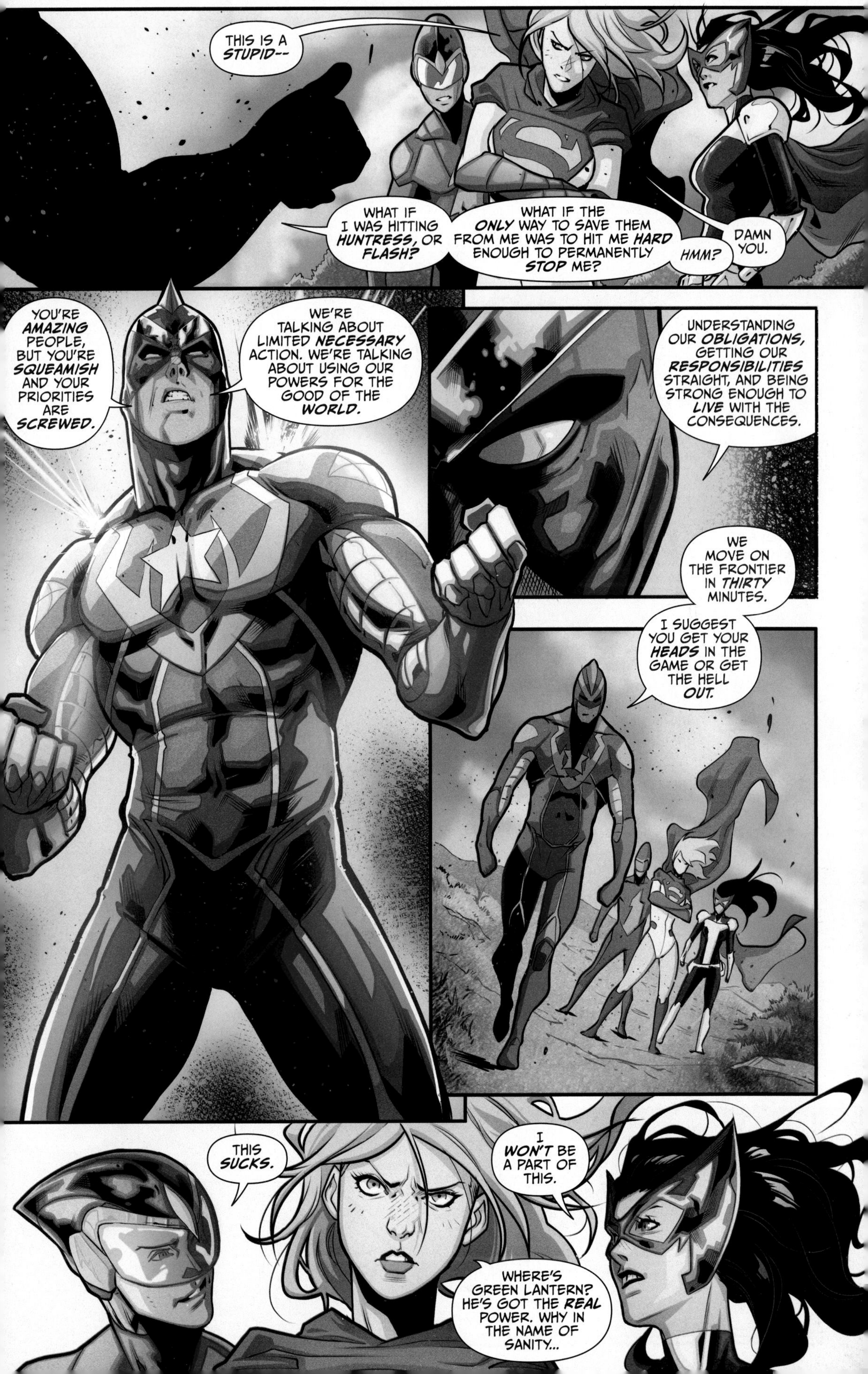

THIS IS A STUPID--
WHAT IF I WAS HITTING HUNTRESS, OR FLASH?
WHAT IF THE ONLY WAY TO SAVE THEM FROM ME WAS TO HIT ME HARD ENOUGH TO PERMANENTLY STOP ME?
HMM?
DAMN YOU.
YOU'RE AMAZING PEOPLE, BUT YOU'RE SQUEAMISH AND YOUR PRIORITIES ARE SCREWED.
WE'RE TALKING ABOUT LIMITED NECESSARY ACTION. WE'RE TALKING ABOUT USING OUR POWERS FOR THE GOOD OF THE WORLD.
UNDERSTANDING OUR OBLIGATIONS, GETTING OUR RESPONSIBILITIES STRAIGHT, AND BEING STRONG ENOUGH TO LIVE WITH THE CONSEQUENCES.
WE MOVE ON THE FRONTIER IN THIRTY MINUTES.
I SUGGEST YOU GET YOUR HEADS IN THE GAME OR GET THE HELL OUT.
THIS SUCKS.
I WON'T BE A PART OF THIS.
WHERE'S GREEN LANTERN? HE'S GOT THE REAL POWER. WHY IN THE NAME OF SANITY...

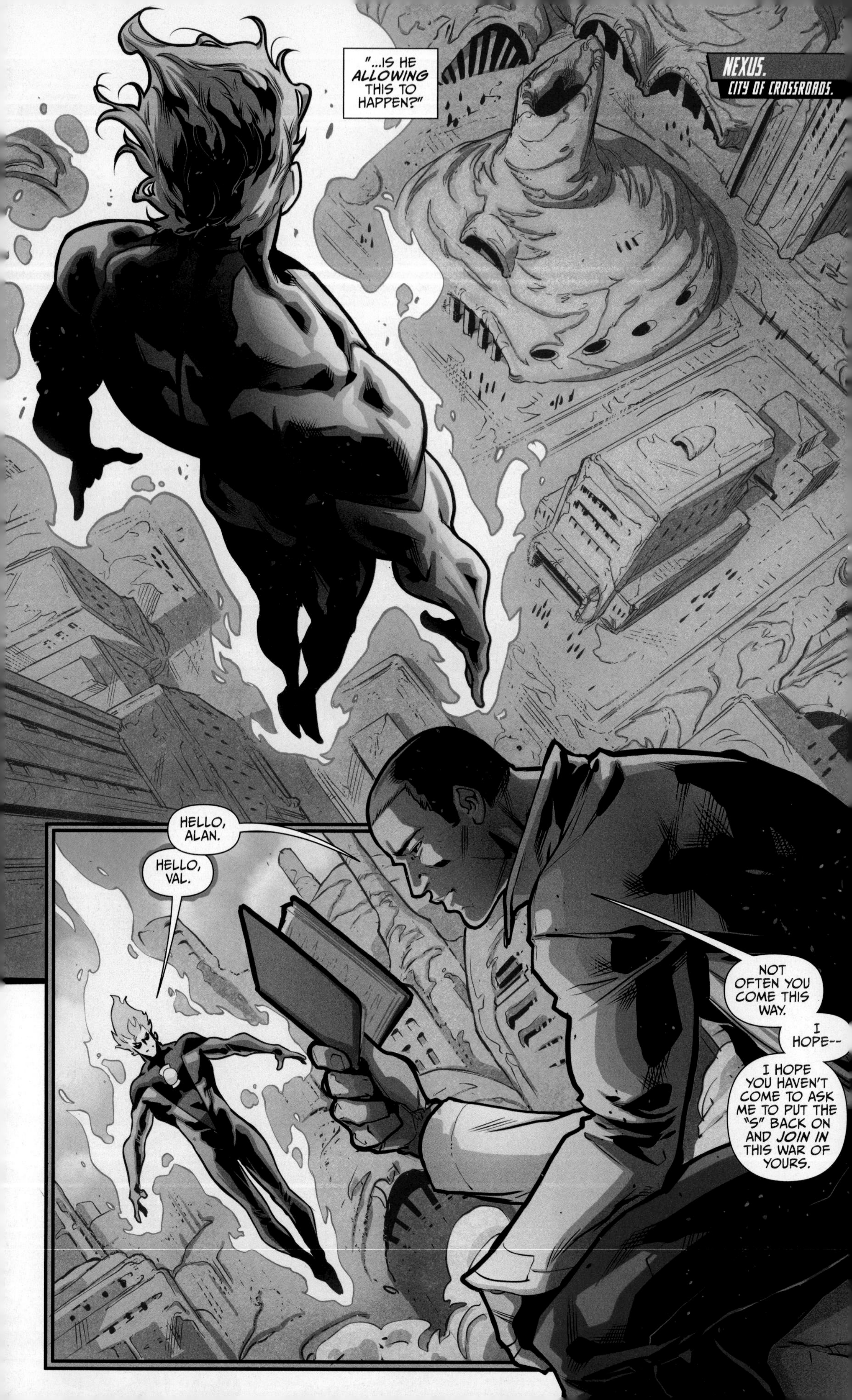

"...IS HE ALLOWING THIS TO HAPPEN?"
NEXUS.
CITY OF CROSSROADS.
HELLO, ALAN.
HELLO, VAL.
NOT OFTEN YOU COME THIS WAY.
I HOPE--
I HOPE YOU HAVEN'T COME TO ASK ME TO PUT THE "S" BACK ON AND JOIN IN THIS WAR OF YOURS.

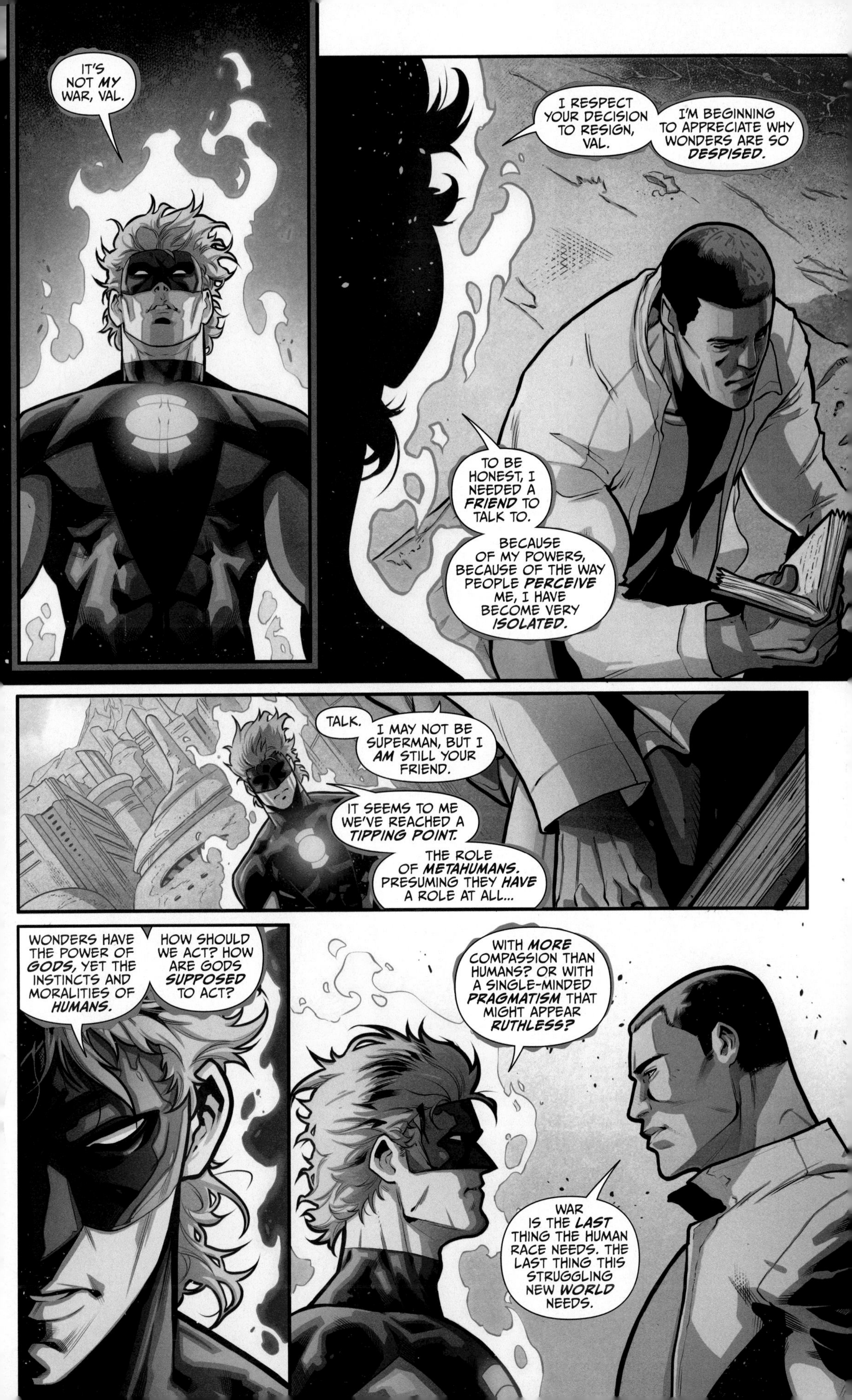
IT'S NOT MY WAR, VAL.
I RESPECT YOUR DECISION TO RESIGN, VAL.
I'M BEGINNING TO APPRECIATE WHY WONDERS ARE SO DESPISED.
TO BE HONEST, I NEEDED A FRIEND TO TALK TO.
BECAUSE OF MY POWERS, BECAUSE OF THE WAY PEOPLE PERCEIVE ME, I HAVE BECOME VERY ISOLATED.
TALK.
I MAY NOT BE SUPERMAN, BUT I AM STILL YOUR FRIEND.
IT SEEMS TO ME WE'VE REACHED A TIPPING POINT.
THE ROLE OF METAHUMANS. PRESUMING THEY HAVE A ROLE AT ALL...
WONDERS HAVE THE POWER OF GODS, YET THE INSTINCTS AND MORALITIES OF HUMANS.
HOW SHOULD WE ACT? HOW ARE GODS SUPPOSED TO ACT?
WITH MORE COMPASSION THAN HUMANS? OR WITH A SINGLE-MINDED PRAGMATISM THAT MIGHT APPEAR RUTHLESS?
WAR IS THE LAST THING THE HUMAN RACE NEEDS. THE LAST THING THIS STRUGGLING NEW WORLD NEEDS.

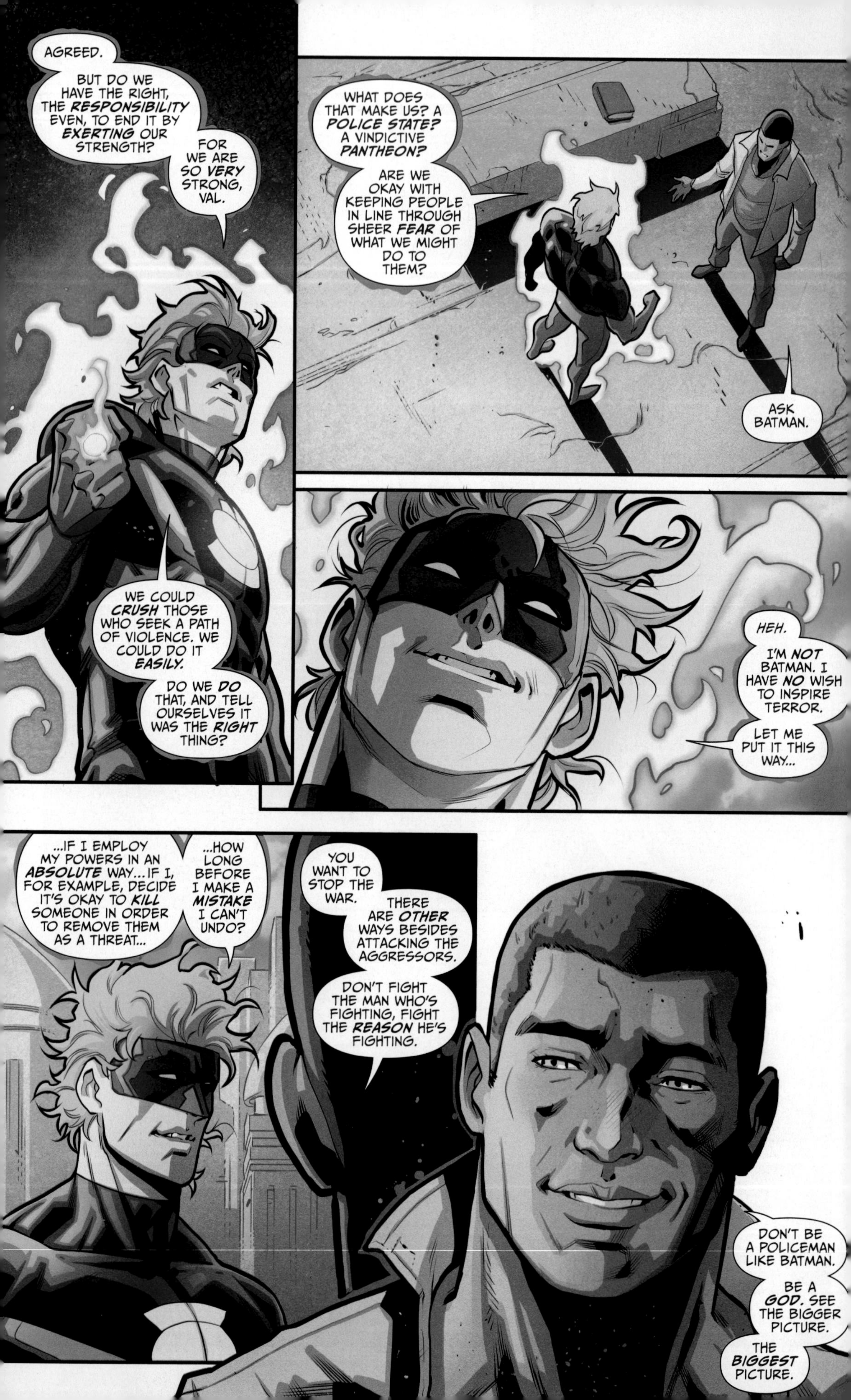
AGREED.
BUT DO WE HAVE THE RIGHT, THE RESPONSIBILITY EVEN, TO END IT BY EXERTING OUR STRENGTH?
FOR WE ARE SO VERY STRONG, VAL.
WE COULD CRUSH THOSE WHO SEEK A PATH OF VIOLENCE. WE COULD DO IT EASILY.
DO WE DO THAT, AND TELL OURSELVES IT WAS THE RIGHT THING?
WHAT DOES THAT MAKE US? A POLICE STATE? A VINDICTIVE PANTHEON?
ARE WE OKAY WITH KEEPING PEOPLE IN LINE THROUGH SHEER FEAR OF WHAT WE MIGHT DO TO THEM?
ASK BATMAN.
HEH.
I'M NOT BATMAN. I HAVE NO WISH TO INSPIRE TERROR.
LET ME PUT IT THIS WAY...
...IF I EMPLOY MY POWERS IN AN ABSOLUTE WAY... IF I, FOR EXAMPLE, DECIDE IT'S OKAY TO KILL SOMEONE IN ORDER TO REMOVE THEM AS A THREAT...
...HOW LONG BEFORE I MAKE A MISTAKE I CAN'T UNDO?
YOU WANT TO STOP THE WAR.
THERE ARE OTHER WAYS BESIDES ATTACKING THE AGGRESSORS.
DON'T FIGHT THE MAN WHO'S FIGHTING, FIGHT THE REASON HE'S FIGHTING.
DON'T BE A POLICEMAN LIKE BATMAN.
BE A GOD. SEE THE BIGGER PICTURE.
THE BIGGEST PICTURE.

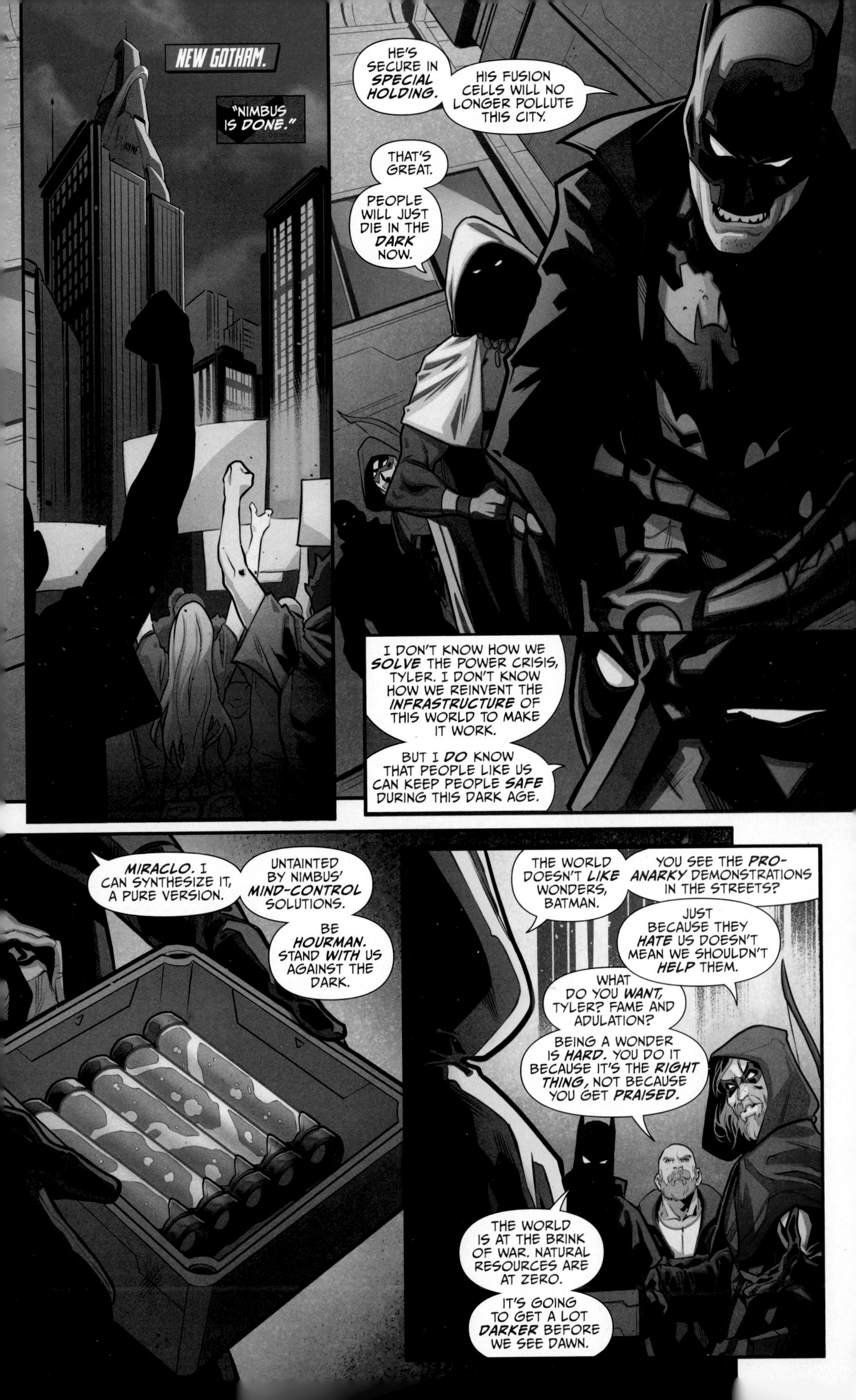
NEW GOTHAM.
"NIMBUS IS DONE."
HE'S SECURE IN SPECIAL HOLDING.
HIS FUSION CELLS WILL NO LONGER POLLUTE THIS CITY.
THAT'S GREAT.
PEOPLE WILL JUST DIE IN THE DARK NOW.
I DON'T KNOW HOW WE SOLVE THE POWER CRISIS, TYLER. I DON'T KNOW HOW WE REINVENT THE INFRASTRUCTURE OF THIS WORLD TO MAKE IT WORK.
BUT I DO KNOW THAT PEOPLE LIKE US CAN KEEP PEOPLE SAFE DURING THIS DARK AGE.
MIRACLO. I CAN SYNTHESIZE IT, A PURE VERSION.
UNTAINTED BY NIMBUS' MIND-CONTROL SOLUTIONS.
BE HOURMAN. STAND WITH US AGAINST THE DARK.
THE WORLD DOESN'T LIKE WONDERS, BATMAN.
YOU SEE THE PRO-ANARKY DEMONSTRATIONS IN THE STREETS?
JUST BECAUSE THEY HATE US DOESN'T MEAN WE SHOULDN'T HELP THEM.
WHAT DO YOU WANT, TYLER? FAME AND ADULATION?
BEING A WONDER IS HARD. YOU DO IT BECAUSE IT'S THE RIGHT THING, NOT BECAUSE YOU GET PRAISED.
THE WORLD IS AT THE BRINK OF WAR. NATURAL RESOURCES ARE AT ZERO.
IT'S GOING TO GET A LOT DARKER BEFORE WE SEE DAWN.

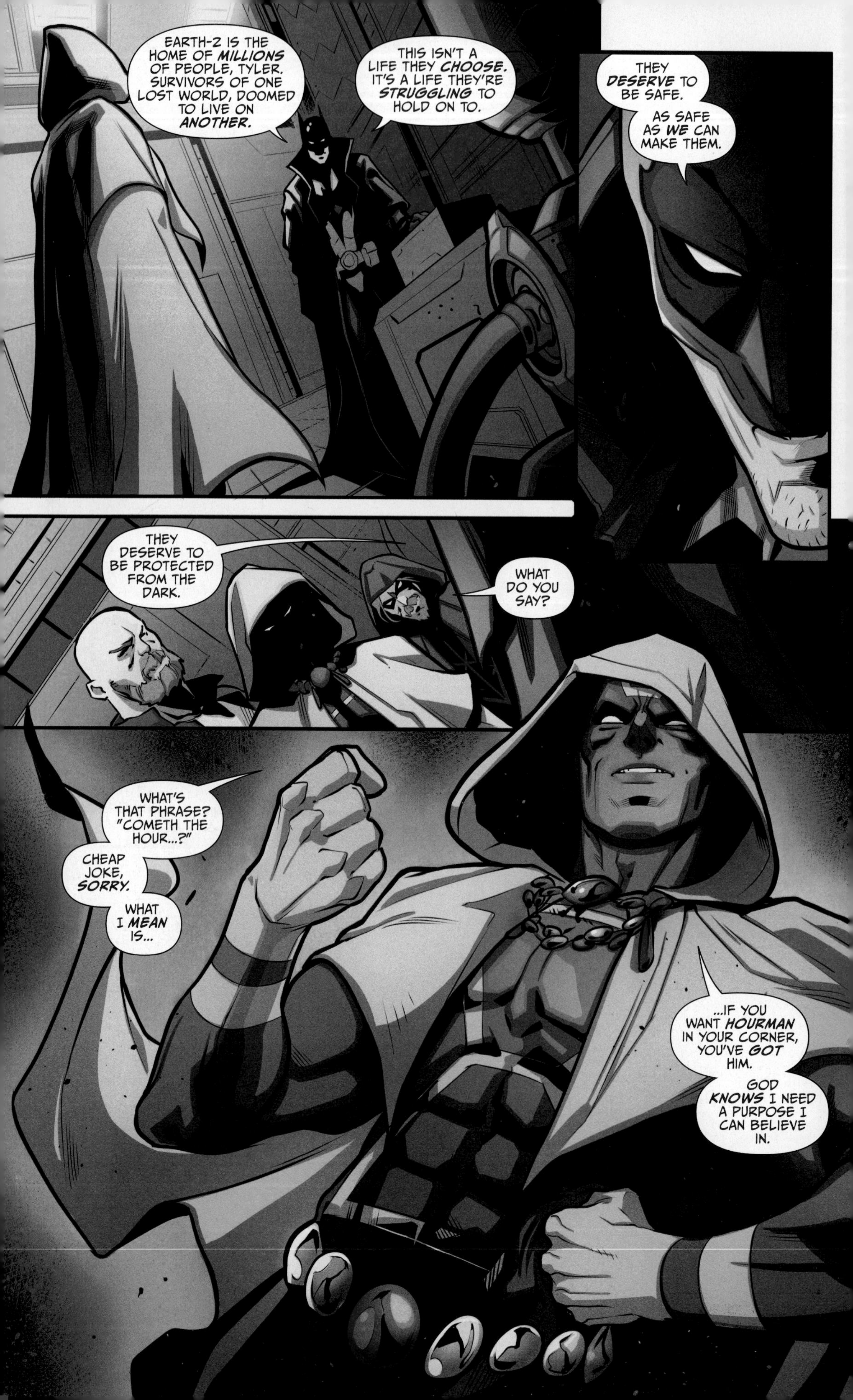
EARTH-2 IS THE HOME OF MILLIONS OF PEOPLE, TYLER. SURVIVORS OF ONE LOST WORLD, DOOMED TO LIVE ON ANOTHER.
THIS ISN'T A LIFE THEY CHOOSE. IT'S A LIFE THEY'RE STRUGGLING TO HOLD ON TO.
THEY DESERVE TO BE SAFE.
AS SAFE AS WE CAN MAKE THEM.
THEY DESERVE TO BE PROTECTED FROM THE DARK.
WHAT DO YOU SAY?
WHAT'S THAT PHRASE? "COMETH THE HOUR...?"
CHEAP JOKE, SORRY.
WHAT I MEAN IS...
...IF YOU WANT HOURMAN IN YOUR CORNER, YOU'VE GOT HIM.
GOD KNOWS I NEED A PURPOSE I CAN BELIEVE IN.

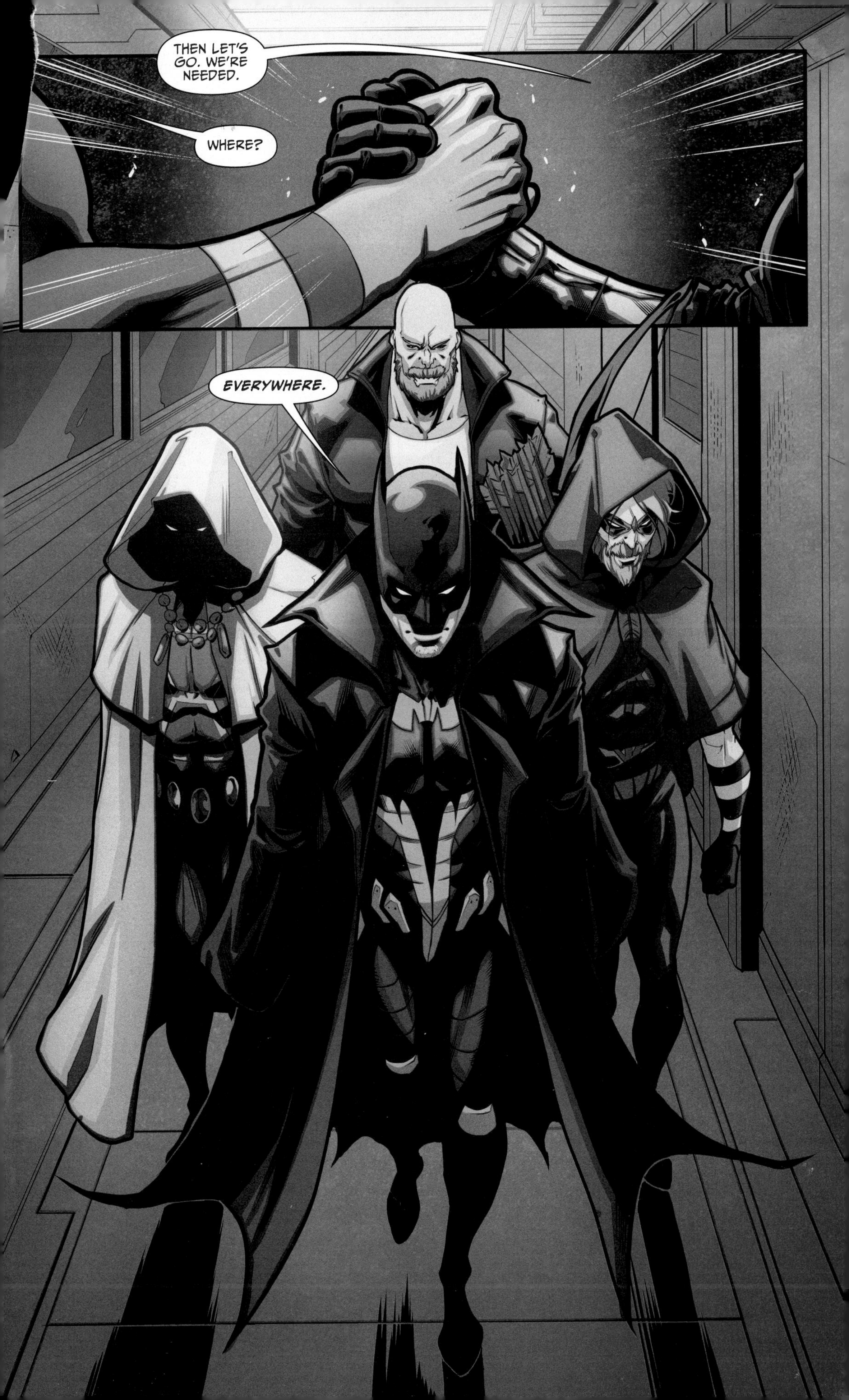
THEN LET'S GO. WE'RE NEEDED.
WHERE?
EVERYWHERE.

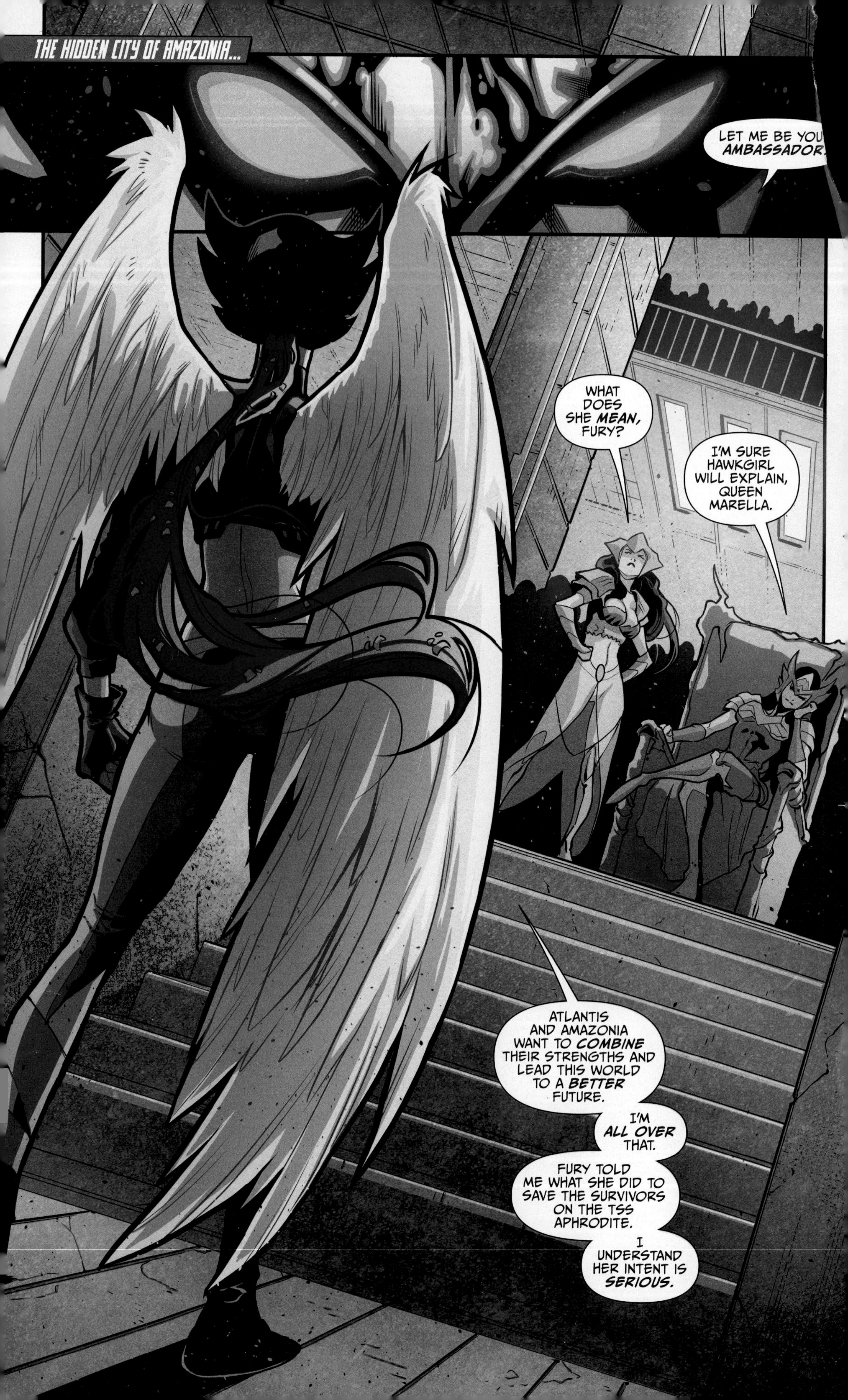
THE HIDDEN CITY OF AMAZONIA...
LET ME BE YOUR AMBASSADOR!
WHAT DOES SHE MEAN, FURY?
I'M SURE HAWKGIRL WILL EXPLAIN, QUEEN MARELLA.
ATLANTIS AND AMAZONIA WANT TO COMBINE THEIR STRENGTHS AND LEAD THIS WORLD TO A BETTER FUTURE.
I'M ALL OVER THAT.
FURY TOLD ME WHAT SHE DID TO SAVE THE SURVIVORS ON THE TSS APHRODITE.
I UNDERSTAND HER INTENT IS SERIOUS.

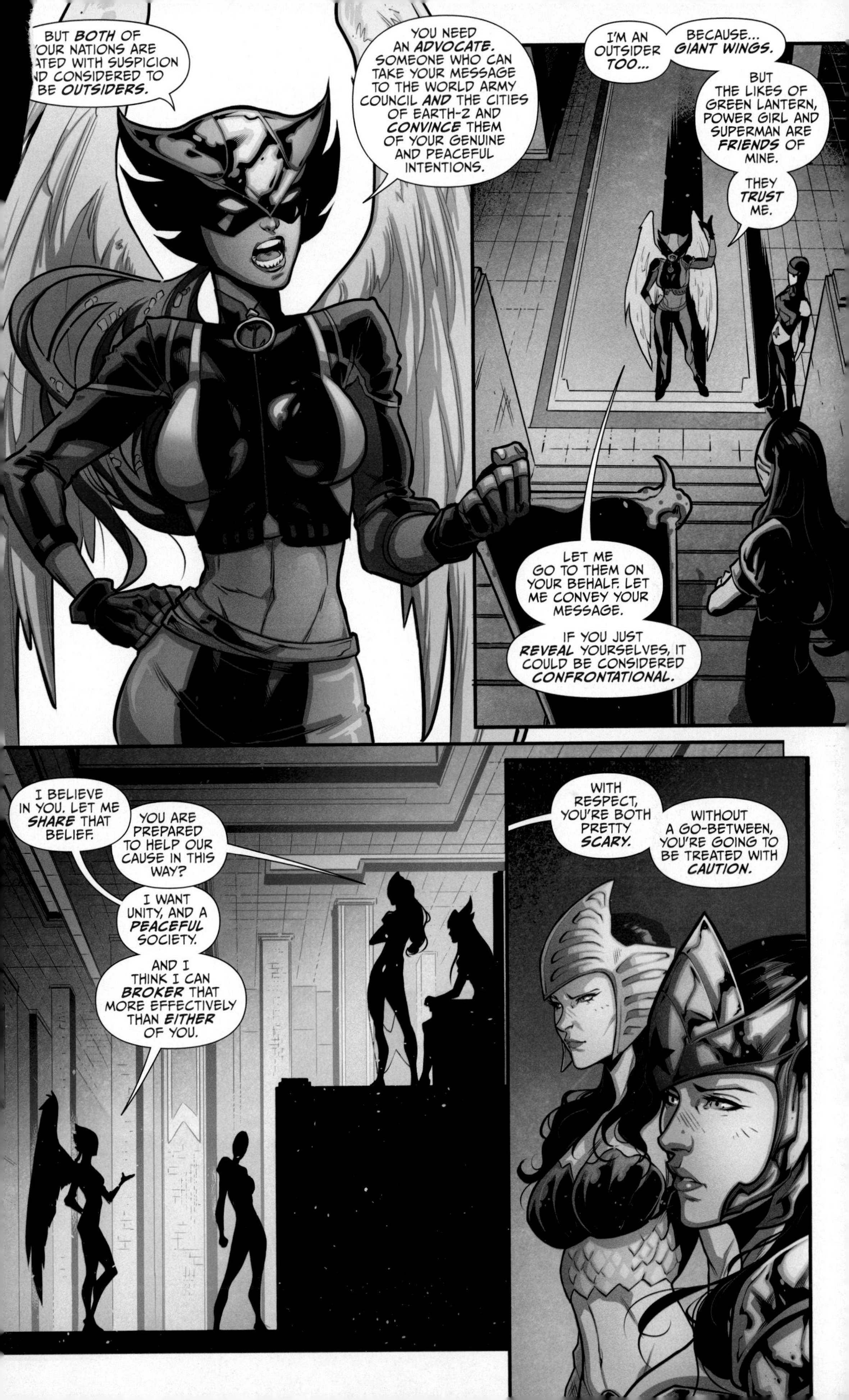
BUT **BOTH** OF YOUR NATIONS ARE ATED WITH SUSPICION ND CONSIDERED TO BE **OUTSIDERS.**
YOU NEED AN **ADVOCATE.** SOMEONE WHO CAN TAKE YOUR MESSAGE TO THE WORLD ARMY COUNCIL **AND** THE CITIES OF EARTH-2 AND **CONVINCE** THEM OF YOUR GENUINE AND PEACEFUL INTENTIONS.
I'M AN OUTSIDER **TOO...**
BECAUSE... **GIANT WINGS.**
BUT THE LIKES OF GREEN LANTERN, POWER GIRL AND SUPERMAN ARE **FRIENDS** OF MINE.
THEY **TRUST** ME.
LET ME GO TO THEM ON YOUR BEHALF. LET ME CONVEY YOUR MESSAGE.
IF YOU JUST **REVEAL** YOURSELVES, IT COULD BE CONSIDERED **CONFRONTATIONAL.**
I BELIEVE IN YOU. LET ME **SHARE** THAT BELIEF.
YOU ARE PREPARED TO HELP OUR CAUSE IN THIS WAY?
I WANT UNITY, AND A **PEACEFUL** SOCIETY.
AND I THINK I CAN **BROKER** THAT MORE EFFECTIVELY THAN **EITHER** OF YOU.
WITH RESPECT, YOU'RE BOTH PRETTY **SCARY.**
WITHOUT A GO-BETWEEN, YOU'RE GOING TO BE TREATED WITH **CAUTION.**

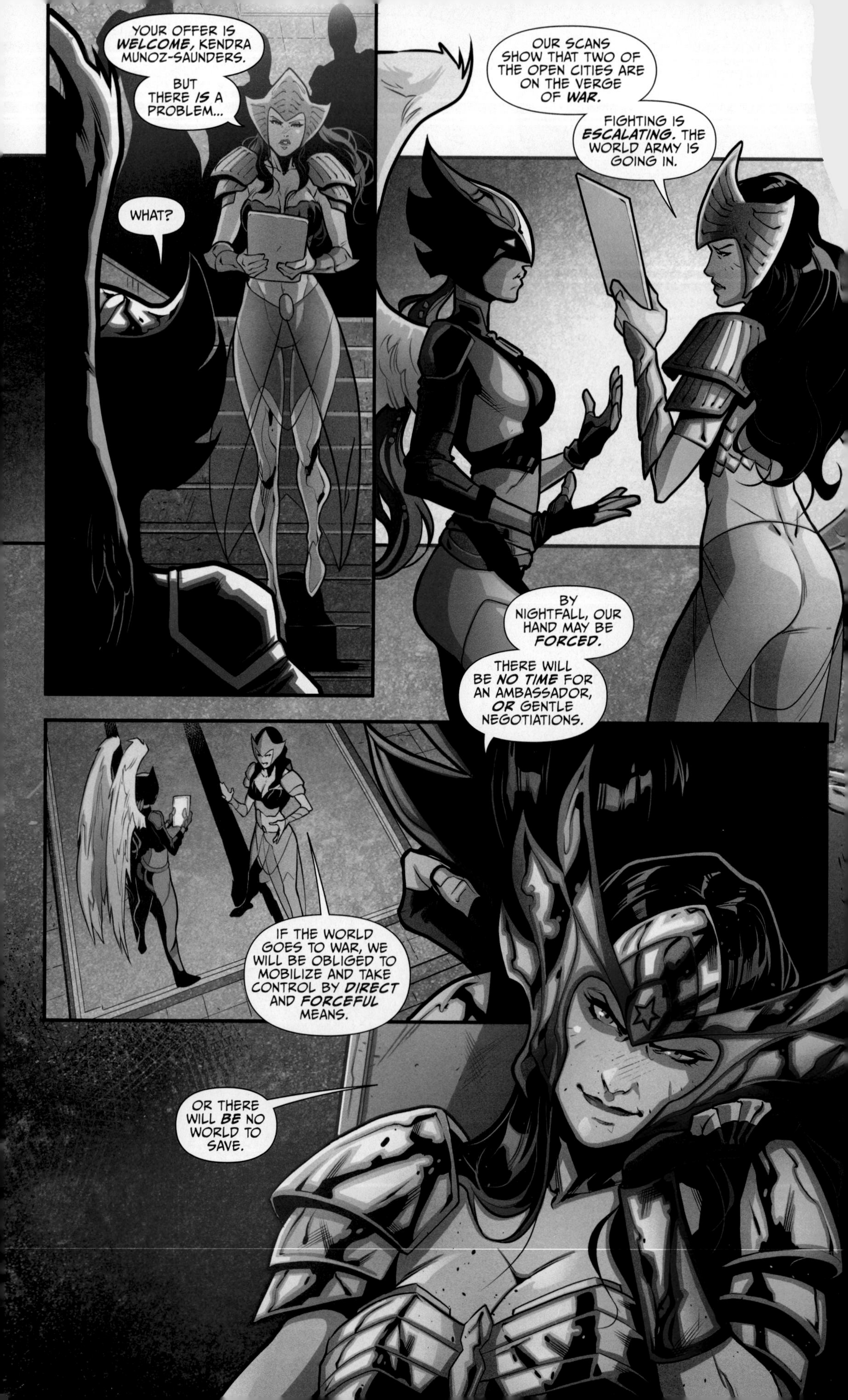
YOUR OFFER IS WELCOME, KENDRA MUNOZ-SAUNDERS.
BUT THERE IS A PROBLEM...
WHAT?
OUR SCANS SHOW THAT TWO OF THE OPEN CITIES ARE ON THE VERGE OF WAR.
FIGHTING IS ESCALATING. THE WORLD ARMY IS GOING IN.
BY NIGHTFALL, OUR HAND MAY BE FORCED.
THERE WILL BE NO TIME FOR AN AMBASSADOR, OR GENTLE NEGOTIATIONS.
IF THE WORLD GOES TO WAR, WE WILL BE OBLIGED TO MOBILIZE AND TAKE CONTROL BY DIRECT AND FORCEFUL MEANS.
OR THERE WILL BE NO WORLD TO SAVE.

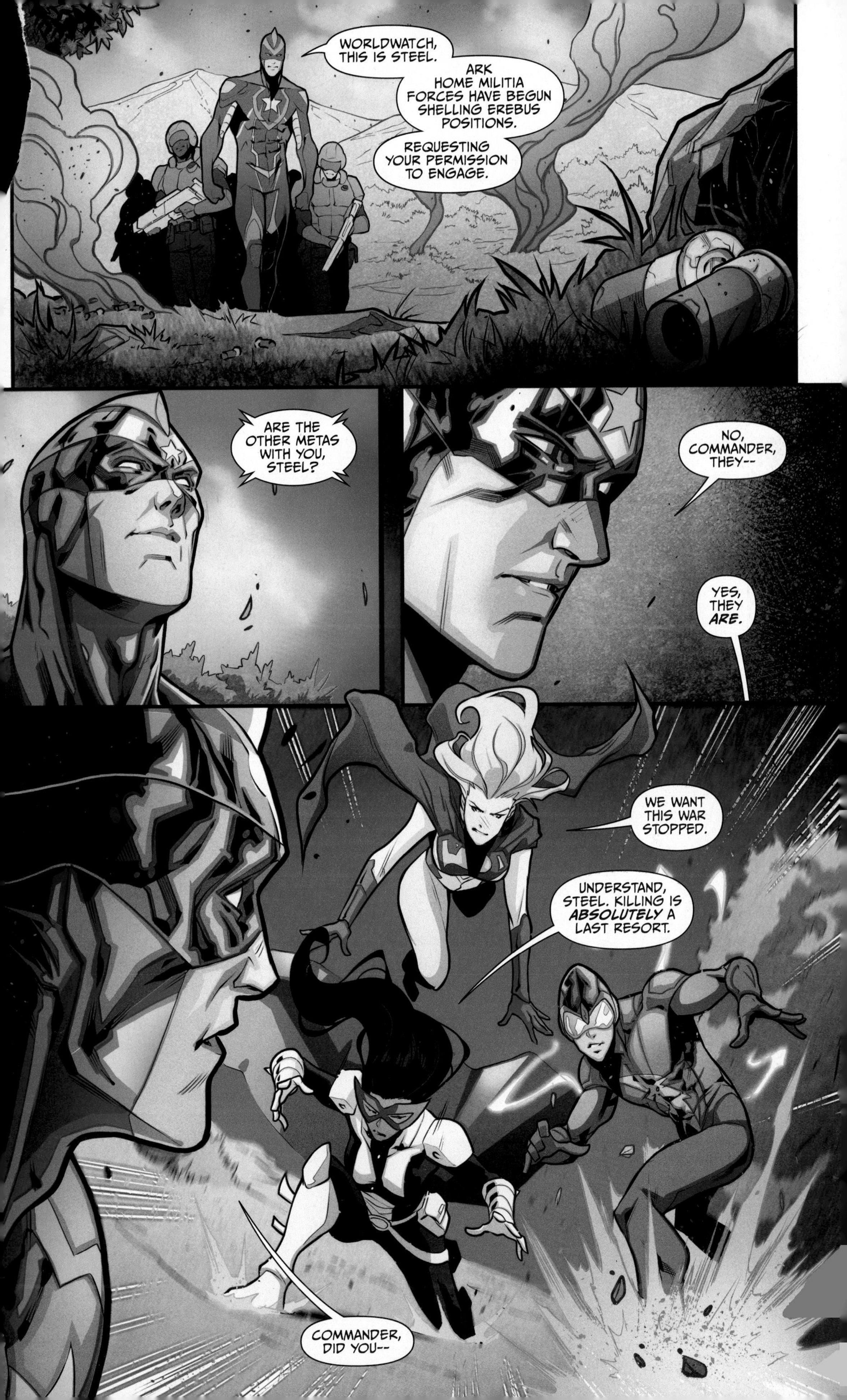
WORLDWATCH, THIS IS STEEL.
ARK HOME MILITIA FORCES HAVE BEGUN SHELLING EREBUS POSITIONS.
REQUESTING YOUR PERMISSION TO ENGAGE.
ARE THE OTHER METAS WITH YOU, STEEL?
NO, COMMANDER, THEY--
YES, THEY *ARE.*
WE WANT THIS WAR STOPPED.
UNDERSTAND, STEEL. KILLING IS *ABSOLUTELY* A LAST RESORT.
COMMANDER, DID YOU--

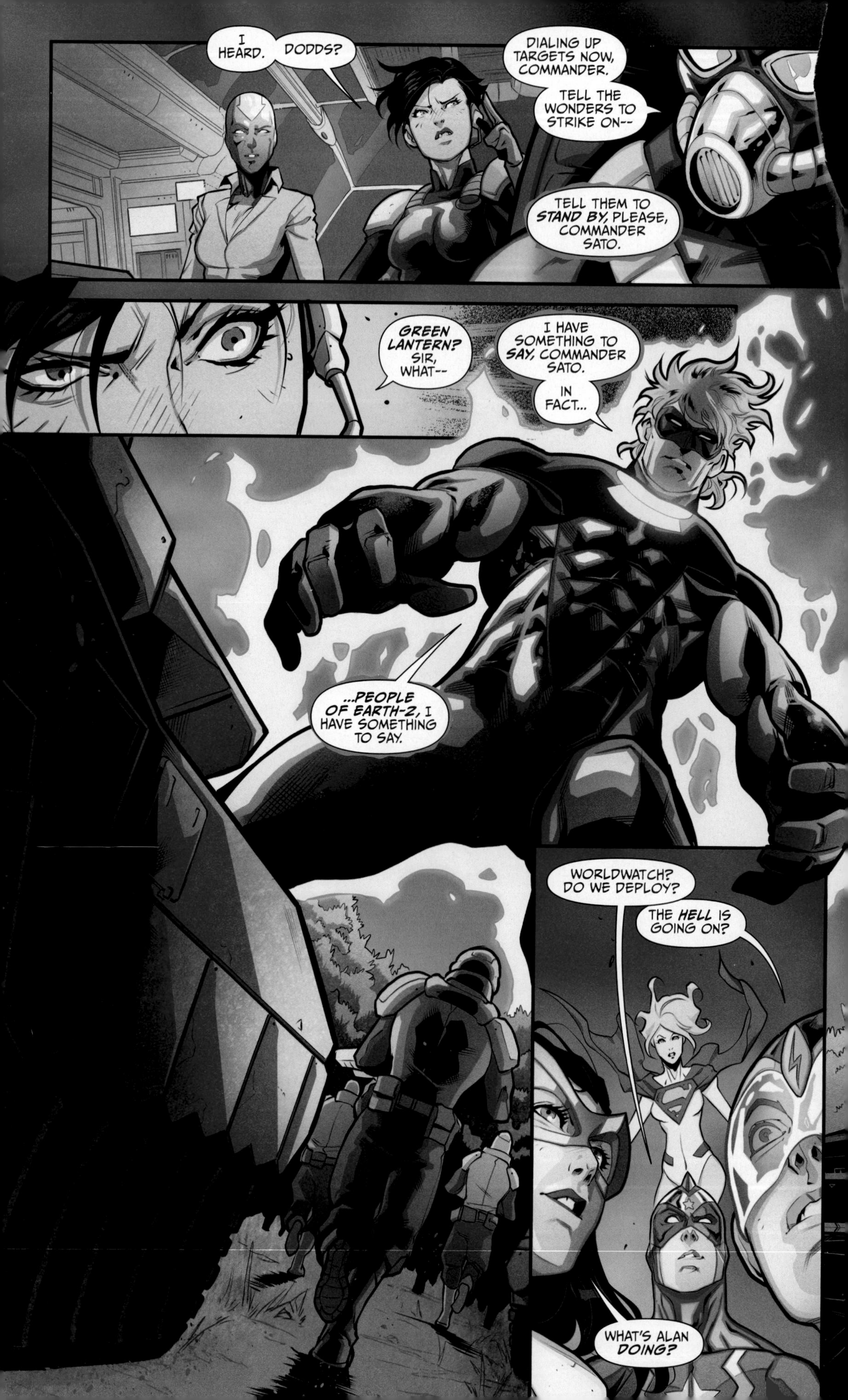
I HEARD.
DODDS?
DIALING UP TARGETS NOW, COMMANDER.
TELL THE WONDERS TO STRIKE ON--
TELL THEM TO STAND BY, PLEASE, COMMANDER SATO.
GREEN LANTERN? SIR, WHAT--
I HAVE SOMETHING TO SAY, COMMANDER SATO.
IN FACT...
...PEOPLE OF EARTH-2, I HAVE SOMETHING TO SAY.
WORLDWATCH? DO WE DEPLOY?
THE HELL IS GOING ON?
WHAT'S ALAN DOING?

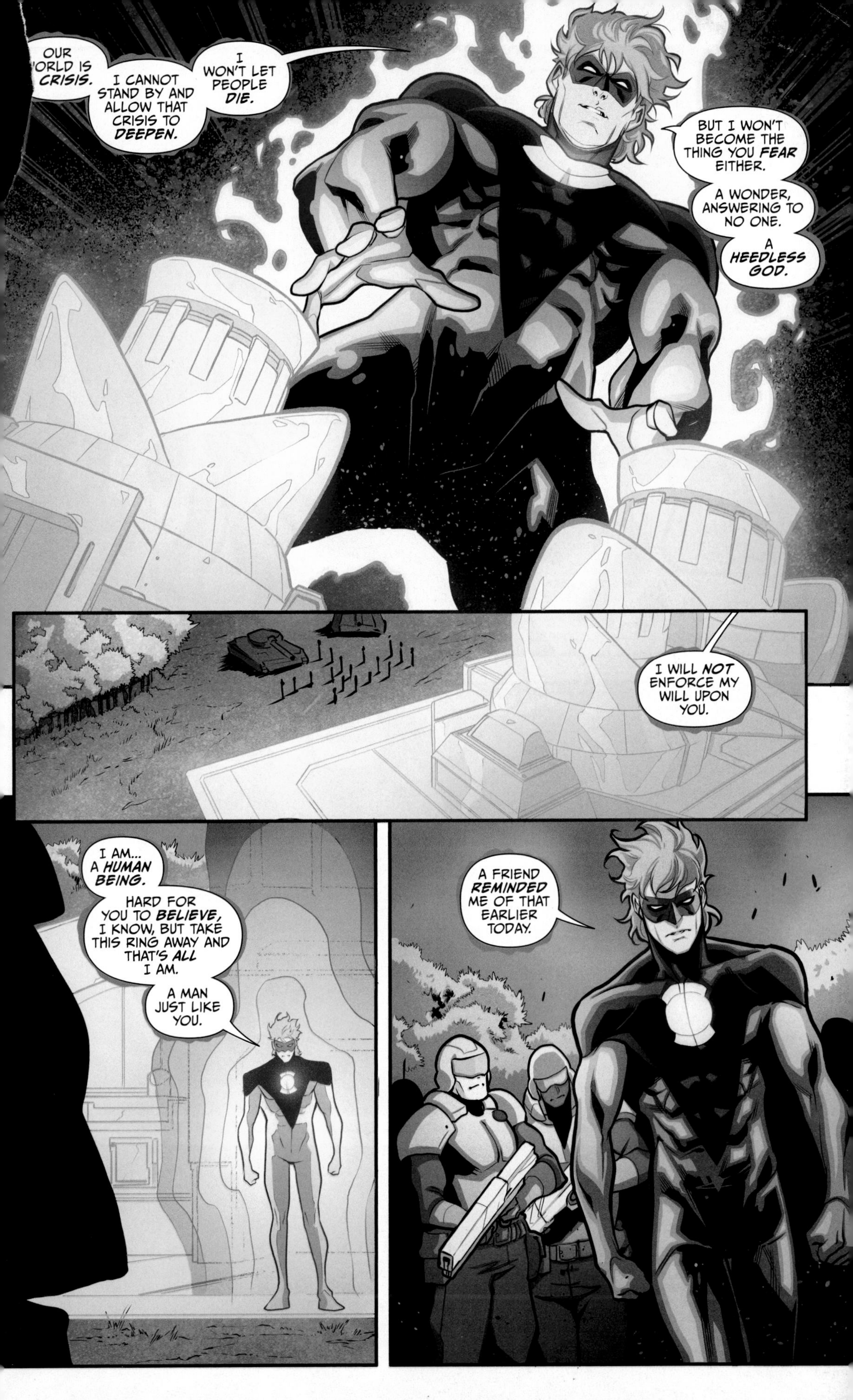
OUR WORLD IS CRISIS.
I CANNOT STAND BY AND ALLOW THAT CRISIS TO DEEPEN.
I WON'T LET PEOPLE DIE.
BUT I WON'T BECOME THE THING YOU FEAR EITHER.
A WONDER, ANSWERING TO NO ONE.
A HEEDLESS GOD.
I WILL NOT ENFORCE MY WILL UPON YOU.
I AM... A HUMAN BEING.
HARD FOR YOU TO BELIEVE, I KNOW, BUT TAKE THIS RING AWAY AND THAT'S ALL I AM.
A MAN JUST LIKE YOU.
A FRIEND REMINDED ME OF THAT EARLIER TODAY.

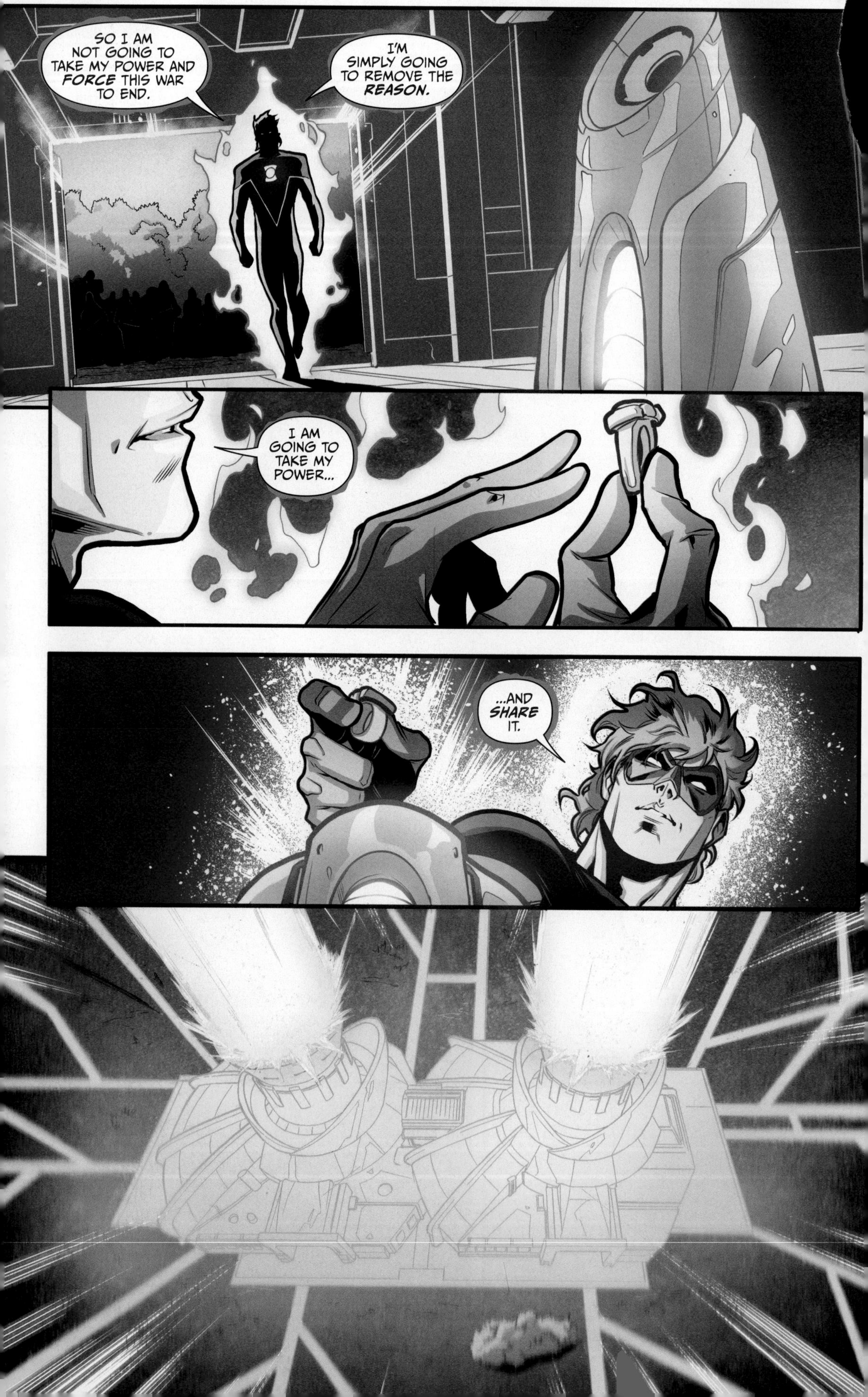
SO I AM NOT GOING TO TAKE MY POWER AND *FORCE* THIS WAR TO END.
I'M SIMPLY GOING TO REMOVE THE *REASON.*
I AM GOING TO TAKE MY POWER...
...AND *SHARE* IT.

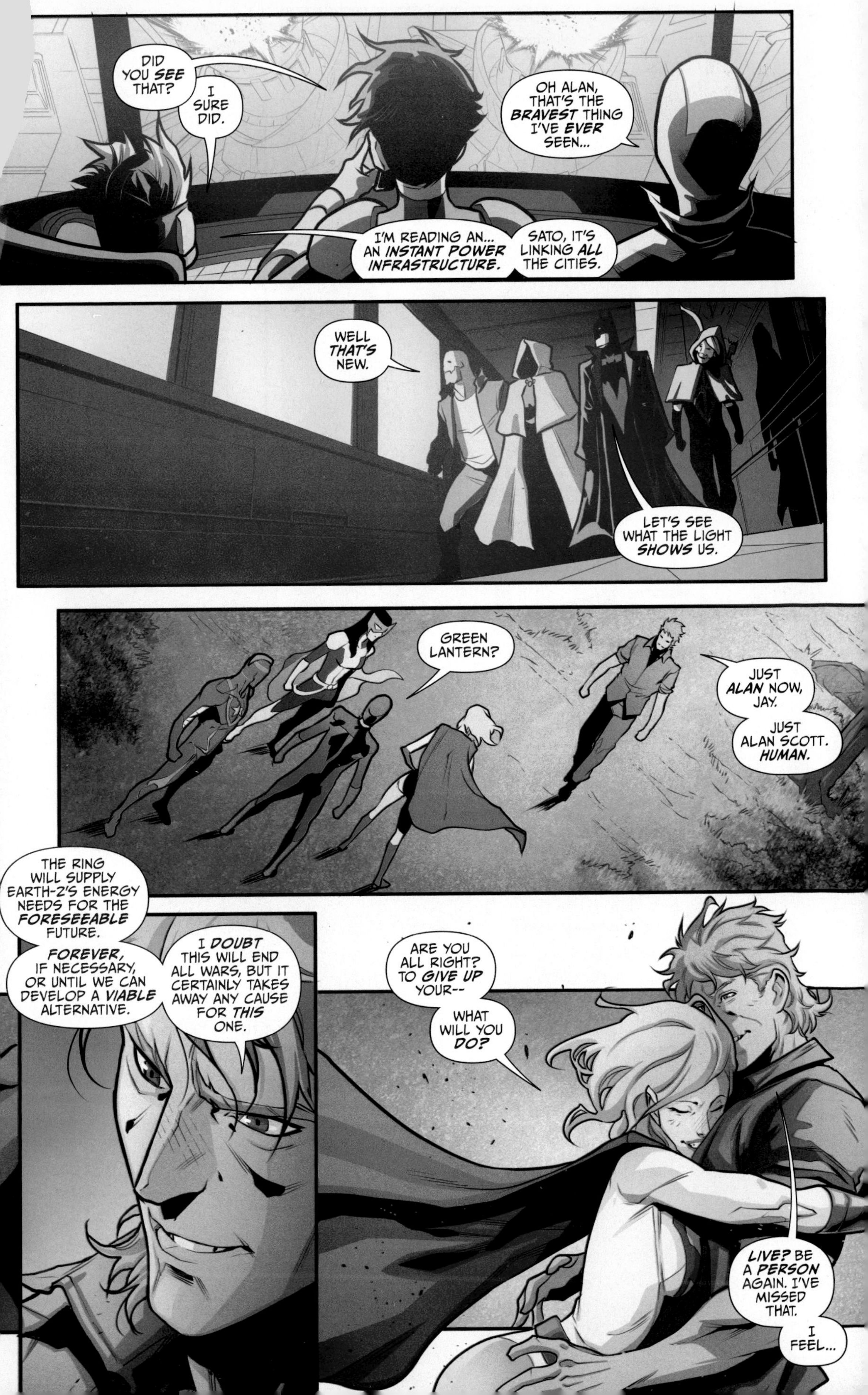
DID YOU SEE THAT?
I SURE DID.
OH ALAN, THAT'S THE BRAVEST THING I'VE EVER SEEN...
I'M READING AN... AN INSTANT POWER INFRASTRUCTURE.
SATO, IT'S LINKING ALL THE CITIES.
WELL THAT'S NEW.
LET'S SEE WHAT THE LIGHT SHOWS US.
GREEN LANTERN?
JUST ALAN NOW, JAY.
JUST ALAN SCOTT. HUMAN.
THE RING WILL SUPPLY EARTH-2'S ENERGY NEEDS FOR THE FORESEEABLE FUTURE.
FOREVER, IF NECESSARY, OR UNTIL WE CAN DEVELOP A VIABLE ALTERNATIVE.
I DOUBT THIS WILL END ALL WARS, BUT IT CERTAINLY TAKES AWAY ANY CAUSE FOR THIS ONE.
ARE YOU ALL RIGHT? TO GIVE UP YOUR--
WHAT WILL YOU DO?
LIVE? BE A PERSON AGAIN. I'VE MISSED THAT.
I FEEL...

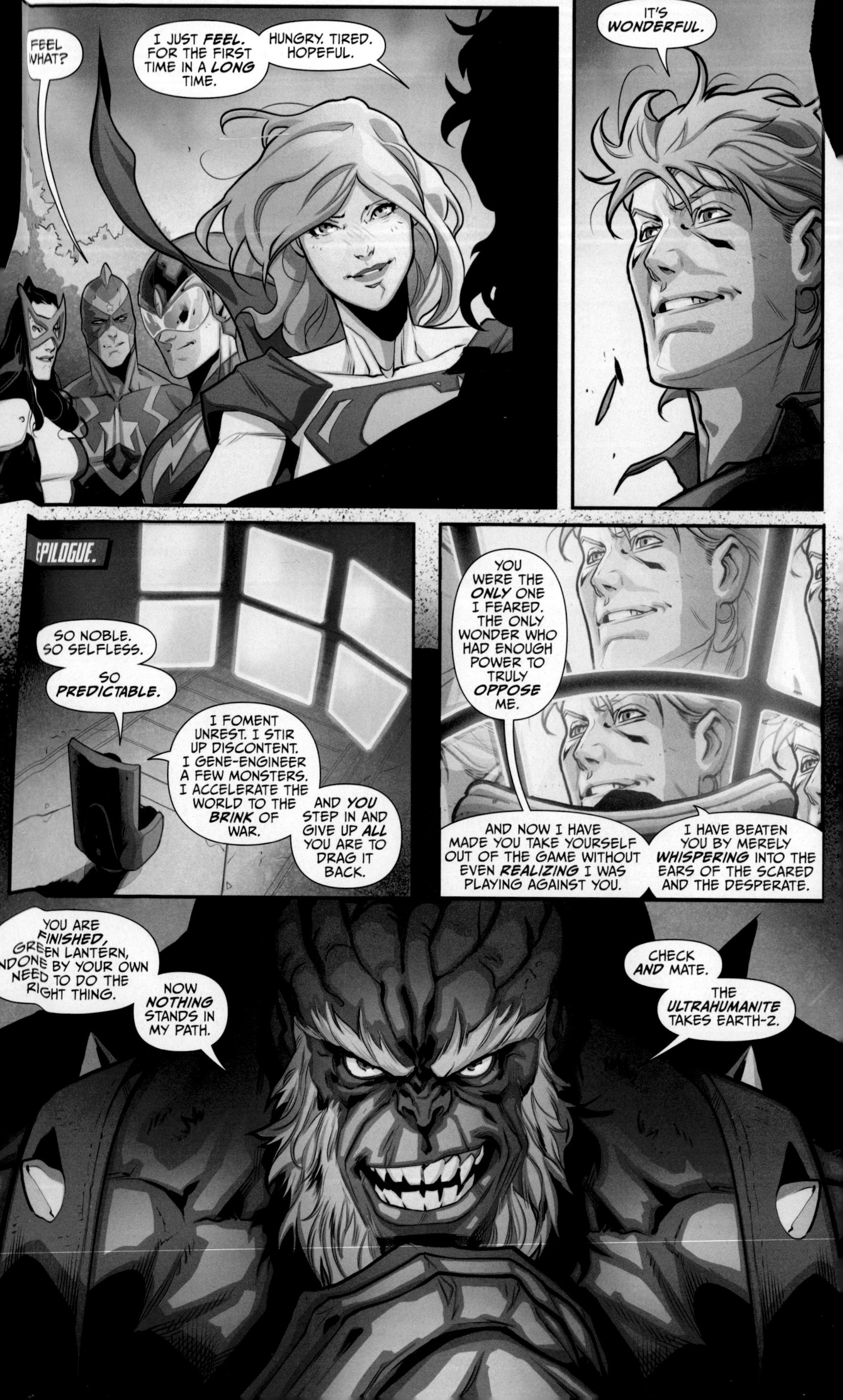
FEEL WHAT?
I JUST FEEL. FOR THE FIRST TIME IN A LONG TIME.
HUNGRY. TIRED. HOPEFUL.
IT'S WONDERFUL.
EPILOGUE.
SO NOBLE. SO SELFLESS.
SO PREDICTABLE.
I FOMENT UNREST. I STIR UP DISCONTENT. I GENE-ENGINEER A FEW MONSTERS. I ACCELERATE THE WORLD TO THE BRINK OF WAR.
AND YOU STEP IN AND GIVE UP ALL YOU ARE TO DRAG IT BACK.
YOU WERE THE ONLY ONE I FEARED. THE ONLY WONDER WHO HAD ENOUGH POWER TO TRULY OPPOSE ME.
AND NOW I HAVE MADE YOU TAKE YOURSELF OUT OF THE GAME WITHOUT EVEN REALIZING I WAS PLAYING AGAINST YOU.
I HAVE BEATEN YOU BY MERELY WHISPERING INTO THE EARS OF THE SCARED AND THE DESPERATE.
YOU ARE FINISHED, GREEN LANTERN, NDONE BY YOUR OWN NEED TO DO THE RIGHT THING.
NOW NOTHING STANDS IN MY PATH.
CHECK AND MATE.
THE ULTRAHUMANITE TAKES EARTH-2.

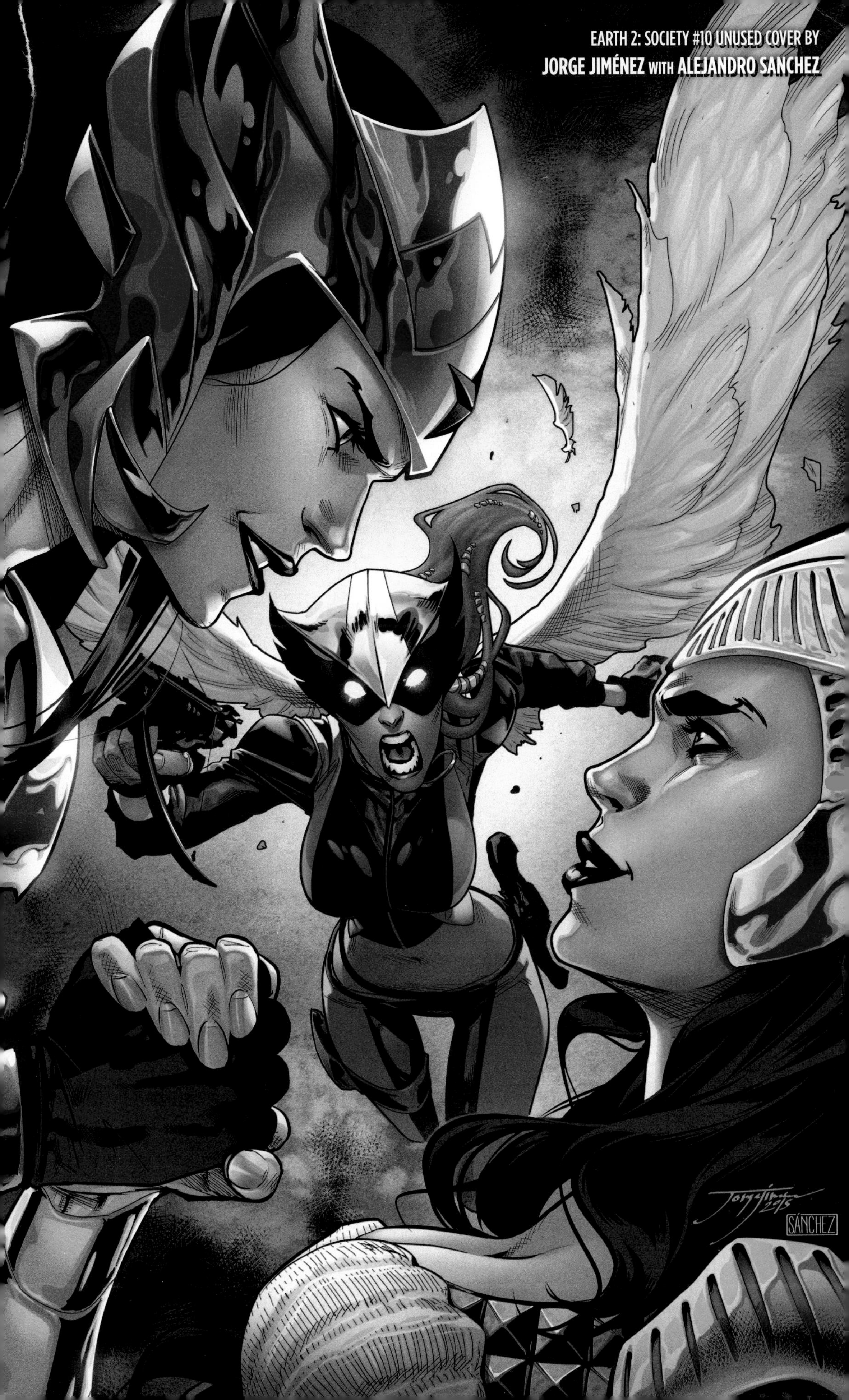
SÁNCHEZ

EARTH 2: SOCIETY #10 UNUSED COVER BY
JORGE JIMÉNEZ WITH **ALEJANDRO SANCHEZ**

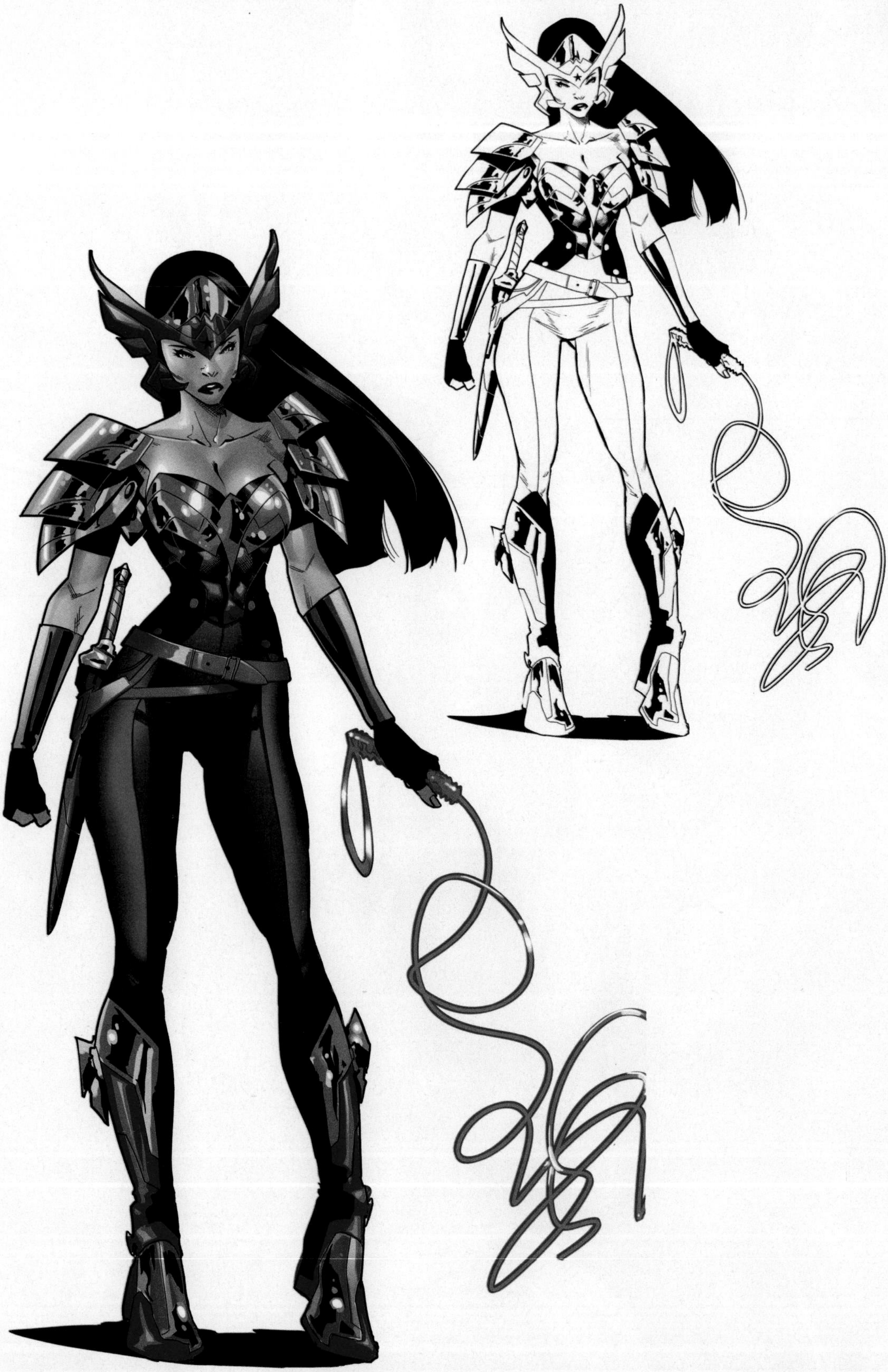

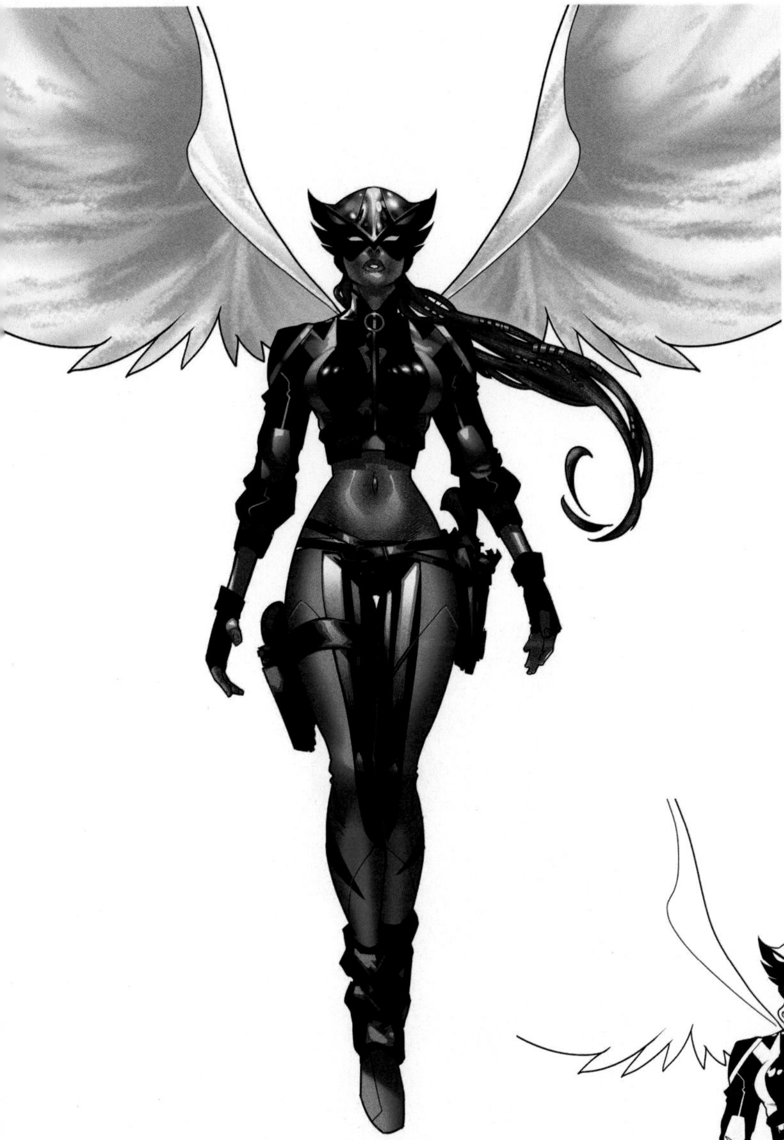

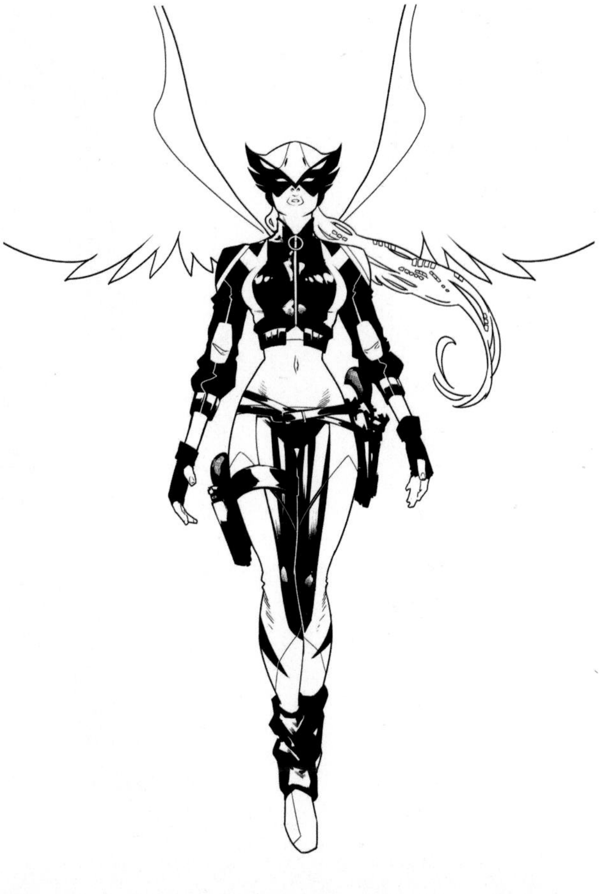

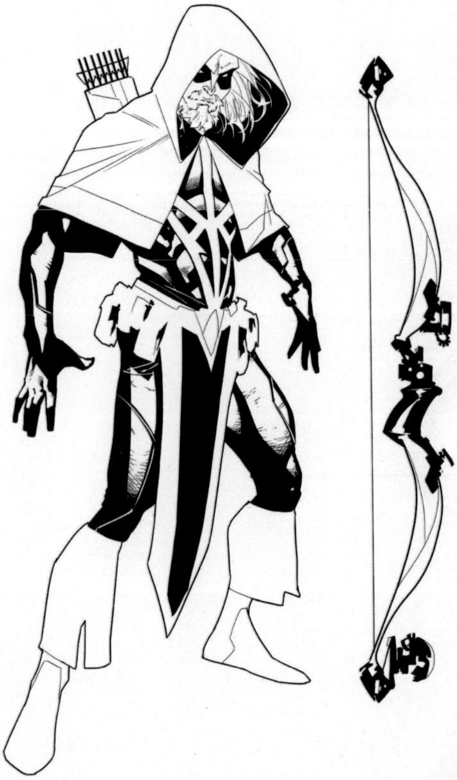

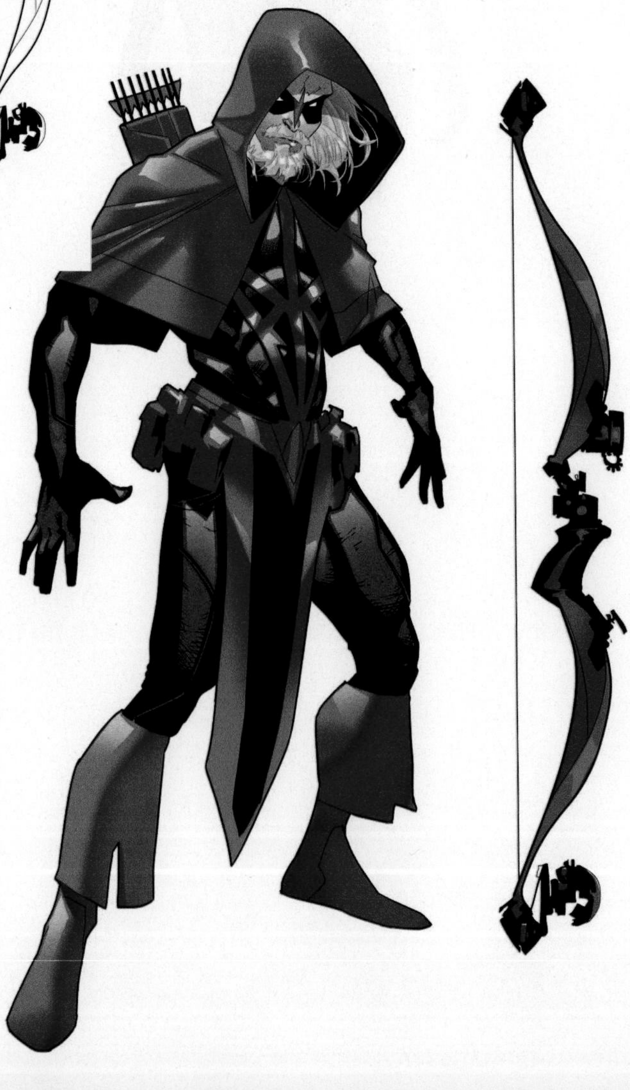

COVER LAYOUTS BY
JORGE JIMÉNEZ

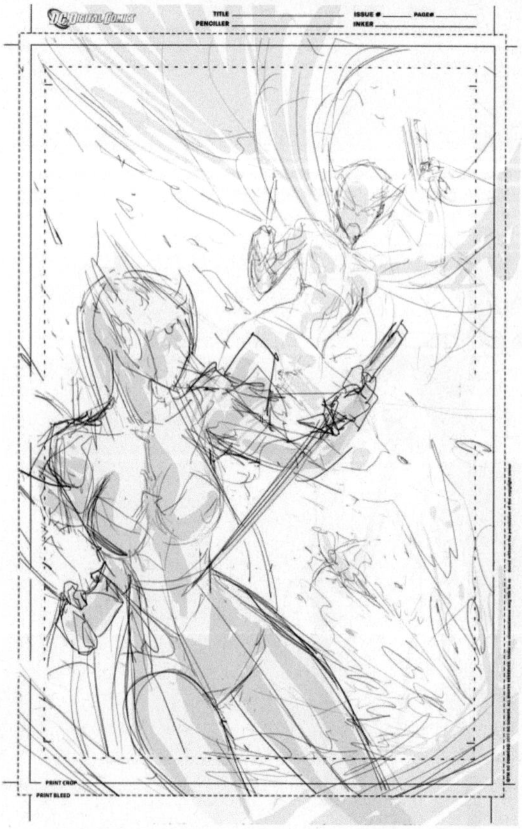

TITLE
PENCILLER
ISSUE #
PAGE#
INKER
PRINT CROP
PRINT BLEED

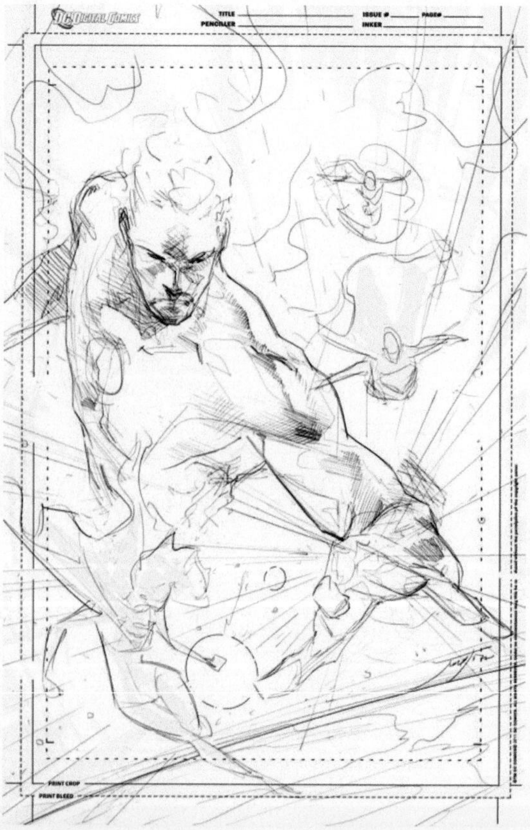

TITLE
PENCILLER
ISSUE #
PAGE#
INKER
PRINT CROP
PRINT BLEED

PAGE ONE

Full page splash.

Gorgeous "Spirit title page" style shot of BATMAN perched on the top of a massive art deco corporate sign that reads NIMBUS SOLUTIONS. It's a huge, 3D, scaffolding-supported sign decorating the top of the Nimbus headquarters in Gotham, very sculptural and very 1940's. It's like he's perched on an ornate version of the Hollywood sign. Night sky behind him. Very dramatic, quite close in so we get the sign and him, very archetypal and "Frank Miller/Will Eisner" in its design

LOC CAP

New Gotham

BATMAN

It's wartime.

(joined)

Start the clock.

TITLE

One Nation Indivisible

SUB

Chapter three: Running on Empty

CREDITS

EARTH 2 SOCIETY #10 INKS BY
JORGE JIMÉNEZ

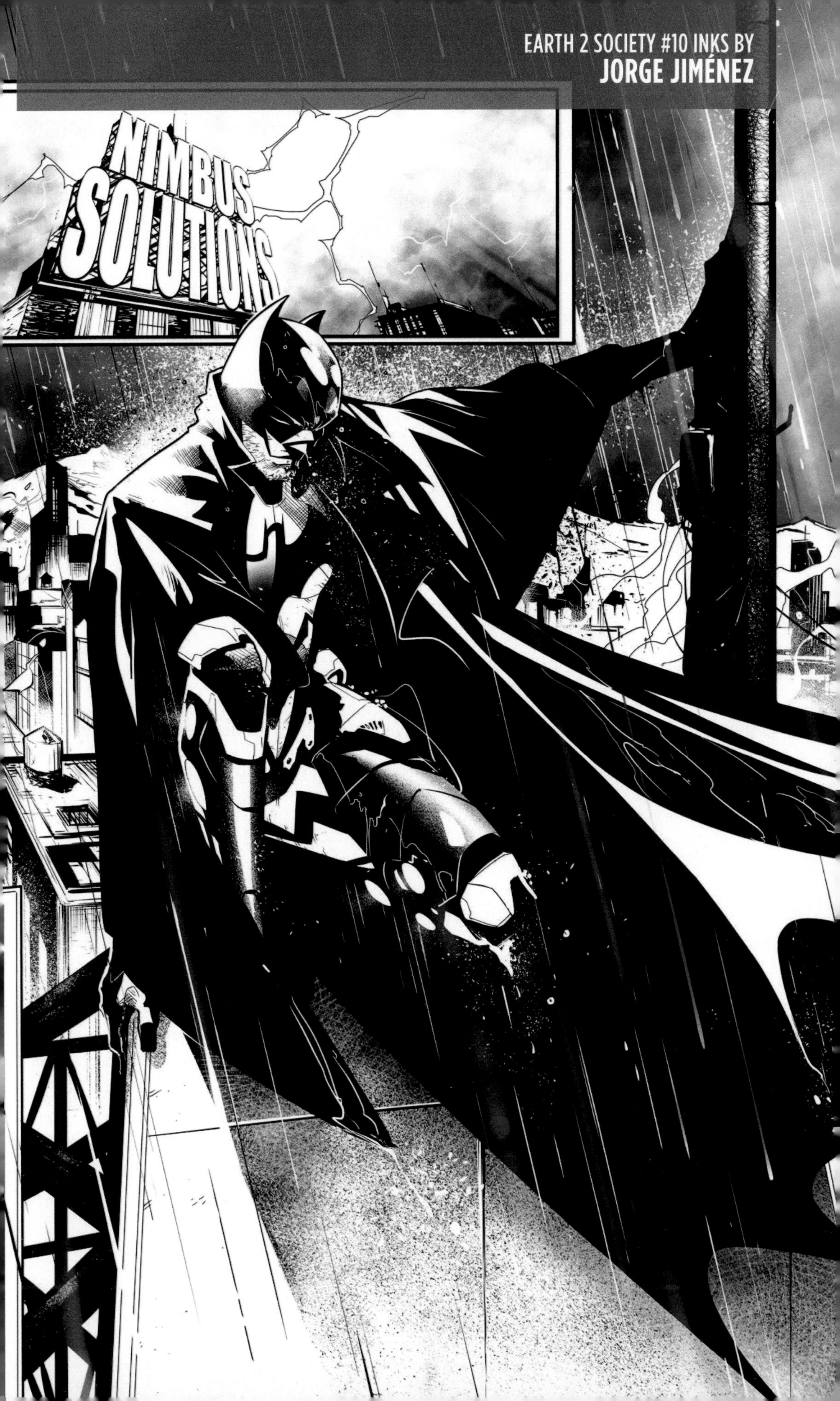
NIMBUS SOLUTIONS

PAGE TWO

1. Page wide. Cut to a dynamic shot of TED GRANT and RED ARROW vaulting athletically over the top of a very high chain-link security fence, coming down at us. Night all around. They are breaking into a secure compound off of a darkened street. Red Arrow is in full costume, bow in hand, and Ted is dark sweats and a leather jacket, like a gangland enforcer. Ted also has an ear-piece mic on. Very agile and dynamic.

> TED
> This is Ted, Batman. Reading you loud and clear.
> (joined)
> We're moving into the warehouse compound.

> ARROW
> Tell him there could be trouble.

2. Page wide. We're behind them, looking through the fence, as they land side by side. Ahead of them are dark warehouses. DIRECTLY ahead of them, a dozen or so thuggish hoodlums (night club bouncer types) are rushing at them, wielding clubs and chains. Red Arrow is raising his bow. Ted is hunching, raising his brawler fists. Very dynamic.

> TED
> Red Arrow says—

> ARROW
> Correction. Tell him there is trouble.

> TED
> Security, Batman. Bunch o' them.

3. Page wide. Now we're in front of them. The fight has started. Dynamic and meaty. Ted is brutally punching out one attacking thug, maybe fending off another. He looks amused. Beside him, Red Arrow is firing a 'stun' arrow point blank into the stomach of another thug, doubling him over as it explodes in a shock of electric discharge. Other thugs rushing in from all sides.

> JAG
> You okay there, Ted?

> TED
> Dandy. Nothing I like better than a wildcat brawl.

> FX ARROW
> KZZZGT

4. Page wide, continuous. Ted smacks another thug flying. Red Arrow has spun FAST and fired another stun arrow ACROSS THE FRAME BEHIND TED, hitting (shock flare again) another big thug who was about to smack Ted around the back of the head with a chair leg. Very dynamic.

> TED
> Hey! Maybe I should mask up like you guys and call myself Wildc—

> FX
> KZZGT

> ARROW
> Maybe you should watch your back, big guy.

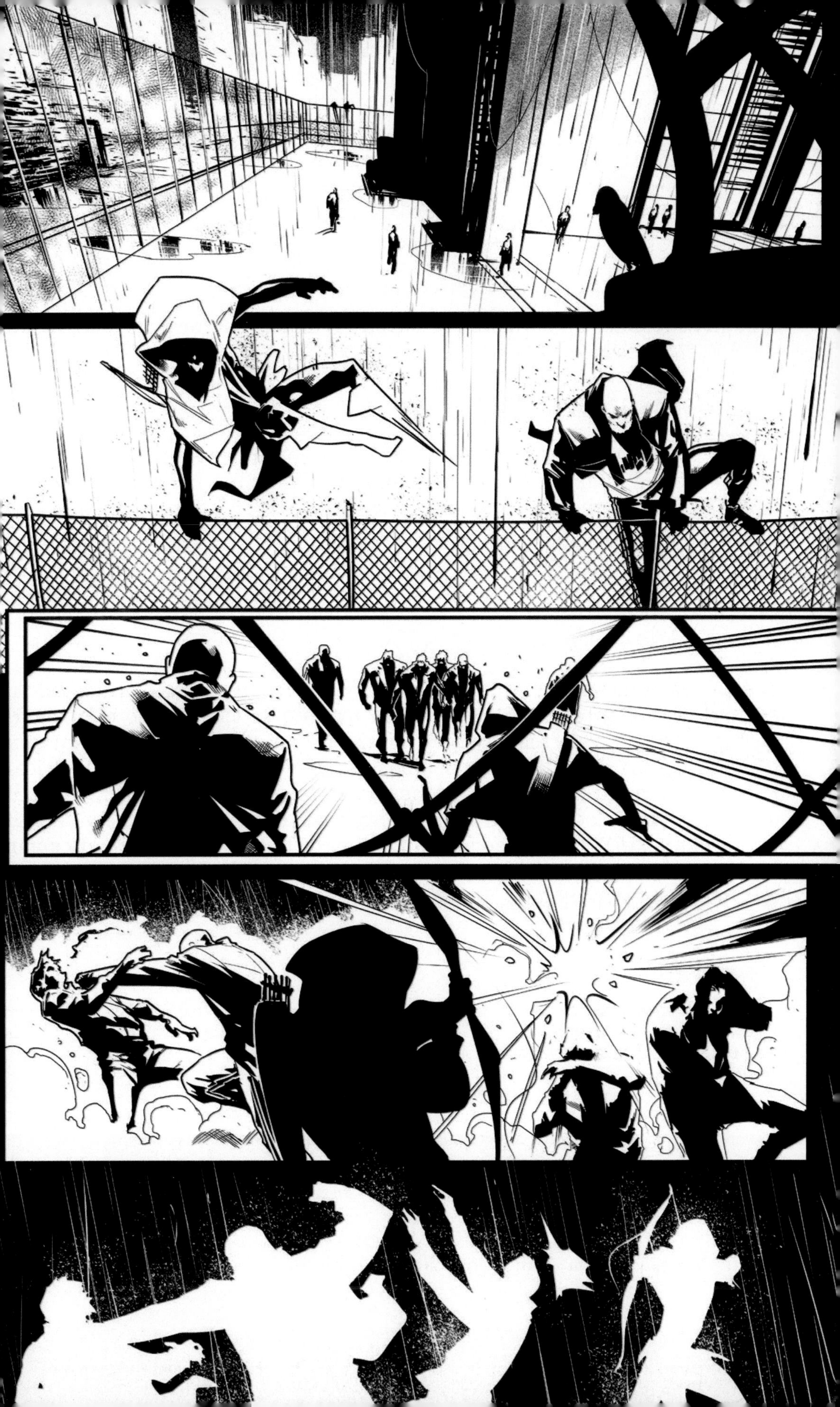

1. Page wide. Back on Batman, tight in on his mask, just the eyes, narrowing.

BATMAN
If you guys are getting it done, I'll move in.

2. BIG PAGE WIDE PANEL, SPLASHY (dominating page). Batman leaps down through a large skylight into a well-lit chamber below. This is from ABOVE HIM, framed by the darkness of the roof. Glass explodes in a blizzard. Batman is dropping elegantly, cape spread in a black BAT SHAPE. Very David Mazzucchelli.

FX
KRAAAATISSSHHH!

3. Page wide. Interior, a large double-height office. Arm chairs, rugs, drinks cabinets etc. Center panel, Batman is landing in the middle of the rug, facing us, glass from the skylight raining down all around. He is landing DYNAMICALLY, cape swirling in a bat shape, very ominous and theatrical. Foreground, a big desk, a big leather chair, facing Batman. KYLE NIMBUS sits in the chair, looking at Batman across the desk. Nimbus (new version of this character) is a handsome man in his thirties, dressed in a very smart suit. I'm picturing someone like Neal McDonough - handsome, arrogant, wry, superior, white blond. He does not react in surprise.

FX
WHUMMPP

NIMBUS
Really? Is there something wrong with doors?

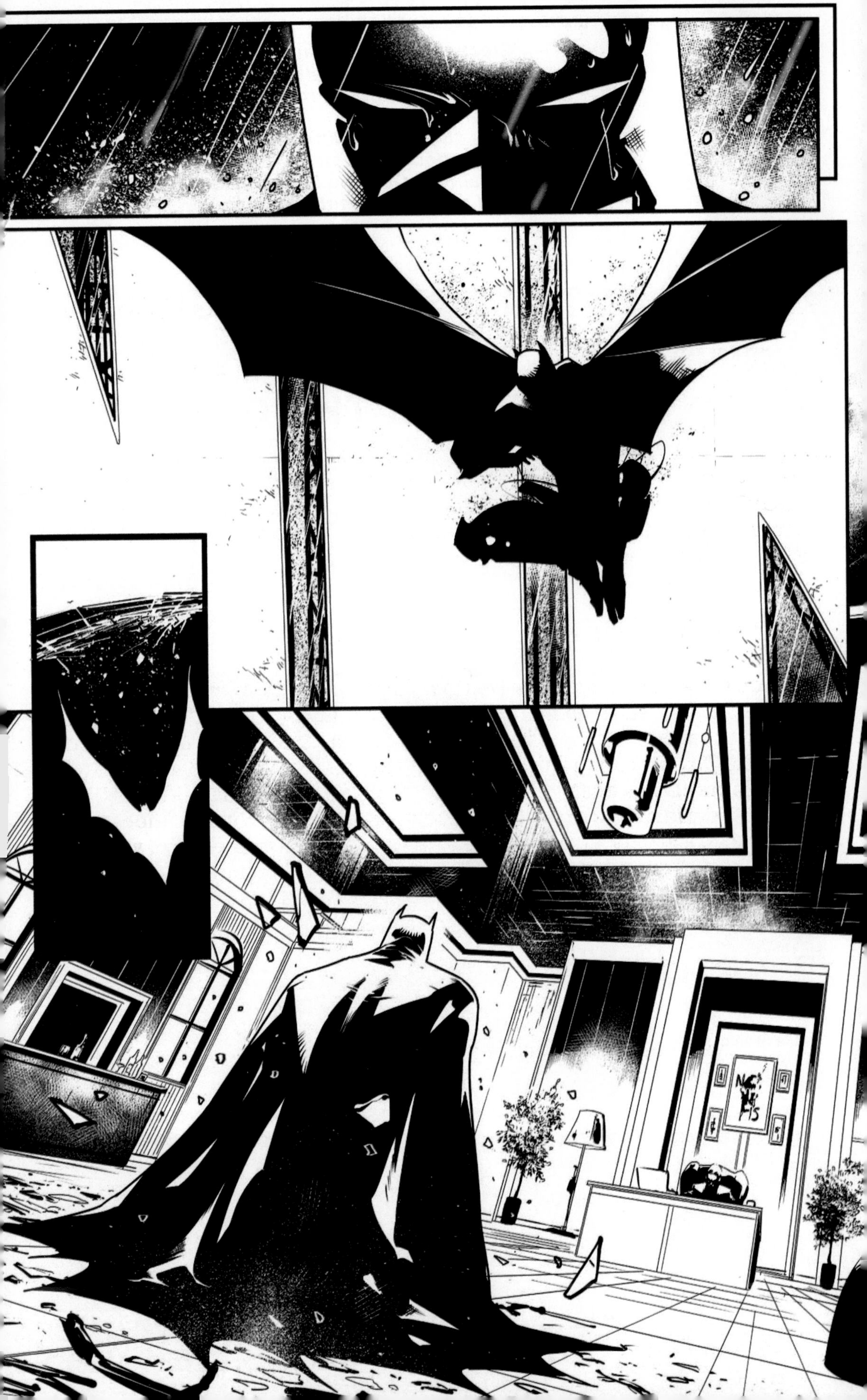

DC
COMICS™

"Great characterization and exciting action sequences
continue to be the hallmarks of this series, along with
some interesting meta commentary as well."—IGN

"EARTH 2 is an incredibly entertaining ride. The
freedom to create a world from the ground up has
allowed it to be one of the most exciting, diverse,
and entertaining titles DC puts out." –CRAVEONLINE

START AT THE BEGINNING!
EARTH 2
VOLUME 1: THE GATHERING

**EARTH 2 VOL. 2:
THE TOWER OF FATE**

with JAMES ROBINSON,
NICOLA SCOTT and
YILDIRAY CINAR

**EARTH 2 VOL. 3:
BATTLE CRY**

with JAMES ROBINSON,
NICOLA SCOTT and
YILDARAY CINAR

**EARTH 2 VOL. 4:
THE DARK AGE**

with TOM TAYLOR and
NICOLA SCOTT

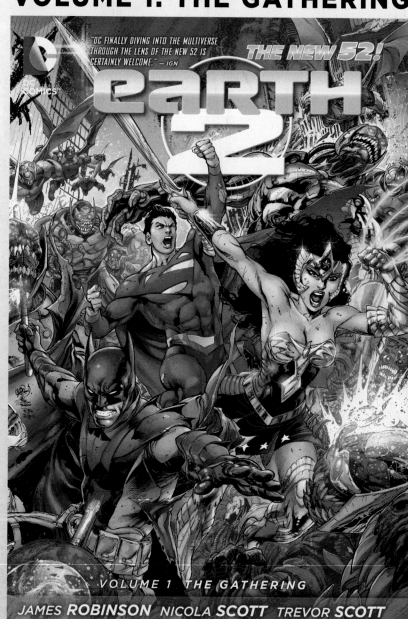

VOLUME 1 THE GATHERING

JAMES **ROBINSON** NICOLA **SCOTT** TREVOR **SCOTT**